T0002657

WHEN THE SUN FELL OUT OF THE SKY

This beautifully illustrated, therapeutic picture book tells the story of Stan the Giraffe. Stan loves the sun and to feel its warmth on his long back; but one day it suddenly and unexpectedly falls from the sky and disappears from his life. Stan experiences many different and difficult emotions throughout the story, reflecting the seven stages of grief. The story aims to normalise these feelings, which for children and those around them, can be frightening.

This storybook has been written to support key adults in helping bereaved children to find a way to cope, manage and make it through their grief.

The resource *Guide to Supporting Children through Bereavement and Loss* has been written to accompany the storybook, providing information, guidance and ideas for anyone supporting a grieving child, in school or at home.

Hollie Rankin is a counsellor who has worked with and supported children, young people and their families within schools in the North East over the last ten years. Her recent books on trauma and bereavement were prompted by a noticeable gap in resources to help to guide adults when supporting children in emotionally challenging circumstances.

For Nancy Peters MBE

Forever in our hearts

Marcus x

First published 2019
by Routledge
2 Park Square, Milton Park, Abingdon, Oxon OX14 4RN

and by Routledge
52 Vanderbilt Avenue, New York, NY 10017

Routledge is an imprint of the Taylor & Francis Group, an informa business

British Library Cataloguing-in-Publication Data
A catalogue record for this book is available from the British Library

Library of Congress Cataloging-in-Publication Data
Names: Rankin, Hollie, author.
Title: When the sun fell out of the sky : a short tale of bereavement and loss / Hollie Rankin.
Description: Abingdon, Oxon ; New York, NY : Routledge, 2019. | Summary: When the sun disappears from the sky, Stan the Giraffe goes through all of the stages of grief, then finally notices the moon and sees that he can go on.
Identifiers: LCCN 2018051792 | ISBN 9781138360440 (pbk.) | ISBN 9780429433146 (ebk)
Subjects: | CYAC: Loss (Psychology)—Fiction. | Grief—Fiction. | Sun—Fiction. | Giraffe—Fiction.
Classification: LCC PZ7.1.H3714 Whe 2019 | DDC [E]—dc23
LC record available at https://lccn.loc.gov/2018051792

ISBN: 978-1-138-36044-0 (pbk)
ISBN: 978-0-429-43314-6 (ebk)

Typeset in Calibri
by Apex CoVantage, LLC

When the Sun Fell Out of the Sky

A Short Tale of Bereavement and Loss

Hollie Rankin

Illustrated by Marcus Peters

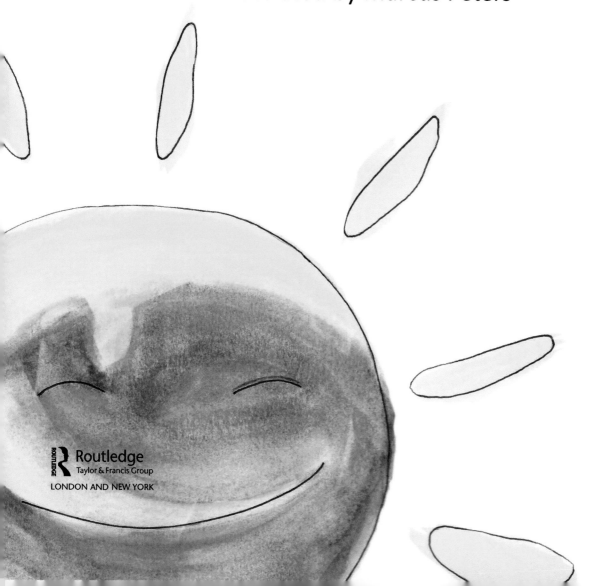

Routledge
Taylor & Francis Group

LONDON AND NEW YORK

Stan was a giraffe.

Like all giraffes, he had long, spindly

legs, and an extremely long neck.

Stan loved nothing more than to eat the greenest leaves from the tallest trees, and to feel the warm sun on his face as he crunched and munched.

One morning, Stan awoke with a start.

A strange feeling in his tummy told him that

something wasn't right.

All around him was darkness!

Stan hurried outside.

It was dark out there too.

The other animals stared up into the ink-black sky.

The sun was nowhere to be seen.

It was as if the sun had fallen out of the sky.

Stan couldn't believe what had happened.

Wouldn't believe it.

"The sun can't just fall out of the sky."

He decided it must be hiding.

He was going to find it and put it right back

where it belonged.

Off he marched.

Stan was sure it was all a big mistake.

He searched and searched and searched some more.

He hunted behind trees, under bushes, in the stream.

He stretched his neck as high as he could to see

if the sun was hiding behind the clouds.

It was nowhere to be seen.

It really was as if the sun had fallen out of the sky.

Stan felt cross.

Really angry in fact!

He clenched his teeth.

He stamped his hooves.

Stan was furious.

He spotted a grey rock on the ground. Stan kicked it with all his might into the dark sky where the sun used to sit. "Stupid sun, I hate you! You left me, and now the whole world has changed."

Stan felt guilty for being so angry with the sun.

He cried.

Big angry tears rolled off his face and down his long neck.

He knew it wasn't the sun's fault.

He felt awful for being so cross.

"I should have done something," Stan sobbed.

"I should have stopped the sun falling out of the sky."

He closed his eyes ever so tightly, and wished and prayed

for the sun to return.

He would give anything for the sun to come back.

Stan had never wanted something more in his whole life.

He was desperate to feel the sun on his face

and for the world to be light again.

Time passed.

Stan realised that wishing wasn't working.

No matter how much he wanted to save the sun,

he knew he couldn't.

Stan felt sadder than ever before.

He felt so sad that his head ached, so sad that his legs ached.

In fact, so sad that his whole body ached, from the top of

his head, to the tips of his hooves.

It was a pain he had never felt before.

A pain that made him more tired than ever before.

Stan was exhausted.

He did the only thing he could.

Eventually, Stan lay down and slept.

The other animals were worried.

They brought Stan the greenest, juiciest leaves to eat.

Stan wasn't interested.

He wanted to be left alone, to sleep, and sleep.

And so he slept.

One night, some time later, Stan was woken

gently by a silver light shining above him.

Slowly, he opened his eyes.

Stan stared at the bright glow of the silver moon.

He had never noticed how beautiful the moon was before.

Stan stood up slowly.

He stretched his neck to take a closer look.

He felt the warm beams on his back.

He saw how it softly lit up the world.

Stan saw a glimmer of hope in that full moon.

He knew it could never replace the sun

that had fallen out of the sky.

The sun that he loved and missed terribly.

The world was very different now, without the sun.

But Stan thought to himself that maybe, just maybe,

there was a chance he could get used to living in this new world.

With that, Stan stood up tall, took a big, deep breath,

and with the moon above him lighting the way, Stan bravely

stepped onto the silver path ahead of him.

The End

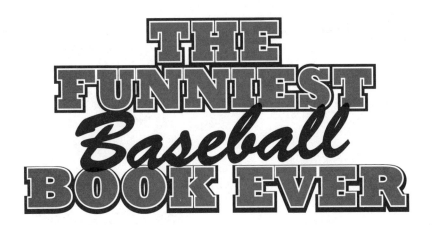

Other Books by Peter Handrinos

Best New York Sports Arguments

The Truth About Ruth (and More)

THE FUNNIEST Baseball BOOK EVER

The National Pastime's Greatest Quips, Quotations, Characters, Nicknames, and Pranks

PETER HANDRINOS

Andrews McMeel
Publishing, LLC

Kansas City • Sydney • London

10 11 12 13 14 MLT 10 9 8 7 6 5 4 3 2 1

ISBN-13: 978-0-7407-9128-4
ISBN-10: 0-7407-9128-1

Library of Congress Control Number: 2009943089

www.andrewsmcmeel.com

Attention: Schools and Businesses
Andrews McMeel books are available at quantity discounts with bulk purchase for educa-
tional, business, or sales promotional use. For information, please write to: Special Sales
Department, Andrews McMeel Publishing, LLC, 1130 Walnut Street, Kansas City, Missouri
64106.

READER'S NOTE

Due to space constraints, not all of the original manuscript is included in this book.
Those interested in reading additional excerpts can find them at this address:
www.UnitedStatesofBaseball.com

**For Sophia,
who makes me smile**

CONTENTS

QUIPS, QUOTATIONS, AND CHARACTERS
Page 1

The 1st • Page 3

Character Profile: *Ralph Kiner*

The 2nd • Page 31

Character Profile: *Jim Bouton*

The 9th • Page 221

Character Profile: *Casey Stengel*

NICKNAMES • Page 251

THE 20
GREATEST BASEBALL PRANKS
EVER PULLED
Page 309

Character Profile: *Moe Drabowsky*

QUIPS, QUOTATIONS, *and* CHARACTERS

The 1st

Dubious Achievements

I've set records that will never be equaled. I hope 90 percent of them don't even get printed.

BOB UECKER

This sets up the possibility of losing 162 games, which would probably be a record. In the National League, at least.

CASEY STENGEL,
on the '62 Mets' starting the year at 0–9

[The Cubs] scored 13 runs, a playoff record. We scored zero, which tied another playoff record.

DICK WILLIAMS, on Game One of the
'84 National League Championship Series

Agents

A complete ballplayer today is one who can hit, field, run, throw, and pick the right agent.

BOB LURIE

Baseball fights are to fighting what artificial turf is to grass—it looks like a fight and sounds like a fight, but it isn't really a fight. For instance, nobody insults anybody's mother or heritage, primarily because so many of the players are related by agent.

RON LUCIANO

On a good day, he's merely indifferent, on others he's as downright nasty as anyone making $3 million can possibly be. But his agent loves him.

BOB KLAPISCH, on Vince Coleman

All the old guys get here early. We need to make sure we wake up.

TOM GLAVINE, on spring training

I don't mind turning 50. It's just that at the beginning of the season I was 43.

HANK GREENWALD

I've given the Cardinals some of the best years of my life. Now I'm going to give them some of the worst.

JACK BUCK

I thought you were dead, but you look good.

ANONYMOUS FAN, on 80-something coach Eddie Popowski

That's the hell of it. You get smart only when you begin getting old.

ALLIE REYNOLDS

We've had hits from time to time, but they weren't timely hits at the right time.

GARY CARTER

I hit it out, but it didn't go out.

RICKEY HENDERSON, on a long single

I did my job. The ball didn't do its job.

COCO CRISP

I lost it in the shade.

FRENCHY BORDAGARAY,
on misplaying a ball on a cloudy day

YOGI BERRA: I lost it in the sky.
CASEY STENGEL: The sky's been there for years.

The only thing that keeps this organization from being recognized as one of the finest is wins and losses at the major league level.

CHUCK LAMAR, on the Devil Rays

Dick Allen

He sported long muttonchop sideburns, a mustache, and tinted aviator glasses. It was like having Super Fly at first base.

RICHARD ROEPER

He didn't like to practice. Always felt it wasn't in his contract. He just signed up for the games.

BOB UECKER

I can play anywhere; first, third, left field. Anywhere but
Philadelphia.

ALLEN, on his future plans

It was a relationship based on mutual respect. [White Sox manager Chuck Tanner] thought a superstar like Allen had a divine
right to play by his own rules. Allen thought Tanner was right.

DIEGO MUSILLI

Attendance Woes

It was the first time in history that everyone in the stands got a
foul ball.

DAVE LaPOINT, on a Giants game with 1,632 fans

300,000 free tickets.

GRAIG NETTLES, on what it would take to attract 75,000 to the Indians' home opener

If I were a young man in Cleveland and I wanted to take my
girlfriend out for a nice quiet evening, someplace dark where we
could be alone, I'd take her to an Indians game.

KEN LEVINE

In this town, a scalper could starve to death.

DICK YOUNG, on Baltimore

This would have been a good year to paint the ballpark seats.

GERALD PERRY

Autographs

I'll sign anything but veal cutlets.

CASEY STENGEL

I've got to sign this. These people came all the way from Texas.

YOGI BERRA, giving autographs at a convention in Houston

I enjoyed signing autographs. Until the major leagues, the only people who'd seem interested in my autographs were my bank manager and the power company.

RON LUCIANO

When I was a little kid, teachers used to punish me by making me sign my name 100 times.

WILLIE WILSON, on why he refused to sign autographs

No autographs.

RUBEN SIERRA, after a stranger approached and said, "Hi, Ruben, I'm Phil Rizzuto"

SIGN HERE

For almost as long as fans have followed baseball action on the field, they've asked for baseball signatures on paper.

The most interesting autograph stories come from unusually timed requests. Once, a fan jumped out of the stands in the middle of a game, ran to outfielder Ken Griffey, Jr., produced a ball and a pen, and, as the security guards closed in on him, asked the startled star for an autograph. Another time, Yogi Berra was recognized by a fan while the two of them were doing their business at adjoining urinals; when the fan suddenly turned to ask for an autograph, Yogi found himself with a wet pair of shoes.

Barry Bonds got an autograph request from the judge presiding over his divorce proceedings, and Tim Raines took a request from the arbitrator who was ruling on his salary request, but the most unusual autograph request of all time was probably fielded by Ted Williams. While serving as a combat pilot in the Korean War, Williams was forced into a fiery, death-defying plane crash at his air base and, just as he staggered away from the flaming wreck, an air force officer rushed up to Teddy Ballgame, checked to see if he was all right and . . . asked for his autograph.

The moral of all these stories? It pays for seekers to be bold: The loitering fan, urinal guy, judge, arbitrator, and colonel all ended up with their prize momentos.

Ballparks

Baker Bowl had the charm of a city dump but not the size. If the right fielder had beer on his breath, as he frequently did, the first baseman could smell it.

RED SMITH

The Grand Canyon with seats.

ED ROEBUCK, on the L.A. Coliseum

The biggest hair dryer in the world.

JOE PEPITONE, on the Astrodome

If, in some distant century, it becomes necessary to transport thousands of earth colonists to Alpha Centauri, I picture them making the trip in something that looks rather like Olympic Stadium.

ART HILL

All around you could see rust and dripping asbestos and exposed wires that would occasionally spark. The floor stuck like flypaper. It would have been a good place to interrogate people.

JOE POSNANSKI, on Municipal Stadium

I don't think there are any good uses for nuclear weapons, but then, this may be one.

DAN QUISENBERRY, on the Metrodome

Ernie Banks

Without Ernie Banks, the Cubs would finish in Albuquerque.

JIMMY DYKES

The greatest man to play on a wretched team since Robert E. Lee.

SCOTT SIMON

I used to say to Ernie, "Look at the dark sky. It's cloudy. It's not a great day." And he'd say, "There's a sun behind those clouds, my man."

JOHNNY ROSEBORO

The Cubs lost over 2,000 ball games with Ernie Banks on the roster. I strongly suspect that the "Let's play two!" thing was a plea for revenge.

DIEGO MUSILLI

Bars

The Last Place You Stop Before Going Home.

Motto for Boston's "Third Base Saloon"

I never took my troubles home with me. I left them in bars along the way.

BOB LEMON

[Don] Gullett will go to the Hall of Fame and I'll go to the Eliot Lounge.

BILL LEE, after losing to the Reds' pitcher in the '75 World Series. (He was only half right.)

The Basement

On a clear day they could see seventh place.

FRESCO THOMPSON, on the '20 Phillies

When I think of some of those other teams I had, I was wondering whether I was managing a baseball team or a golf course. You know what I mean—one pro to a club.

CASEY STENGEL, on the mid-1930s Dodgers

Back when I managed the Boston Braves in 1941 and '42, it took me both years to win over 100 games.

CASEY STENGEL, on the Yanks' winning 103 games

We had a rainout and held a victory party.

JOE GARAGIOLA, on the 112-loss Pirates of 1952

If you wanna see the Mets in first, turn the 'paper upside down.

New York adage, early 1960s

After the Iran hostage crisis ended with the Americans coming home, several of them were given free lifetime passes to Met games, and that might not have been the best of decisions, given their 100-loss seasons. I heard at least one reporter murmuring "Haven't they suffered enough?"

DIEGO MUSILLI

GO BRAVES! AND TAKE THE FALCONS WITH YOU!

Early '80s fan banner

Rochester, Baltimore. It's all the same. It's all Triple-A.

JEFF BALLARD,
on his minor league demotion

They say "win some, lose some," but in the case of the '03 Tigers, they were only half right.

DIEGO MUSILLI

PITTSBURGH BASEBALL: REBUILDING SINCE 1992

Recent fan banner

Most people would never understand how someone could love a team that has never won anything of much consequence. The Rangers are like the Cubs without the history.

GREG SINDELAR

Just a few years ago, the Mariners were mediocre or slightly below average in every phase of the game. Looking back, those were the good old days.

DIEGO MUSILLI, on the Mariners' 101-loss season in 2008

[Ted Williams] was always asking questions, looking for new theories on hitting, telling his own theories. One time, he started asking me which was my power hand. When I left him, I started thinking about all the things he told me and I didn't get a hit for about 25 at-bats.

MICKEY MANTLE

How can you think and hit at the same time?

YOGI BERRA

You know you're going bad when your wife takes you aside and tries to change your batting stance. And you take her advice.

THOMAS BOSWELL

Beanballs

Some people give their bodies to science; I gave mine to baseball.

RON HUNT,
on his 243 career hit-by-pitches

I think he's still waiting for that ball to break.

GRAIG NETTLES,
on Ron Cey's beaning in the '81 World Series

That's what happens when you don't wear a batting helmet.

CHARLIE HOUGH,
after a seagull was struck dead by a thrown ball

All that jumping around, tipping hats, shaking hands—I wouldn't waste a pitch hitting them. I'd hit 'em in the dugout.

EARLY WYNN,
on today's showboating hitters

Bed Checks

Curfews and bed checks are time-honored baseball traditions, and they met with a certain amount of success with our ball club. I can honestly say that every time a bed check was held, they found all the beds.

BILL LEE

Suppose somebody told Johnny Sain to conduct a bed check. He'd tell them to take the phone and stick it up their receivers.

JIM BOUTON

Beer

I worry about all those foul balls. Those baseballs are more expensive than you'd think, but I've noticed that people knock over three or four cups of beer in the scramble and then buy more beer, so I guess we just about break even.

AMON CARTER, JR.

The late Senator Edward Kennedy was honored before the game with a solemn ceremony and "Taps" and all of that. With all due respect to the recently departed, however, don't you think he would much rather have been honored by the allowance of beer sales past the seventh inning?

CRAIG CALCATERRA

If we'd known that was gonna happen, we'd have said we liked women and beer.

HOMELESS MAN/RED SOX FAN "JOHN,"
after a newspaper profile prompted his
fellow fans to donate game tickets

Albert Belle

Let's try to find ten good things to say about Albert Belle:

10. So far as we know, he's never killed anyone. . . .

 7. He has never appeared on *The Jerry Springer Show*. . . .

 5. He hasn't been arrested in several years. . . .

 2. He has never spoken favorably about Adolf Hitler, Saddam Hussein, or any other foreign madman. . . .

BILL JAMES

He just put his name on a new breakfast cereal, "Albert Belle's Slugger Cereal." It should be released in Baltimore under the name "Albert's Not-So-Cheerios."

PETER SCHMUCK

Bench Warmers

Ballplayers all say they "take things one day at a time." Some mean it more than others.

KEN LEVINE

I'll stay here so I never forget how close I am to the highway.

JIM BOUTON, on lockering next to the clubhouse door

This is the best pennant race I've ever watched.

GEORGE THOMAS, on 1967

Play me or keep me.

PHIL LINZ

He likes to complain about not playing, which is what he does best.

PAT GILLICK, on Mike Marshall

Bench Warmers: Kurt Bevacqua Division

I think I hold the record for most games watched, career.

BEVACQUA

The guy played so little during the regular season, he probably didn't know where third base was.

DICK WILLIAMS, on Bevacqua's failed triple attempt in the '84 World Series

I experienced a fantasy of my own—I got to play an entire game.

BEVACQUA, on participating in a fantasy camp

This deal indicates that Major League Baseball is healthy, Kevin Mitchell is wealthy, and the Giants are wise.

JOE SROBA, on his client's
$15 million deal with San Francisco

For me, a $84 million contract would have to be for 168 years. My kids would have to work for the Twins, too.

MIKE TROMBLEY, on Mike Piazza's
turning down a big contract offer

$91 million is an awful lot of money, but don't kid yourself—it's not an easy paycheck. This man, for the next seven years, has to attend every single Mets game.

DAVID LETTERMAN, on Mike Piazza's new contract

Big Outs

Frank Howard used to scare home runs out of the park.

JOE POSNANSKI, on the 6'7" slugger

Fighting him is like fighting a two-story building.

BILLY MARTIN, on 6'8" Gene Conley

You know, I'm beginning to like it, too, Gene.

TOMMY DAVIS, on 6'6" Gene Brabender's
preference for country music in the clubhouse

Biography Titles

Fowl Tips: My Favorite Chicken Recipes by Wade Boggs . . . *It Pays to Steal* by Maury Wills . . . *Planet of the Umps* by Ken Kaiser . . . *Some of My Best Friends Are Crazy* by Jay Johnstone . . . *Sox and the City* by Richard Roeper . . . *The Umpire Strikes Back* by Ron Luciano . . . *Veeck as in Wreck* by Bill Veeck . . . *The Catcher in the Wry* by Bob Uecker . . . *The Wrong Stuff* by Bill Lee . . . *The Zen of Zim* by Don Zimmer.

The most accurately titled book since Anne Heche's *Call Me Crazy*.

JIM CAPLE, on David Wells's *Perfect I'm Not*

PLAYING BY THE BOOK

Many major leaguers are obsessed with books. Unfortunately, they're mostly interested with record books and checkbooks, and that usually doesn't leave a lot of time for literary tomes.

A lack of book learning isn't a particularly big secret within the game. When Johnny Pesky was asked about his favorite book, he cited *The Boston Red Sox Media Guide*, while Yogi Berra named comic books. A playboy named Bo Belinsky said his favorite book was . . . *Playboy* magazine.

Others aren't even that ambitious; When a California junior high school named its library after Tommy Lasorda, one beat writer wondered if the Dodgers manager had ever read a book. Pete Rose's ex-wife claimed that Pete had, indeed, read one, and it was entitled *The Pete Rose Story*.

You'd think that disinterested ballplayers wouldn't necessarily make for the greatest book writers. And you'd be right. But at least they don't put on airs.

Babe Ruth used to tell people that his favorite scribe was Christy Walsh, the ghostwriter who handled most of the columns and books that came out under the "Babe Ruth" byline. David Wells once claimed that he was misquoted in a book, which wouldn't be all that surprising except for the fact that Wells supposedly wrote the book in question. Is it possible to misquote yourself?

One way or the other, it can be a world of surprises for player "authors." One beat reporter claims that he once came across Johnny Damon in the Red Sox clubhouse, asked him to sign his *Idiot* autobiography, and then, when the reporter returned a few minutes later, he found Damon sitting back, reading along and nodding as if perusing the pages for the first time.

If baseball isn't a business, General Motors is a sport.

JIM MURRAY

Baseball owners would have you believe that they are more sportsmen than businessmen, and it is true that money's the last thing they ever think about—just before they fall asleep at night.

JOE MORGAN

For more than a century the sport has been home to more dug-in, backward, stone-headed traditionalists than any other subset of American society; baseball owners make the Republican Party seem like the Paris Commune.

MATT TAIBBI

It was like hearing that the church had sold out.

BABE RUTH, on the "Black Sox" gambling scandal

They ought to put bleachers in here and charge admission.

BUCK WEAVER, on the courtroom's overflow crowds

Barry Bonds

Here are the only things that could tarnish Barry Bonds's reputation, at this point:

1. Committing double murder of Tom Brokaw and Dame Judi Dench.
2. Defecting to Afghanistan, joining Taliban, leading Afghan baseball team to gold medal over American team in Beijing.
3. Running high-end dog-fighting ring where the dog fights take place on Princess Diana's grave.

Blogger **"KEN TREMENDOUS"**

What the ultra-diplomatic [Bruce] Bochy said of Bonds was, "He learned. That's why you go down the line. They caught him." He learned? He learned? That was Bonds's 2,970th major league game. Learning to hustle at that point in your career is like Hugh Hefner taking a sex-education class.

SCOTT OSTLER

Books

Every chapter in the book is Chapter 11.

BILL SCHEFT, on Pete Rose's latest biography

Before he writes a book, he should read one.

DALLAS GREEN, on Rickey Henderson's upcoming autobiography

Booooo

In Cleveland, you couldn't root for [the Yankees], but you would boo them in awe.

GEORGE STEINBRENNER, on growing up in Ohio

What's Frank trying to do, steal all my fans?

MARVELOUS MARV THRONEBERRY,
on Frank Thomas's two-error game

I never heard my last name the whole time I pitched [in Boston]. I'd hear, "Now pitching for the Red Sox, Tom Boooooo."

TOM HOUSE

These are the kinds of people who stand in your way in supermarket aisles and cut you off on the Southern State Parkway and boo their cats for not being dogs.

GREG W. PRINCE, on Met fans

Bouncing Back

Look, we can't lose 'em all.

FRANK THOMAS, on the '62 Mets

REPORTER: Are you always this downhearted after you lose a World Series game?
BILL LEE: Why be downhearted? I did my best. I'll still be alive tomorrow, barring a traffic accident.

Brawls

[Bill] Lee said that the Yankees fought like a bunch of Times Square hookers, that we used our purses. Lee ended up with a broken shoulder and two black eyes. He must've run into some pretty rough hookers.

GRAIG NETTLES

[Graig] Nettles came over, picked me up, and dropped me on my shoulder. He later claimed that he was only trying to keep me out of the fight. He did do that. I guess Graig's idea of keeping the peace was to arrange for me to get a lot of bed rest in a quiet hospital.

BILL LEE

You have to love when moron reporters ask pitchers questions like, "Were you trying to hit him?" after one of those retaliation/beanball brawls. What kind of answers are they expecting? "Yes, I was trying to hit him. I was actually aiming for his head, because I was hoping to put him into a coma. Could you suspend me for ten games instead of two? And could you triple my fine? Thanks."

BILL SIMMONS

BASEBRAWLS

Umpire Ron Luciano once said that today's ballplayers don't really brawl and fight, mostly because they're related by agent. That might be true nowadays, but it wasn't always true.

During the 1973 National League Championship Series, for instance, the Mets' Bud Harrelson and the Reds' Pete Rose tussled at second base as their teams' benches cleared. The confrontation was emotional enough in itself—several haymaker punches were thrown—but the Reds' Pedro Borbon put a capper on the experience as he slowly walked back to his dugout; Pedro absentmindedly picked up a cap, discovered it belonged to a Met opponent, and then, newly enraged, took a bite out of it. Believe it or not, Borbon some-how ripped the blue cloth into three ragged pieces.

About ten years later, Bob Horner was on the disabled list when he witnessed a brawl involving his Braves teammates. He responded by racing from the press box down to the clubhouse, hastily putting on his Atlanta uniform, then coming out to join the fight in progress.

For my money, one of the most memorable fights involved the sometimes unstable, always interesting Jimmy Piersall.

In 1961, Piersall was minding his own business, playing center field for the Indians, when two young spectators climbed out of the Yankee Stadium stands and ran out to his position. Piersall saw the duo coming, scored a single knockout punch on the first attacker, then turned to the other one, who promptly turned tail and ran away. Piersall very nearly managed to, quite literally, kick the kid's ass before he ran into the clutches of late-coming security guards.

The Bronx fans, ever impressed by tough guys, even those wear-ing opponent uniforms, gave Piersall a big, spontaneous cheer as he trotted off at the end of the inning.

The Bright Side

99 more like that and we win the pennant.

> **CASEY STENGEL**, on the
> '62 Mets' first win after nine straight losses

It's a partial sellout.

> **SKIP CARAY**, on a Braves crowd of 6,000

Anyone with a bat in his hands is dangerous.

> **VINCE LLOYD**, on the Cubs' lame hitting

Without losers, where would the winners be?

> **BILL VEECK**

The Bright Side: Boos

Fans don't boo nobodies.

REGGIE JACKSON, on why he didn't mind them

When I'm on the road, my greatest ambition is to get a standing boo.

AL HRABOSKY

It's an honor to get booed by 30,000 fans in Boston. I was booed by 2,000 at Candlestick Park.

JACK CLARK

When it's ten years later and they still hate you, that's what you call charisma.

RON DAVIS, on being booed
long after his retirement

The Bright Side: Hitting

We played well. We just didn't hit.

JIMY WILLIAMS

Well, we did keep out of the double play.

DENNIS LAMP, on the
Red Sox hitting into two triple plays

The Bright Side: Numbers

At this rate, I'll be a 20-game winner in 18 years.

MATT BEECH, on his 1–11 record

It could just as easily have gone the other way.

DON ZIMMER, after a 4–4 road trip

The Bright Side: Pitching

The way I look at it, a home run is just a fly ball that goes a little farther.

RON DARLING

We had a lot of good exercise chasing those balls in the outfield today.

BILL VIRDON, on losing a World Series game 12–0

At least they all had their off-days on the same day.

JOE TORRE,
on his pitching staff's giving up 15 runs

Hey, at least no one blew a save in this one.

CRAIG CALCATERRA, on the Nationals' 7–1 loss

They've been ineffective lately. But, from the other side, it has been exciting.

TOM TREBELHORN

The Bright Side: Records

Those other 60 guys helped that record, too.

TRACY STALLARD, on giving up
Roger Maris's 61st home run

I was just in the right place at the right time.

CESAR GERONIMO, on being Nolan Ryan's 3,000th strikeout victim

All I have to do is talk. Some people have to think as well.

BOB WOLFF

Just how far should an announcer go in criticizing his team? A number of factors come into play. Do you have the background or experience to support your criticism? Are you employed by the radio station or the team? Do you have integrity? How big are the ballplayers? Can they hurt you?

KEN LEVINE

Ballplayers as Broadcasters

I'm very, very speechless.

JOHNNY LOGAN, on being hired as a broadcaster

He quit baseball to become a star.

LOU PINIELLA, on reserve-catcher-turned-broadcaster Fran Healy

Maybe now he'll get a complete game.

RICH DONNELLY, on Bob Walk's new career

I heard doctors revived a man who had been dead for four and a half minutes. When they asked him what it was like to be dead, he said it was like listening to Phil Rizzuto during a rain delay.

DAVID LETTERMAN

He announces the games as if he's a Little League dad and every single player on the roster is his son.

RICHARD ROEPER, on Ken "The Hawk" Harrelson

The Bronx

I like when the stadiums have promotional nights. They give stuff away, T-shirts, badges, but they don't always go well. Back in the

1970s, the Yankees, at Yankee Stadium, gave away free baseball bats—thousands of drunk guys in the South Bronx at night . . . "Let's give them all weapons! What could possibly go wrong?!" It's like giving Dick Cheney a martini and a handgun. There's a very predictable result.

CRAIG FERGUSON

It was my favorite name of all: The Bronx. It was the toughest, most perfect word I'd ever heard. It sounded like a punch in the gut. It grabbed you by the collar. Bronx. And what kind of place had "the" in front of it? Whatever it was, there could only be one. After all, it wasn't "A Bronx."

DAYN PERRY

The Bronx Zoo

The crazy times really began after Reggie [Jackson] announced that he was "the straw that stirred the drink" and, of course, Billy [Martin] right away wanted Reggie to know that he, Billy, was the straw. And all the while, there was George [Steinbrenner], sitting in his office, thinking he was stirring the drinks. I'll tell you, for a couple of years there, there was an awful lot of stirring going on. Something crazy was going on every single day.

GRAIG NETTLES

Rooting for the Yankees once was like rooting for U.S. Steel. Now it's like rooting for Ringling Bros. and Barnum and Bailey.

FRANK DOLSON on the "Bronx Zoo" era

I can't wait to see what happens next.

BOB LEMON, on the '77 Yankees

Before [Bob] Lemon took over, the only times the word "character" was used in the Yankee clubhouse it was followed by the word "assassination."

PETER GAMMONS

Brooklyn

The borough of churches and bad ball clubs, many of which I had.

CASEY STENGEL

All they cared about was their family, their job, and the Dodgers. And I don't know which one was the most important.

DOLPH CAMILLI, on the Brooklyn fans

Brothers

Joe was the best hitter, Dom had the best arm, and Vince had the best voice.

ANONYMOUS REPORTER, on the DiMaggio brothers

When brothers played in the majors, the Phillies usually wound up with the one who produced less. We had Frank Torre instead of Joe, Ken Brett instead of George, Mike Maddux instead of Greg, Rick Surhoff instead of B.J., and Jeremy Giambi instead of Jason. If there had been a Zeppo Alou, the Phillies would have signed him.

HAROLD HERMAN

There I was trying to play high school baseball and I've got one brother starting in right field for the Red Sox and the other brother starting in center field. When I would strike out they would yell, "Hey, Conigliaro, you're a bum just like your brother Tony and your brother Billy."

RICHIE CONIGLIARO

Andy and Adam LaRoche are like the modern-day Cal and Bill Ripken, only they're both Bill Ripken.

ESPN PAGE 2

Brushbacks

If they're thinking of living through the at-bat, it takes their minds off hitting a little bit.

MITCH WILLIAMS

In situations when a pitcher might throw at a batter, it's up to the umpire to decide when an inside pitch is actually an attempt to hit a batter. The problem with that rule is that I'm not a mind reader; I can barely read my mail.

KEN KAISER

Brushbacks: Early Wynn Division

His idea of an intentional walk is four pitches at the batter's head.

ANONYMOUS PLAYER, on Wynn's style

Some day I may get all nine of 'em.

WYNN

HIT THE DIRT!

They're sometimes called purpose pitches. Or chin music. Or bow ties. Or brushbacks.

Whatever the name, pitchers have always found ways to deliver inside pitches designed to not-so-gently remind opponents that they shouldn't get too, too comfortable in the batter's box. Often, the fastballs come far enough inside that the hitters have to leave their feet, hit the dirt, and maybe contemplate what it would be like to get hit by a future pitch.

Certain individuals have always gone farther than others, though. It's said that Hugh Casey, a hard-throwing Dodger in the 1940s, once took a dubious balk call, then started aiming his fastballs at George

Magerkurth, the offending home plate umpire. Stan Williams, a latter-day Dodger, kept a book on those hitters who had victimized him in the past; he'd tuck a "hit list" inside his cap during a game, then go after 'em. Managers Birdie Tebbetts and Alvin Dark were known to fine their pitchers for not hitting batters on orders.

When it came to brushbacks, the all-time "hit king" may have been Early Wynn. Wynn was so mean that they said he'd brush back his own grandmother, and he admitted it was true ("My grandma could really hit the curveball," he explained). He'd knock down anybody for anything, too: It was said he would try to hit runners during pickoff attempts at first base, he brushed back guys for taking aggressive swings during exhibition games, and he once threw at a guy who was standing too close to the on-deck circle.

Character Profile: RALPH KINER

Award-winning sportswriter Leonard Koppett once estimated that the typical broadcasting team can utter tens of thousands of words during the course of a two-and-a-half-hour ball game, more than enough verbiage to fill a good-sized novella.

That's a whole lot of talk and, of course, there has to be some quality for all the quantity, too. Apart from a working knowledge of the game and a grasp on the ever-evolving facts of the on-field situation, a broadcaster is expected to find all the right words, string them together in grammatical sentences, and then try to weave them into enough paragraphs and chapters for a game story that's, hopefully, both informative and diverting. When you think about it, the basic challenges in off-the-cuff, fast-as-life broadcasting are almost enough to make a linguistics professor weep with frustration.

And Ralph Kiner was no linguistics professor. He was a base-ball man.

Kiner first gained fame as a slugger for the Pittsburgh Pirates, winning seven straight National League home run titles in a Hall of Fame playing career that stretched from the 1940s to the 1950s. Not long after retiring, in 1962, Kiner was invited into the booth for the debut season of the New York Mets, teaming with Lindsey Nelson and Bob Murphy in what became one of the longest lasting announcing teams in the national pastime's history. In many ways, he was the real "Mr. Met"—for his outgoing personality, fan-friendly ways, and offbeat ("Kiner's Korner") interviews, he's been honored as one of the most influential figures in franchise history.

The accolades made no mention of Kiner's adept grasp of English grammar, though, which was understandable. You see, for better and for worse, he didn't have one; as a broadcaster, he was still an old ballplayer. Ralph provided plenty of inside-baseball insights, but when it came to a whole range of broadcasting mistakes, he could also flub it all.

Stating the Obvious: This ever-popular maneuver pads a sentence with extra info. ("Sutcliffe was Rookie of the Year in his first year." "All of the Mets road wins against L.A. this year have been at Dodger Stadium.")

The Ol' Switcheroo: This is a verbal gaffe in which one concept is introduced, then followed up with completely unrelated material. ("The Mets are winless in the month of Atlanta." "Jay Bell is 0 for 6 in this series with 10 homers and 52 RBIs.").

The Ol' Switcheroo, Part Two: Pretty straightforward—your brain switches words in midsentence. ("Rookie Wilson was a candidate for Mookie of the Year.")

The Impossibility: This is when you say one thing, do a midsentence flip, then say the exact opposite. ("Jones allowed four earned runs, three unearned." "Some quiet guys are inwardly outgoing.")

The Name Game: The old-timer's perennial trick, where a latter-day player is introduced by a name from a previous generation. ("Dwight Gooden" becomes "Greg Goossen." "Darryl Strawberry" becomes "Darryl Throneberry.")

Come Again? Pretty self-explanatory. ("It's Father's Day, so to all you fathers out there, Happy Birthday!" "The Hall of Fame ceremonies will be held on July 31st and 32nd.")

It didn't take too long for the Kiner faux pas to make the rounds, all of them provoking a fair amount of head-scratching and chuckles among the general public. "Kiner-isms" gradually became the "Yogi-ism" malaprops of the New York "err" waves, but, unlike some of the quips attributed to Mr. Berra, all of Kiner's gems were 100 percent verifiably, undeniably authentic.

The jocular Kiner, for his part, mostly took his quite unintentional wordsmithing in stride, conceding that, in his line of work, some mistakes were inevitable. As Ralph once said, "That's the great thing about baseball—you never know what's going on."

The 2nd

Missed Calls

You called him out, but the 50,000 people here know he was safe!

BILL VIRDON

I've seen the films of that play maybe fifty times, and Robinson is out every time.

YOGI BERRA, on Jackie Robinson's (successful) steal
during the '55 World Series

Friday nights Red Sox–Orioles game, home plate umpire gives the full, dramatic strike three call against Coco Crisp. The only problem is that it is only strike two, leaving the umpire with a little egg on his face. Coco almost gets run when he tells the umpire, "And it still wasn't a strike!"

ANONYMOUS BLOGGER

When the players make mistakes and try to put the pressure on us, we just have to handle it, not let our emotions get in the game, and stay steady. Even when we're wrong we're right.

ERIC GREG

If you don't think you're out, read the morning paper.

BILL McGOWAN

It might not be right, but that's the way it is.

KEN KAISER

Oh, Canada

The Expos stayed on the field, so I went up to bat. I figured maybe they do things differently in Canada.

PHIL NEVIN, on coming to the plate
after the third out in the inning

We had him throwing 88 on the radar gun, but with the Canadian exchange rate, it was only 83.

MIKE FLANAGAN,
on Mike Boddicker's fastball in Toronto

I like Jason Bay. I'm not saying anything disparaging against Canadians because I've married two of them.

BILL LEE

Jose Canseco

Nolan Ryan recorded his 5,000th strikeout on a 96 mph fastball. It's ironic it was against the A's, since that's the speed Jose Canseco drives through a school zone.

MARK PATRICK

40 home runs, 40 steals, 40 moving violations.

JIM LEFEBVRE, on Canseco's '88 season

Cards

Hey, if you can make money off me defacing a baseball card, good luck.

ROD BECK, on autographs

I prefer to remember Mickey as he is.

YOGI BERRA, on Mickey Mantle's invaluable rookie card

CARDED

For a young boy, getting his picture on a baseball card can be a dream come true. For some ballplayers, it can be a license to be a kid again.

Sometimes the joke's a bit lewd. While serving as Tigers manager in 1972, for instance, Billy Martin posed for his Topps card while placing his middle finger down the bat handle, secretly giving the world the ol' one-finger salute. Billy Ripken did Martin one better for his card shot in the late '80s, as his bat had a clearly visible obscenity scrawled on its knob.

On other occasions, mistaken identity was the name of the game. In 1969, the "Aurelio Rodriguez" card actually depicted Angels batboy Leonard Garcia. Gary Pettis pulled the same ruse in '85, only he had his younger brother stand in for the pic; it was a good deed for the family, as it turned out, since the kid never made it to the majors on his own.

Cards have also provided subtle exercises in self-mockery. Duane Kuiper, owner of a minuscule .316 career slugging percentage, once posed with a broken bat over his shoulder, and chronic defensive liability Mickey Hatcher was once depicted wearing a fielding glove about the size of a serving tray. Bob Uecker went into a left-handed stance in a mid-'60s card, as if it wasn't hard enough for him to hit .200 while batting righty.

Rod Carew

He's the only guy I know who can go 4 for 3.

ALAN BANNISTER

When we get hot, we go up to .300. When he gets hot, he goes up to .500.

DOUG DECINCES

He can't miss. If I were him I'd go looking for wallets.

JERRY McNERTNEY

Chatter

YOGI BERRA: Have a good dinner last night?
TED WILLIAMS: The food is all bad here in New York.
BERRA: If you leave a tip, the food gets better.
WILLIAMS: Shut up, you ugly bastard.
(Pause.)
BERRA: Done any good fishing lately?

Never met a microphone he didn't like.

BILL REYNOLDS, on George Scott

When we have closed-door meetings we want to tape his mouth shut. He always has to put in his two cents and it isn't worth two cents.

MIKE LaVALLIERE, on Andy Van Slyke

His strong point? He gives good TV interviews.

JIM FREGOSI, on Steve Lyons

If you ask him what time it is, he'll tell you how to make a watch.

BOB LEMON, on Tommy John

Sheff had one of the quickest swings I've ever seen. Maybe it was trying to catch up to his mouth.

DIEGO MUSILLI, on Gary Sheffield

Cheating in baseball is just like hot dogs, french fries, and cold Cokes.

BILLY MARTIN

If you can cheat, I wouldn't wait one pitch longer.

GEORGE BAMBERGER, to a struggling hurler

CHEATIN'

There's an old expression in the national pastime: If you ain't cheatin', you ain't tryin'.

Major league competitors have always known that most opponents are willing to do just about whatever they can to get ahead, which is a prime reason why they rarely get too worked up by cheaters' plying their trade.

Gaylord Perry, for one, featured one of the great spitballs of all time and, unable to either stop the pitcher or hit the illegal pitch, some opponents simply chose to make light of it. Hank Aaron once gave him a baseball marked with an "X" and an inscription reading "Spit here." Reggie Jackson once took a full Gatorade cooler over to the diamond, suggesting that Gaylord dip the ball in it. Don Sutton, who was known to scuff a few baseballs in his time, once gave Perry a small tub of Vaseline, only to receive a sheet of sandpaper in return.

Roger McDowell once showed up before a game wearing a carpenter's belt stocked with emery boards, files, rasps, and several other tricky tools of the trade, but the Niekro brothers probably topped him in the mid-1980s. Shortly after Joe Niekro was suspended for taking a nail file with him out to the mound, Phil Niekro reportedly sent him a power sander with a 50-foot extension cord.

Chemistry

How can a player have one full year so far above and beyond his natural talents? As a man who has spent his entire life in baseball I can tell you, without fear of contradiction, that I don't have the slightest idea. Other baseball men will look wise and say, "Momentum!" That means they don't have the slightest idea, either.

BILL VEECK

A pinch-hit double with the bases loaded.

JIM FREY, on his "chemistry" definition

Yeah, and we're missing a little geography and arithmetic around here, too.

WHITEY HERZOG, on the Cardinals' lack of chemistry

Dear Chicago

Nelson Algren once wrote that Chicago was "an October sort of city even in spring." Please note that he was referring to the weather, not the playoffs.

DIEGO MUSILLI

It's been said that in Chicago there are two seasons, winter and construction. For Cub fans, there is only one, and it always comes next year.

RICK TALLEY

The Church of Baseball

Baseball is like church—many attend but few understand.

WES WESTRUM

Stadiums are the cathedrals of baseball. Or, in my case, synagogues.

BILLY CRYSTAL

In some respects, it could be likened to our gatherings. . . . It had its own ritual—they began with a song. . . . There were times we all stood up and then sat down. . . . There was a featured soloist [Harry Caray]. . . . Many attempts were made to take our money. . . . There were moments of extreme elation and deep depression. . . . I'm not sure, but I think I even heard a prayer or two whispered.

Reverend **JOHN AKER**, on the similarities between the church and the church of baseball

Cincy

It's possible to spend money anywhere in the world if you put your mind to it, something I proved conclusively by running up huge debts in Cincinnati.

LEO DUROCHER

It's a good thing I stayed in Cincinnati for four years—it took me that long to learn how to spell it.

ROCKY BRIDGES

Hello, Cleveland!

Real Clevelanders. They all seemed to have incomprehensible jobs like bending refrigerators or crushing carburetors into dust with their bare hands. They lived hard lives. They drank beer that smelled like gasoline out of wax paper cups and they smoked Marlboros and Kents without filters and would take a nip now and again from a flask containing schnapps powerful enough to burn through metal and they believed that this time, definitely this time, Rick Manning would come through.

JOE POSNANSKI, on Indian fans of the '70s

There's a nice symmetry there. The team's driven people to drink for 40 years now, and the liquor tax was used to build a new stadium.

BUD SHAW

Cleveland and Geography

That's what you get when you build a ballpark by the ocean.

DENNIS "OIL CAN" BOYD,
on Municipal Stadium (which was located on Lake Erie)

It's in Ohio. Friday, it'll be in Boston.

JIMY WILLIAMS, on "the state of your pitching rotation"

To the modern-day player, a foreign country is Cleveland. A foreign phrase is, "My turn to buy."

DICK WILLIAMS

THE MISTAKE BY THE LAKE

The mid-1970s were a difficult time in this country. There was a gas crisis, the Watergate scandal, the loss in Vietnam. For some reason, people insisted on wearing bell bottoms and flair collars, sometimes at the same time. Things were difficult.

In Cleveland, it was worse. After all, they had all those problems . . . plus the Indians, the lowest of low-rent baseball clubs.

The Tribe's plentiful losses and scarce dollars led to game-watching situations that were, let's say, unique. There was the fact that they frequently drew only a few thousand fans per contest, leaving nearly 70,000 seats empty in cavernous Municipal Stadium, the infamous "Mistake by the Lake." Rain or shine, there were so few Clevelanders at the games that, it's said, players could identify individual hecklers; some swore that they could make out spectator conversations between innings, too.

The Indians were a low-budget team. They stiffed hotels with unpaid bills so many times that, at one point, the club stopped making road reservations, instead driving around to as many as three hotels before they could find one where their credit was still good. They had a home clubhouse with a heater that worked only in the summertime and junky charter planes that looked like something out of *Major League*. They couldn't hire enough security for "10 Cent Beer Night" in 1974, so when the promotion, predictably enough, devolved into an on-field riot, the Indians' opponents held off would-be attackers by wielding their own baseball bats. Things were dire.

You wouldn't believe the players' off-field clothes. Now I know why the league insists that they wear uniforms.

KEN LEVINE

A ballplayer should stay on a reporter's good side. Say nice things. Admire his clothes. Compliment him on his T-shirt.

ANDY VAN SLYKE

We'll leave the Bermuda shorts for the Beach Boys.

DICK WILLIAMS, on his team's new dress code

Clubhouses

The conditions were lousy, but it had a great big lawn out back.

KEVIN HICKEY,
on living in a minor league clubhouse

The clubhouse in the Astrodome is so big you could almost have infield practice in it. I noticed because the Seattle clubhouse was too small for chess.

JIM BOUTON

The Blue Jays' clubhouse is unbelievable. Imagine the swankiest health club you possibly can—the plushest locker rooms, the finest training equipment—and you've pictured the downtown Y compared to the Skydome. I don't understand how a player can be demoted to Triple-A and not kill himself.

KEN LEVINE

THE NAKED TRUTH

Baseball men spend anywhere from seven to eight months out of the year together, playing, working, traveling, and living with one another every day. With all that time and togetherness, there are occasions when very little comes between them.

Not even clothes.

Players become so used to showering together that shower rooms tend to become just another part of the clubhouse; they've been known to sing, debate, smoke cigars, and eat in the buff. Once, when a naked John Kruk learned that he and a teammate were traded away from San Diego, the two of them hugged in the showers—it was a spontaneous gesture that drew only a few sideways glances from their fellow ballplayers.

Casey Stengel would have had an even more memorable experience when he served as a Boston manager in the later 1930s; he was ejected from a game and taking an early shower when he found that his star pitcher had also been tossed by the umpire. Casey, completely nude and dripping wet, was ticked off enough to start back to the field, only to have an alarmed attendant hold him back at the last minute.

A fully clothed Larry MacPhail, who ran the Dodgers in the early 1940s, once walked under a running shower in order to console a grieving pitcher for a late-inning loss. Vice President Richard Nixon had much the same experience when he dropped by the Washington Senators' postgame clubhouse in the late 1950s; Nixon didn't bat an eye as he shook hands with several naked players. (Evidently he recognized them, even out of uniform.)

And then there was at least one time when a ballplayer treated nudity as something other than completely natural. It seems that when female reporters were first allowed into major league clubhouses in the late 1970s, the ever-exhuberant Sparky Lyle took to walking around the ladies while wearing a single, strategically placed sanitary sock—and it wasn't on his foot.

Coaches

In six major league seasons Billy Muffett won 16 games while losing 23. He had a 4.33 lifetime ERA, gave up 407 hits, 132 walks,

and had one shutout. In 1966, he was named pitching coach by the St. Louis Cardinals. You figure it out.

BRENDAN C. BOYD and **FRED C. HARRIS**

It's frustrating. Your job is not to get in the way of a rally.

RICH DONNELLY, on coaching third base

The Mets fired Willie Randolph as the manager. Given the way they've played, I can see it. They fired Rick Peterson as pitching coach. Given the way they've pitched, OK. But they also fired Tom Nieto as first base coach, but why, exactly? A first base coach is the baseball equivalent of an innocent bystander. Firing one is like coming on to an accident scene and punching the witness.

DIEGO MUSILLI

He does all the pitching, I do all the talking. I'd call it a good relationship.

TOM HOUSE, on coaching Randy Johnson

Coaching Advice

"Quit walking people." "Throw more strikes." What the hell do you think they were going to tell me—"Get wilder"?

STEVE DALKOWSKI, on his coaches' advice

He don't say much, but that don't matter much, because when you're out there on the mound, you got nobody to talk to.

CASEY STENGEL, on pitching guru Johnny Sain

Absolutely not. Except, of course, I'm gonna call him "sir."

Coach **WHITEY FORD**, on whether
Catfish Hunter would get special treatment

Cold Water

Omar Minaya was quick to point out after the Mets lost six of their last seven games of the season, "We spent more days in first place than any other team in baseball." Yeah. And Billy Conn was leading Joe Louis after 12 rounds, the *Titanic* sailed beautifully for three days, and didn't Abraham Lincoln just love the first two hours of the play?

WALLACE MATTHEWS

[Javier] Lopez called the seven-run inning "disappointing," which is a bit like calling Chernobyl an industrial energy mishap.

JIM CAPLE

I remember one game when he gave up six runs in five innings, all of the runs coming on four homers. He said to us, "I pitched very well. I just made four bad pitches." I guess he didn't take into account that those four pitches traveled almost 2,000 feet.

MARK FEINSAND, on Esteban Loaiza

Collapses

It was like swimming in a long, long lake, and then you drown.

COOKIE ROJAS, on the Phillies' '64 collapse

I can't believe that the Angels lost and O. J. Simpson won.

ANONYMOUS FAN, after the team finished blowing an 11-game lead on the same day of the October 1995 not-guilty verdict

Comebacks

Baseball and malaria keep coming back.

GENE MAUCH

The problem with being Comeback Player of the Year is it means you have to go somewhere before you can come back.

BERT BLYLEVEN

It was like watching a movie you've seen a hundred times, only they snuck in an alternate ending.

BILL SIMMONS, on the Red Sox winning the 2004 World Series

Comiskey Park

Not exactly sterile, but it has roughly the charm of a clean utensil drawer.

RICK TELANDER, on the new Comiskey Park

The World's Largest Outdoor Tavern.

Unofficial nickname

Commissioners

Happy [Chandler] left office for reasons of health; that is, the owners got sick of him.

RED SMITH

[Ford] Frick had a slogan of his own, a slogan that has served him throughout the years. It goes, "You boys settle it among yourselves." For that he gets paid $65,000 per year.

BILL VEECK

The nation's idiot.

CHARLIE O. FINLEY, on Commissioner Bowie Kuhn
(he explained that Kuhn was too famous to be a "village idiot")

[Bud] Selig's the kind of guy who fixes his muffler by getting a louder stereo.

KING KAUFMAN

Complaints

Don't tell people your troubles. Eighty percent of the people don't care and the other 20 percent are glad you're having them.

TOMMY LASORDA

If you want to quit, I know a bricklaying company back in Columbus.

DON ZIMMER, to complaining players

Retire.

THURMAN MUNSON'S standard response to player complaints

Conditioning Conditions

Red Auerbach used to tell me after the last game, "Now go get out of shape so you can pitch."

Former NBA player and major leaguer **GENE CONLEY**

The only reason I don't like to run is that it makes me tired.

ART FOWLER

A waist is a terrible thing to mind.

TERRY FORSTER

About as long as it takes a pitcher to warm up.

DICK ALLEN, on how long it takes for him to get into condition

Mickey Lolich didn't believe in training. He has run, that's true, but it was just once, and he only did it to flag down a passing Good Humor truck, so I'm pretty sure that doesn't count.

DIEGO MUSILLI

He seemed to prepare for games by burping.

JOE POSNANSKI, on Sidney Ponson

He's been called the hardest-working man in throw business.

MIKE WALLACE, on Roger Clemens

By 1980, I was down to one sit-up a day—half when I woke up and half when I went to bed.

ERIC GREGG

Wait until he sees me hit.

Rookie **TED WILLIAMS**, when told "wait until you see [Jimmie] Foxx hit"

It's not easy being a man who is embarrassed by short home runs.

THOMAS BOSWELL, on Reggie Jackson

I want to tell you guys something—we're gonna win this thing. . . . If you don't think so, if you don't believe it, let me know so I can get you to one of the other teams we're gonna beat.

BILLY MARTIN'S self-introduction to the '76 Yankees

When the leaves turn brown, I'll be wearing the batting crown.

DAVE PARKER'S prediction for 1977 (he was right)

The first 3,000 were easy.

PETE ROSE, on his 4,000+ career hits

Confusion

There are three types of baseball players: those who make it happen, those who watch it happen, and those who wonder what happens.

TOMMY LASORDA

There is one word in America that says it all, and that word is "You never know."

JOAQUIN ANDUJAR

The Yankees are only interested in one thing, and I don't know what that is.

LUIS POLONIA

[Manager] Lou [Piniella] has three rules for us: Be on time, play heads-up, and, uh, I forget the third.

TODD BENZINGER

Right now I have the three C's: comfortable, confident, and seeing the ball well.

JAY BUHNER

We are making a run. I don't know which way we're running.

FELIPE ALOU, on the Giants' playoff chances

Control Issues

I'm working on a new pitch. It's called a strike.

JIM KERN

Jack Hamilton could throw a strawberry through a brick wall. If he could only hit the wall.

HARRY CARAY

Trying to think with me is a waste of time. Hell, most of the time I don't know where it's going.

"SUDDEN" SAM MCDOWELL

Cooperstown

This is as close as I'll ever get to Cooperstown.

KEN BRETT, on receiving the key to the city in Utica, New York

Difficult to reach, either by car or by career.

JIM CAPLE, on the Hall of Fame

The Cubbies

The only good thing about the past is that the Chicago Cubs would occasionally win the World Series. But that's it. Everything else was Nazis and disease.

STEPHEN COLBERT

At Wrigley Field yesterday, the Big Red Machine ran over the Little Blue Bicycle.

BOB VERDI, on a mid-'70s game between the Reds and Cubs

It's hard to be a Chicago Cubs fan. Everyone gets that. There have been so many close calls, like in 1962, when they missed the postseason by 42½ games.

KING KAUFMAN

Declaring that the Cubs had the nucleus of a good team, Leo said, "This is not an 8th-place ball club." He was right. The Cubs finished 10th in 1966.

EDDIE GOLD and **ART AHRENS**

Is it a coincidence that at the O'Hare Airport parking garage, the Cubs level is located on the bottom floor?

GENE WOJCIECHOWSKI

People always come up and ask me if the Cubs are going to win in their lifetime, and I always give them the same answer: "How long are you planning on living?"

STEVE STONE

Tinker to Evers to Not a &#&'ing Chance.

JIM BAKER'S suggested Cubs motto

The longest running daytime soap opera in history, and the only one without a doctor in it.

ARNE HARRIS, on Cub broadcasts

The late Washington Redskins owner Jack Kent Cooke once said after a disappointing season that he had learned that "no matter how bad things get, they can always get worse." This is a truism Cub fans of the 1960s knew well.

DAVID CLAERBAUT

We came out of the dugout for Opening Day and saw a fan holding up a sign saying, "Wait 'Til Next Year."

MOE DRABOWSKY, on the late-'50s club

It's like rooting for the Italian Army.

SCOTT SIMON, on being a Cubs fan

Another century, and we're done with
'em.

THOMAS BOSWELL, on the Cubs

Cubs vs. Sox

The way it works in Chicago, either you're a Cubs fan or you're a
White Sox fan. There's no in-between. If you say that you're a fan
of both, it means you're not a fan at all. You're a bi-Sox-ual.

RICHARD ROEPER

They were never lovable.

ANONYMOUS WHITE SOX FAN,
on the Cubs' reputation as "lovable losers"

Cub fans stand up to sing "Take Me Out to the Ballgame." White
Sox fans stand up when they're about to storm the field to tackle
an umpire.

RICHARD ROEPER

We have to win for the people to show up. [The Cubs] have to
show up for the people to show up.

EDDIE EINHORN, White Sox owner

Unkind Cuts

It's kind of like, "All those who are going to New York City, please
step forward. Not so fast, Johnson."

JIM BOUTON, on spring training's roster cuts

I can remember walking in the clubhouse and Luman Harris, who was the Braves' manager, came up and said, ''No visitors allowed.''

BOB UECKER, on his last day as a ballplayer

You know, I didn't think I was that bad a ballplayer, but they're making a believer out of me.

JIM GOSGER, on his demotion to the minors

Dating

One percent of ballplayers are leaders of men. The other 99 percent are followers of women.

JOHN J. McGRAW

Well, it's like this—I'm not married, but I'm in great demand.

SATCHEL PAIGE

I had only one rule about these broads: They had to come highly recommended.

BO BELINSKY

If diamonds are a girl's best friend, why do so many girls get mad when you want to go to the ballpark?

BOB DYLAN

Bad Days

It was like ''Meet the Cardinals Day'' at first base.

JOHN KRUK, after losing to St. Louis 14–5

By the fifth inning, we were selling hot dogs to go.

KEN BRETT, on the '76 White Sox

That's not even a close score for a football game.

RICHARD ROEPER, on a 16–0 White Sox loss

Bill Mazeroski threw out the first pitch. Two innings later he suited up and hit a two-run double off of Darrell Rasner because, hey, everyone else was doing it.

CRAIG CALCATERRA

[Tom] Gordon coughed up more than his lunch.

TOM VERDUCCI, on the reliever's
pregame vomiting and late-inning blown save

I had a day in the life of Babe Ruth.

REGGIE JACKSON, on his
three-homer game in the '77 World Series

I'd say he just had a hell of a week.

DON ZIMMER, on Will Clark's six-RBI game

Next time, I'll throw him the resin bag.

JOHN MONTEFUSCO, on Reggie Smith's two-homer game

There's Bucky Dent, with another line drive to the catcher.

JERRY GIRARD

It was roughly equivalent to losing your softball league's title after the token girl on the opposing team knocked a pop fly over the left fielder's head. Only, your life depended on the game.

BILL SIMMONS, on Dent's
game-winning homer in the '78 playoff

Denver

You think Cub fans have suffered? Please. At least they had a team. Ours was the cruelest kind of suffering—the hopeless kind. Our motto was: Maybe Next Century.

RICK REILLY, on pre-expansion Denver

Everyone seemed so surprised that the pope outdrew the Rockies in Denver. They're forgetting that this is not an expansion pope.

SCOTT OSTLER

Detroit

The most unstoppable force to come out of Detroit since Motown singles and urban blight.

DIEGO MUSILLI, on Magglio Ordonez's '07 season

My first thought was, "Some of these guys have better control than my starting pitchers." My second thought was, "We're dead."

DICK WILLIAMS, on rock-throwing
Tiger fans after the '84 Series

The Detroit Tigers are going to the ['06] World Series and not a single car was toppled and burned. Doesn't anyone care about tradition anymore?

JERRY GREENE

The DH

He bats for drunk players.

ANONYMOUS SIX-YEAR-OLD FAN,
on the "designated hitter"

We could question its stars, but nothing could permanently undermine the game itself. Nothing could stop it from bouncing back. Not racism, drugs, wars, depressions, or earthquakes. Not even the designated hitter.

RICK KAPLAN

Who says there's no DH in the National League? The Mets have three in their starting outfield.

JIM ARMSTRONG

He does everything better than anyone else.

TOMMY HENRICH

He makes the rest of 'em look like plumbers.

ART PASSARELLA

I want to thank my teammates, who scored so many runs, and Joe DiMaggio, who ran down my mistakes.

LEFTY GOMEZ, at his Hall of Fame induction

Joe had ulcers. Ted gave them.

ED LINN, on the differences between DiMaggio and Williams

Diminutives

He could wear shorts and still be in long pants.

CASEY STENGEL, on 5'5" Nick Tremark

Character Profile: JIM BOUTON

Sometimes, in baseball, controversy and comedy can go hand in hand. Jim Bouton's *Ball Four* is conclusive proof.

When Bouton published his book-length player's diary back in 1970, it unleashed a backlash that was both fast and furious. Former Yankee teammates charged that the pitcher's secretly penned memoirs betrayed conversations they had intended to keep private. Baseball's establishment figures, Commissioner Bowie Kuhn among them, believed the book's portrayal of drinking and skirt chasing unfairly chipped away at ballplayers' personal reputations. The detractors ended up banning Bouton from Yankee Old-Timers' Day and, often, shunning his company. To them, his book was to clubhouse confidentiality what Saddam Hussein was to good government.

Some of the criticism around *Ball Four* still hasn't dissipated, but it should never obscure what the book has always been: hands down, the most raw and real baseball book of all time.

In today's controversy-obsessed society it may be hard to remember, but, in its time, Bouton's book was an absolute revelation. It came along in an era when beat reporters were virtually ball club employees who, not surprisingly, treated major leaguers like a collection of cardboard gods, figures above hard questions or impartial reporting, much less investigation and revelation. That was true even when the columns were entitled "Clubhouse Confidential."

Bouton changed all that. From its self-deprecating title to its last words, *Ball Four* exposed an existence recognizable to anyone who's ever been around a bunch of jocks with more testosterone and tension than they needed; in its pages were dozens of bemused tales of clubhouse lawyering, personality clashes, two-faced executives, clueless coaches, cheating competitors, and grasping groupies. Bouton's reporting on the Yankees of the early to mid-1960s debunked generations of bland coverage on ballplayers, providing an unprecedented look at the game's roller-coaster highs and lows.

The astonishing gap between baseball's soaring expectations and sometimes lowly realities was actually the key to the book's humor. Time and again, Bouton's brash words gave a sense that real-world baseball could be a bit too painful to take with a completely straight face, and that was true whether he was describing a slump ("I was 1–9. With any luck I'd have been 2–7"), his minor league call-down ("Meal money in Triple-A is $7.50 a day. In the big leagues it's $15. I don't know if they mean to have you eat half as much or half as well"), or a grizzled skipper's somewhat limited tactics ("Joe Schultz would have been a better manager if he understood more. Of course, if he understood more, he might not have been a manager"). In another passage, Bouton wrote:

"Other things that draw a team together: You're riding down the street in the team bus and you see a guy hanging on to a lamp-post, a wino in a drunken stupor, severely defeated by life. 'That's what happens when you can't hit the curveball,' someone says."

Sometimes, with enough wit, even topics like failure, demotion, incompetence, and shattered dreams can prompt a little bemusement.

To be sure, fans didn't necessarily delight in learning that Mickey Mantle could be a little lewd, sometimes rude, and often crude, but baseball fans were already savvy enough to realize that even a Hall of Famer could be imperfect, so Bouton's irreverent, down-to-earth comments on the Mick's flaws only humanized a man millions had long admired but barely known. For the first time, they were invited in to laugh along, to imagine what it might be like to pal around with Mickey Mantle in the real world, and that only boosted his popularity in the long run.

It was much the same when it came to the world of baseball as a whole. Any adult with half a brain and a nodding acquaintance with reality already knew that jocks could sometimes indulge a bit too much and think a bit too little, but, hey, that's a part of life. Most everybody's been there and done that. The book invited the general public to see ballplayers as ordinary guys who happen to be in extraordinary situations, a perspective that, again, only worked to make the national pastime funnier (and fascinating) over the years. Bowie Kuhn and the rest didn't know it at the time, but the guy who once called himself "the first fan to make it to the majors" was destined to recruit thousands of new fans.

It was a lot to stuff into fewer than 200 pages. Whatever else it may have been, Jim Bouton's *Ball Four* was a pitch that made baseball finally fully human and hilarious.

The 3rd

There was never any question about his courage. He proved it by getting married four times.

JACK BRICKHOUSE, on Enos "Country" Slaughter

This just proves that no man can be a success in two national pastimes.

OSCAR LEVANT, on Joe DiMaggio's split from Marilyn Monroe

I've given him more chances than I gave my first wife.

EARL WEAVER, on Mike Cuellar

This was like having a wedding reception after a divorce.

DENNIS HAMILL, on 2008's Shea Stadium farewell ceremony/Mets collapse

Drinking Men

Scotch and soda.

RALPH KINER, on his contribution to a Mets recipe book

When I lose, I drink. When I win, I celebrate.

BO BELINSKY

Ninety percent I'll spend on good times, women, and Irish whiskey. The other 10 percent I'll probably waste.

TUG McGRAW, on his salary

The Yankees should have been easy to stalk because, being a high-class club, they drank martinis and left a trail of olives.

JOHN LARDNER

I can tell you Billy [Martin] has a great heart, but I can't vouch for his liver.

WHITEY FORD

CURT GOWDY: Casey, I've never seen anyone drink beer as fast as you do.
CASEY STENGEL: Well, it's been that way since my accident.
GOWDY: What accident?
STENGEL: Somebody knocked my glass over.

Zim sort of took me under his wing, and one night he put me under the table.

RON SANTO, on Don Zimmer

It could be the scotch. It numbs the pain.

BILL LEE, on the source of Carl Yastrzemski's longevity

10:30? I'm not even done throwing up at that hour.

JIM PAGLIARONI, on morning batting practice

I'm old school. I was taught that ice was for bourbon, not for your arm.

ROD BECK

Drinking Men: Mickey McDermott Division

I had a lot of friends in Detroit. And not just bartenders.

It was injured. I bent it in the cocktail lounge.

On why his legendary arm never produced a 20-win season

I told him he had a five-cent head on a ten-dollar arm.

After being told he had "a ten-cent head and a million-dollar arm"

Drinking Men: Babe Ruth Division

Santa Claus drinking his whiskey straight.

JIMMY CANNON, on Ruth

He thought every night was New Year's Eve.

BOB CONSIDINE

[Manager Miller] Huggins had a rule that Ruth had to be in by one o'clock. But he never said if it was 1 A.M. or 1 P.M.

"SAD" SAM JONES

RUTH: I don't want to pitch anymore.
ED BARROW: How come?
RUTH: I'm tired all the time.
BARROW: Have you tried sleep?

BIG POISON

When he was tearing up the National League of the 1920s and 1930s, Paul Waner was widely known as "Big Poison." The nickname was based on his large frame and deadly hitting, but it could just as easily have applied to his staggering alcohol consumption.

Few, if any, major leaguers could ever match Waner's ability to simultaneously drink booze and play ball. Casey Stengel claimed that Waner proved his graceful reflexes through an ability to slide into a base without breaking the bottle in his hip pocket. Dick Bartell told stories of Big Poison's drinking whiskey before, during, and after a Bucs' contest, and at least one ball boy knew that was true: A kid allegedly took a few swigs from Waner's "Coca-Cola" once and immediately became woozy, then came down with a crashing hangover.

It's said that the front office once convinced the future Hall of Famer to give up drinking for a couple of weeks, saw him fall into a deep slump, and then told him to get back to his old habits. He did just that, and never made any bones about it, either; when someone once asked him if an unattended, half-empty whiskey bottle was his, Paul Waner said it wasn't, because if it was, the bottle would've been empty.

Drugs

I can think of a lot worse things in baseball than marijuana, if used in moderation. Things such as walks, designated hitters, and Astroturf.

BILL LEE

She thought I was a drug dealer. I was young, had this big place to live, and didn't work during the day.

TERRY MULHOLLAND, on a girlfriend's first visit to his mansion

Drug Testing

The owners are about to shut down baseball, which is richer than it's ever been. And the players are the ones who have to do drug testing?

RON DARLING, on the '94 strike

I believe in drug testing. All through the '60s, I tested everything.

BILL LEE

Don Drysdale

You had the feeling that guy up there with the bat had just made a nasty remark to his mother, threw a brick through his church window, or voted Communist.

JIM MURRAY

I would have liked to see him do that against Bob Gibson or Don Drysdale. They would have had to surgically remove that ball from his ear.

MARK GRACE, on a preening home run trot

The trick against Don Drysdale is to hit him before he hits you.

ORLANDO CEPEDA

Leo "The Lip" Durocher

The pitch missed by a millimeter, to the profound regret of uncounted millions.

JOHN LARDNER, on a brushback pitch against Durocher

He'd break his elbow if he ever reached for the check.

ERNIE SIMON

What would Leo know about nice guys?

CHARLIE GRIMM, on Durocher's "Nice guys finish last" quotation

BAD GUYS FINISH LAST.

Banner seen at Shea Stadium in 1966,
during a visit from Durocher's 10th-place Cubs

Leo's problem is that he can't stand anyone who's more popular than he is. Of course, that means most of the people in the world.

JACK BRICKHOUSE

Education

[Billy Werber] graduated from Duke University Phi Beta Kappa, which is Greek for "really smart guy."

BILL JAMES

If he could only do what he knows.

CASEY STENGEL, on fringe prospect/engineering genius Jay Hook

Can tell you about the dynamics and physics and gravity of curveballs, but hasn't thrown a decent one in weeks.

STEVE RUDMAN, on Shane Rawley

Ego

BRANCH RICKEY: Can you hit?
HEINE MUELLER: I can hit as good as Tris Speaker.
RICKEY: Can you run?
MUELLER: I can run as fast as Ty Cobb.
RICKEY: Can you steal bases?
MUELLER: As good as Max Carey.
RICKEY: Judas Priest!
MUELLER: I don't know him, but I'm just as good as he is, too.

I wish I could buy you for what you're really worth and sell you for what you think you're worth.

MICKEY MANTLE, to Joe Pepitone

That's pretty good, considering Dave's previous idol was himself.

WILLIE STARGELL, on Dave Parker's naming Stargell as his idol

People who know me know I'm a great guy to be around.

RICKEY HENDERSON

It couldn't have happened to a greater guy. Well, yes it could. It could have happened to me.

TOMMY LASORDA, on Jerry Reuss's no hitter

The problem is that he thinks that the "S" and "D" on our shirts stand for "Storm Davis."

LARRY BOWA, on San Diego's Storm Davis

You guys should have been calling me "Sir" a long time ago.

SIDNEY PONSON, on being knighted by the queen of the Netherlands

Had he known that his New York Mets would play baseball so badly, Bobby Valentine never would have invented the game in the first place.

TOM KEEGAN

I'd eat 'em if they paid me enough.

MOOSE SKOWRON, on endorsing cigarettes

The sponsors of Met broadcasts were Kool cigarettes and Rheingold, the dry beer. Only Casey [Stengel] could explain how something on fire could be cool and how a liquid could be dry.

WILLIAM RYCZEK

My players made me a real big celebrity in Chicago. How big? I was doing commercials for both a diet center and a fried chicken chain. I had all the bases covered.

DON ZIMMER,
on managing the '89 Cubs

'Roids and Viagra? I wonder if Palmeiro's wife is still alive.

STEVE SAYAD, on steroid user/Viagra endorser Rafael Palmeiro

Endorsements: Yaz Division

If Ted Williams was the best thing since sliced bread, this was the best sliced bread since Ted Williams.

STEVE RUSHIN, on "Big Yaz" bread

We should feed this stuff to the Orioles, then we'd win the f—ing pennant.

Red Sox infielder **PHIL GAGLIANO,**
on the bread's taste

Executive Decisions

I'm not sure if we're looking in-house or outhouse.

LOU GORMAN, on the team's executive search

The Royals are trying to send a message to their minor league players: Don't embarrass the organization. That's the front office's job.

RANY JAZAYERLI

Raise the urinals.

DARREL CHANEY, on how to keep management "on their toes"

WATCHING THE DETECTIVES

It's the job of the front office to pick, develop, and play the right lineup of winning players. Front office executives have often made it their business to keep an eye on off-duty players, too.

Front offices have hired private detectives to trail their more hard-living players since as far back as the 1910s and, while players don't particularly like the snooping, most take it in stride.

For instance, when a young Casey Stengel learned that he and his running mate Irish Meusel were being trailed by a detective, Case walked up to his boss and, in mock anger, said he didn't deserve that kind of treatment. John J. McGraw asked just what kind of treatment he did deserve and Casey responded, "It's the principle of the thing. I got a right to have a whole detective to myself."

At least a couple of players learned to have more than a little fun with their uninvited guests. It's said that, when he was playing for Detroit, Mickey McDermott actually called a private investigator to come sit down and drink with his friends; the PI did partake but reportedly quit after a couple of weeks, explaining that the early hours carousing was ruining his marriage.

There's another story, one that may or may not be true. It's said that a female detective was hired to tail Joe Page in the late 1940s but suddenly quit; apparently the Yankees' resident womanizer had seduced her, too.

Great Expectations

We didn't believe in this "get 'em tomorrow" crap. We got 'em today.

CHARLIE SILVERA, on the '50s-era Yanks

The Yankees don't pay me to win every day. Just two out of three.

CASEY STENGEL

What is most important to me is that the Red Sox win the World Series, preferably every year, ideally three to five times per year.

MICHAEL SCHUR

We're getting better. It's taking them longer to beat us.

CASEY STENGEL, on an extra-inning loss

They don't pay us to play overtime.

STAN MUSIAL, immediately before a 12th-inning, game-winning home run

SWEEPLESS IN SEATTLE.

Mariner banner seen after
the Yankees lost three straight road games
(and the '95 American League Division Series)

MUCK THE FARLINS.

Cub banner at the '03 National League Championship Series

LOVE IS A MANNY SPLENDORED THING.

Fan banner, seen at Fenway Park
during the '03 American League Championship Series

I WISH I KNEW HOW TO QUIT YOU, GRIFFEY.

Banner on Ken Jr.'s return to Seattle

Fan Relations

Eighty-five percent of the f—in' world is working, the other 15 percent come out here.

> Cubs manager **LEE ELIA**, on Wrigley fans

GEORGE, WE'RE BEHIND YOU ALL THE WAY.

> Fan banner seen after George Bell said booing fans could
> "kiss my purple butt"

Fantasy Baseball

These people have taken a goofy parlor game and turned it into a winner-take-all death match. They don't want to beat you, they want to chew your organs.

> **SAM WALKER**, on fantasy baseball contenders

Pay attention to your wife.

> Fantasy baseball founder **DAN OKRENT**,
> on his best advice to would-be players

Fantasy Camps

He looks like a guy who went to a fantasy camp and decided to stay.

> **DON SUTTON**, on John Kruk

If something happens, just bury me at second base.

> Middle-aged participant **GEORGE GOODALL**

Not-So-Fastballs

Hurt? I never threw hard enough to get hurt.

BILL LEE

My wife has me take out better garbage than he throws.

ROD CAREW, on Mike Boddicker

It's like being bitten by a stuffed panda.

LOU PINIELLA, on striking out against Geoff Zahn

He never threw hard, but now he's throwing as not-hard as he ever did.

JEFF TORBORG, on 44-year-old Tommy John

The outfield scoreboard clocked one of his fastballs at 90 mph. That's sort of like your neighborhood UPS driver winning the Indianapolis 500.

JERRY CRASNICK, on Paul Byrd

I figured I was getting closer to the end when the bullpen catcher started taking his glove off before I was finished throwing.

GREG MADDUX

Fatherhood

I guess he gets it from his mother.

Light-hitting **JOSE TARTABULL**, on his son's power

Having another son was a dream. Now I had two-thirds of an outfield.

PAUL O'NEILL

Our similarities are different.

DALE BERRA, on how he compared to his father

That's not unusual. I couldn't get his dad out, either.

RICK SUTCLIFFE, on giving up a homer to Ken Griffey, Jr.

Fatherhood: Steve Garvey Division

STEVE GARVEY IS NOT MY PADRE.

Common San Diego bumper sticker

THE YOUTH MOVEMENT

They say that baseball is a kids' game. The children of major leaguers might know it best of all.

Very often, the kids of pro ballplayers have a national pastime association that goes to their very names. Curt Schilling persuaded his wife to name his son "Gehrig," after his favorite player, and George Brett named his "Robin," after longtime opponent/good friend Robin Yount. It's said that at least a half-dozen of Mickey Mantle's former teammates named their boys "Mickey," and many more named boys after their own famous selves. Phil "The Scooter" Rizzuto's son was dubbed "Scooter, Jr." even as the boy became a grown man, then a senior citizen.

Players have been known to be a bit creative in their naming, too. Eric Gagne's record-breaking tenure as an L.A. reliever inspired him to name his baby daughter "Bluu" (as in the famed "Dodger Blue"), and Chipper Jones hit so well in New York's ballpark that he decided to name his little girl "Shea."

At least one second-generation player wanted to shield his child from the name game, though with little success.

Ken Griffey, Jr., the son of a star player, was proud of his dad but could foresee that his own firstborn would eventually be pressured to follow in the family's footsteps. Well, the proud papa tried to get out of the dilemma by giving the boy "Ken Griffey III" as an official name but calling him "Trey." It was a clever move, but the Mariners' general

> manager still sent the newborn Trey Griffey an official playing con-
> tract. It was dated 18 years into the future.

Daytime baseball in the sunshine of Fenway.

KEN LEVINE, on "the definition of perfection"

In his book on the Red Sox, Rob Neyer writes, "I fell in love twice
this season—with a ballpark named Fenway and with a woman
named Kristien." One can only hope that he didn't end up having
sex with Fenway Park.

DIEGO MUSILLI

That place holds more broken hearts than a cemetery.

BILL LEE

It was a bad day for violence.

CHRIS JAFFE, on John J. McGraw's retirement

Nobody knew how well Dolph [Camilli] could fight because,
quite frankly, no one ever wanted to find out.

LEO DUROCHER

He'd rather fight than eat.

LEW BURDETTE, on Eddie Mathews

You know what this is? It's a Polish joke stopper.

TED KLUSZEWSKI, on his fist

For some reason, [Billy] Jurges and I didn't get along. I don't mean like oil and water. I mean like gasoline and matches.

DICK BARTELL

Instead of the marines, we should have sent [Rick] Burleson and [Rico] Petrocelli over [to Iran]. They would have come back in 48 hours with the hostages, the ayatollah, and a couple million barrels of oil.

BILL LEE

He's better off going out and getting hit by a car.

MEL HALL, on Brian Harper's offer to fight

Well, I wasn't making any progress talking to him.

ROGERS HORNSBY, on why
he slugged an opposing manager

Hit him? I haven't hit anybody all year.

HANK BAUER, on allegations he'd punched a club patron
(Bauer was batting .203 at the time)

Let 'em go. Maybe they'll kill each other.

JOE FERGUSON, during a fistfight
between Steve Garvey and Don Sutton

Cub fans disagree over which moment turned around Chicago's season. Did the switch flip when Carlos Zambrano punched Michael Barrett or was it when Lou Piniella kicked dirt on an umpire? Anyway, if the Cubs are losing in the sixth inning, cover all of your bases by smashing a potted plant over your friend's head.

JUSTIN PETERS

I'm sorry. Principally, I'm sorry about the $250.

TED WILLIAMS'S "apology" for a spitting fine

Make it $1,500 and let me take the weekend off.

BILL LEE, after being fined one day's pay ($500)

A Chicago alderman recently proposed raising the fine for trespassing onto a field during a White Sox game from $100 to $1,000. That sounds high, but does include parking.

BILL SCHEFT

OK, FINE

Fines are like the potholes, cavities, or taxes of the baseball world: annoyances that can't be avoided for too long. But an annoying fact of life isn't always the same as an unfunny fact of life.

When he was playing for the Athletics in the mid-1970s, for instance, Vida Blue's misbehavior prompted a $250 fine from manager Alvin Dark; the ace's rebellious attitude also prompted him to pay the fine by dumping $250 worth of pennies, nickels, and dimes on Dark's desk.

Of course, managers have always been free to display some cleverness of their own.

When manager Zach Taylor of the old Browns came to the mound to yank Tex Shirley, for example, the departing starter was so ticked off that he heaved the baseball into the left field grandstands. The next day, Taylor had Shirley report to the diamond early, stand by as the groundskeeper marked off the distance to the ball's landing spot, and see that it measured about 200 feet. Taylor then fined Shirley $200.

Once, Tommy Lasorda fined Jay Johnstone for the memorable prank described on page 314. Well, the fans loved the stunt and hated the fine, to the extent that they volunteered enough money to cover the penalty and even provide Johnstone with a nifty little profit. It was at that point the chagrined Lasorda decided to issue a new fine, one that had his reserve outfielder picking up the tab for a big dinner out.

The sweetest baseball fining of all may have occurred during spring training in the late 1950s. It seems that Vernon "Deacon" Law, one of the Pirates' most popular and pious players, inadvertently missed a team workout but, true to his rule-abiding nature, still insisted on paying the mandatory fine. Skipper Danny Murtaugh had no choice but to take Deacon's money, but he decided to donate the funds to a local church. He even added a contribution of his own.

Charlie O. Finley

It was a three-year marriage that got damn close to the "til death-do-us-part" bit.

Manager **DICK WILLIAMS**, on working for the owner of the A's

I'm going to write a book about my days with Finley. I'm going to call it *And They Thought I Was Crazy*.

Former mental patient/A's employee **JIMMY PIERSALL**

Unless he changes his ways, he's going to hell.

ALVIN DARK

Fired

It was more like a shooting.

DICK WILLIAMS, on his 1969 firing

I feel like a guy in an open casket at a funeral; everyone walks by and mumbles what a great guy you are, but you stay dead.

TOM TREBLELHORN

THE GREATEST PLAY SINCE THE EMANCIPATION PROCLAMATION

—Inscription on a trophy given to Browns owner Bill Veeck after he fired Rogers Hornsby

I think they're trying to tell me something.

DAVEY JOHNSON, on his four firings

I wish him all the luck in the world. He'll need most of it.

MAX CAREY, on his successor as Dodgers manager

They say you have to fire the manager because you can't fire 25 players, but in this particular case, they should've looked into the possibility, at least.

DIEGO MUSILLI, on Joe Torre's Mets in the late '70s

The worst ways to fire a manager:

3. Announcing the firing on the stadium scoreboard in between the pizza-delivery race and the "Guess the Attendance" game. . . .
6. Giving him the bad news via signs flashed by the third-base coach during the bottom of the sixth inning. . . .
7. Calling up his weekly radio show, identifying yourself as "Omar from Flushing," and announcing that he's been fired. . . .

JIM CAPLE

Firing: Second Thoughts Division

It would be Bobby Cox, if I hadn't just fired him. We need some-one like him around here.

TED TURNER, on the leading candidate
to replace Cox as Braves manager
(Turner rehired him four years later)

The worst mistake I ever made. To get Yogi back, I'd come in a rickshaw across the George Washington Bridge.

GEORGE STEINBRENNER, on firing Yogi Berra in 1985

Firing: Billy Martin Division

Billy always wants to be the boss, which offends the guys who own the team. Unfortunately, he can't fire them. They can fire him, and often do.

SPARKY LYLE

I pass people on the street these days and they don't know whether to say hello or good-bye.

MARTIN, on his multiple firings

He plays as if he were on the Crusades.

EDDIE KASKO

Wouldn't ask out of a game if both his legs were cut off.

BILL LEE

I know my limitations when I run right into them.

FISK

I was in the dirt, too, but I looked cleaner.

FISK, on the difference between him and Thurman Munson

Football

You know what baseball is? It's playing cards, sleeping, watching TV, dress, batting practice, fool around with the fans, joke with teammates. Football is a little different— before the game, everybody sits on the floor, quietly thinking of who's head they're going to take off.

BO JACKSON

Baseball has Blue Moon, Catfish, Spaceman, and Sugar Bear. Football has Lester the Molester, Too Mean, and the Assassin.

THOMAS BOSWELL,
"99 Reasons Why Baseball Is Better Than Football"

I don't know if it's helping, but we do lead the league in third-down conversions.

CHARLIE HOUGH, on the Rangers staff's tossing footballs on off-days

I thought they were going to blitz.

RYAN HOWARD, on the Rays' use of a five-man infield
during the 2008 World Series

Football: Bo Jackson Division

He's in two leagues by himself.

MIKE DOWNEY, on Jackson's football/baseball stardom

Baseball is probably more physical of the two, mentally.

JACKSON, on the difference between the sports

Free-Agent Busts

There's no such thing as a sure thing, and the unsurest of unsure things in baseball is a free-agent pitcher.

KING KAUFMAN

Derek Bell is the ultimate Pirate: He lives on a boat and steals money.

MARK MADDEN, on a Bucs' bust

Free-Agent Busts: Barry Zito Division

The world's most expensive batting practice pitcher.

CRAIG CALCATERRA, on Barry Zito

[Barry] Zito shelled, grass green, sky blue.

CALCATERRA

They should have put a disclaimer on the ticket to the effect that "any resemblance to Major League Baseball is purely coincidental."

RON SWOBODA, on the mid-'60s Mets

It was a seven-year losing streak.

ED KRANEPOOL, on those same Mets teams

The Yankees didn't know how to lose. But they learned.

RALPH HOUK, on the Yanks' slide
from the '64 pennant to the '66 basement

The San Francisco Giants, who won a World Series as recently as 1954 . . .

KING KAUFMAN

There's one thing you have to appreciate about the Royals—they don't tease the fans with false hope.

JOE POSNANSKI

Character Profile: JACKIE PRICE

Want to see some real nifty tricks? Just head over to the nearest major league ballpark.

It's the place where you can see hurlers delivering pitches that can suddenly curve, dip, dive, speed, sink, and slide at every which rate and angle. Where you'll witness hitters turn on those same pitches and, in the blink of an eye, drive them 400 feet or more into the distance. Where you'll find fielders diving, sliding, colliding, and crashing their way to a tiny ball that might travel at speeds over 120 miles per hour.

Remarkable tricks all, but none begin to compare to what Jackie Price could do.

It's not that Jackie was a particularly great ballplayer, at least not in the traditional sense. When he was coming up as a minor leaguer in the 1930s, Price didn't have Bob Feller's stuff or Stan Musial's bat or Charlie Gehringer's glove. Not even close. Price's entire big league playing career consisted of a cup of coffee— at age 33, in 1946, he got three singles (and 13 at bats) for the Indians. That's it.

No, what made Price so astounding weren't so much his performances as his feats. You see, the man was blessed with the hand-eye coordination, ambidexterity, and inventiveness to rank with any world-class acrobat, and he could utilize them to pull off that which other athletes could scarcely imagine.

Have you ever heard that a certain someone could hit while standing on his head? In Jackie's case, it wasn't an overblown figure of speech—it was just about true. He actually did that once, on a teammate's dare, and soon found that he could consistently hit pitched balls while hanging upside down from a gymnastics suspension bar, to boot. Not long after, he discovered that he could also toss a couple balls into the air, then take a single swing to simultaneously hit one ball into a grounder and the other into a pop-up, so he started doing that one on a regular basis, too.

It was the beginning of something. As word of Price's skills started circulating, he soon developed a full-blown theatrical act, and the new tricks promised even more unbelievable sights. Along with expert bat handling, juggling, and backflips, Jackie delivered all-new, believe-it-or-not material to a whole range of ballpark audiences:

- He'd use both hands to make simultaneous pitches to side-by-side catchers, only, somehow, one catcher would receive a fastball and the other got a curve.

- He'd sit down on second base, using the bag as a seat cushion, then take a bag of baseballs and fire one strike after another across home plate.

- He'd borrow one of Pepper Martin's old tricks, taking a ball and bouncing it off his bat, like one of those paddle-ball games, except without the elastic backup. Then he'd walk across the stands, tipping his cap and waving and chatting up the fans, bouncing the ball all the while.

- In a show finale, he'd set up a mini-cannon at home plate, jump into a Jeep, drive the car back and forth in the outfield, have the mini-cannon shoot baseballs into the car's path, then use one hand to steer while using the other to make mid-drive catches.

Price eventually settled into a role as the house act for the Indian teams of the late 1940s, setting out an utterly unique show that never failed to leave packed houses gasping in astonishment. In time, he performed before millions of fans, becoming the inspiration for baseball clowns such as Max Patkin and an early influence on crowd-pleasing mascots such as the San Diego Chicken.

Not a bad legacy for a .231 career hitter, you might think. Jackie Price may not have been a great baseball player, but he was the greatest trickster of 'em all.

The 4th

Eddie Gaedel

Keep it low.

BOB SWIFT'S advice on pitching to the first midget pinch hitter

He used to play shortstop, when he was smaller.

Owner **BILL VEECK'S** "background information" sheet on Gaedel

A CHAMPION OF THE LITTLE GUY

Inscription on Veeck's Hall of Fame plaque

THE SHORTEST CAREER ON RECORD

People know that owner Bill Veeck once sent a midget up to bat in a major league ball game, but they don't know all the layers of comedic detail that went into the stunt.

When the St. Louis Browns sent 3'7" Eddie Gaedel up to bat to pinch-hit for Frank Saucier on August 19, 1951, the club was fully prepared.

For starters, the Browns had an official major league contract at the ready—Eddie was due $100 per game—and had him wearing a regulation, if extra-small, uniform previously used by the batboy. Other than the size involved, the only thing unique about the uniform was the fact that Gaedel was given number "1/8" and wore special elf-type cleats, the kind that curled up at the toes.

As he prepared to enter the batter's box, Gaedel swung several bats for his practice swings, just like anyone else, except that his particular bats weighed 23 ounces and were 17 inches long. Once at the plate, he stood erect, with his toy bat cocked just so, his weight back and feet spread wide—in the famous picture of the at bat, Gaedel is doing a fair approximation of Joe DiMaggio's classic stance. He'd been practicing it before the game, you see.

During the at-bat itself, the opposing Detroit Tigers did their best to go after him—catcher Bob Swift was on his knees—but Gaedel nonetheless took four (high) balls. As he dutifully ran to first base, he tipped his cap to the delighted crowd and, when removed for a pinch runner, Gaedel gave his teammate a playful pat on the behind.

Not long after the stunt, the killjoy commissioner's office declared Eddie Gaedel's playing contract void as "against the best interests of baseball." It was the end of the "shortest career on record" but even then, Veeck wasn't finished with the little guy: During one 1961 contest, Eddie made a comeback, this time as a ballpark vendor. Veeck guaranteed that the midget vendor wouldn't block anyone's view of the game.

I didn't come down here to get a suntan.

BILLY MARTIN, on the Yankees' championship prospects

Real good. I'm sorry I didn't get a chance to strike him out twice.

SPARKY LYLE, on what it felt like to strike out Willie Mays in his last All-Star Game

He's even tempered—he comes to the ballpark mad and stays that way.

JOE GARAGIOLA, on Rick Burleson

Game Times

I've never seen a pitcher lose a game by not throwing the ball.

LEFTY GOMEZ, on his tendency to delay

He pitches as though he's double parked.

VIN SCULLY, on Bob Gibson

People who sing "I don't care if I never get back" always seem to walk out a few minutes later to beat traffic.

JOE POSNANSKI

General Managers

Boston is the only club where I preferred to conduct the negotiations over the telephone—it isn't easy to make the kind of deal you were able to make with the Red Sox without laughing in their face.

BILL VEECK

[Pitcher Bill Walker] is not to be confused with the Cubs general manager of the same name, who is confused enough as it is.

WARREN BROWN

That's easy. [Frank] Lane was an idiot.

MUDCAT GRANT, on why Lane traded Rocky Colavito for Harvey Kuenn

If Gabe Paul was running a hospital, I'd invest in a mortuary.

BILL JAMES

Our plans are long term. Those are our plans. They're long term. And good. We plan on being very good. Long term.

CHUCK LAMAR, on the Devil Rays' long-term plans

General Managers: George Weiss Division

A refugee from the human race.

BILL VEECK, on the Yankees' tight-fisted general manager

He had a strike zone smaller than George Weiss's heart.

BERT RANDOLPH SUGAR, on midget Eddie Gaedel

He wasn't a bad guy to know when he wasn't working. But he was always working.

YOGI BERRA

At birth. I had a baseball instead of a rattle.

ROD DEDEAUX, on his start in the game

Dad felt that a person had the right to develop his own interests without the bias of parental supervision. This somewhat modern approach to parenting caused him to wait until my mother was three months pregnant before he bought me my first fielder's glove.

BILL LEE

I ran into an old friend and I told him, "The difference between us is that you grew up working and I grew up playing."

DICK BOSMAN

Getting Started: Umpiring Division

I couldn't hit a curveball, so I decided to call it.

WALLY BELL

I just had a dream. I told my mom one day, "I'm going to be on TV." She said, "The only way you're going to be on TV is if I pick you up and put you on top of it." But I believed.

ERIC GREGG

In the daytime, you sat in the dugout and talked about women. At night you went out with women and talked about baseball.

WAITE HOYT

I went to an all-boys school, but I'm making up for it now.

FRANK TANANA

The groupie is the ultimate fan. She doesn't just settle for a mere autograph—she wants the hand that signs it and everything that's connected to it.

BILL LEE

According to the *Sporting News*, over the last four years [palimony target] Wade Boggs hit .800 with women in scoring position.

DAVID LETTERMAN

JEFF HORRIGAN, *SPORTS ILLUSTRATED FOR KIDS:* What's your favorite color?

PEDRO MARTINEZ: Green.

HORRIGAN: Favorite book?

MARTINEZ: Whatever.

HORRIGAN: Favorite actress?

MARTINEZ: Sandra Bullock.

HORRIGAN: Secret ambition?

MARTINEZ: I would like to f—k Sandra Bullock.

HORRIGAN: Pedro, this is a magazine for kids.

MARTINEZ: OK.

HORRIGAN: What's your secret ambition?

MARTINEZ: I would like to *sleep* with Sandra Bullock.

The place where triples go to die.

TY COBB, on "Shoeless" Joe Jackson's glove

Anything the batter grounds, lines, or pops in the direction of [Phil] Rizzuto.

VIC RASCHI, on his best pitch

He played second base, short center field, and part of right field.

BUCKY HARRIS, on Joe Gordon

He can play all three outfield positions. At the same time.

GENE MAUCH, on Cesar Geronimo

He may be crazy, but not in the outfield.

LARRY DOBY, on former mental patient / Gold Glover Jimmy Piersall

Wally Joyner played like he taught first base at Stanford.

BILL JAMES

I was taught to trust my hands.

KEVIN MITCHELL, on why he never wore a protective cup

That glove should last him a minimum of six years, because it rarely made contact with the ball.

FRESCO THOMPSON, on Babe Herman's leather

Marvelous Marv was holding down first base. This is like saying Willie Sutton works at your bank.

JIMMY BRESLIN

Yankee fans suspected that second baseman Horace Clarke wore a glove only to keep his hand warm.

PHILIP BASHE

His dad built him a batting cage but forgot to buy him a glove.

ANONYMOUS METS PLAYER,
on hyped hitting prospect Gregg Jefferies

If there was a worse defensive first baseman in the majors than Willie Aikens, somebody must be playing with a machete.

BILL JAMES

Iron Gloves: Reggie Jackson Division

It's not that Reggie [Jackson] is a bad outfielder. He just has trouble judging the ball and picking it up.

BILLY MARTIN

I didn't see the play. I had my glove over my face the entire time.

RON GUIDRY, on Reggie's catch

Brushes with Greatness

During my career, I came close to greatness. My locker was right next to Sandy Koufax.

LARRY MILLER

I helped Willie Mays and Hank Aaron get to the Hall of Fame. I served up a home run to both of 'em. If not for me, they'd both be one short.

GARY WASLEWSKI

Cal Griffith

It's said that swimming was invented when Calvin Griffith was confronted with a toll bridge.

MARVIN MILLER, on the cheapskate Twins owner

I know winning isn't everything, but with Griffith, winning isn't anything.

RON DAVIS

Grinders

He would run through a brick wall to make a catch or slide into a pit of ground glass to score a run.

ARTHUR DALEY, on Enos "Country" Slaughter

It's only a small bone.

PEPPER MARTIN, on playing with a broken finger

I broke my wrist. I didn't break my head.

CASEY STENGEL, on managing with a broken wrist

Yoda says "Do or do not. There is no try." But Yoda's a little green puppet that never saw Carlton Fisk blocking the plate and bracing himself for a collision with a runner half his age, or Aaron Rowand running into walls in the outfield, or Brian Downing slamming his bat down after a strikeout. On the South Side, we appreciate winning, but we respect the never-say-die spirit.

RICHARD ROEPER

It's the liners those hitters hit back to me.

LUIS ARROYO, on his prematurely gray hair

I call it the Watergate: I try to cover up as much as I can.

JOE TORRE, on his hairstyle

Hall of Fame Scouting Reports

The Pitchers

Could throw a lamb chop past a wolf.

BUGS BAER, on Lefty Grove

He threw about 14 different pitches I couldn't hit.

DICK SCHOFIELD, on Juan Marichal

It's like taking an essay contest against Hemingway.

CURT SCHILLING, on pitching against Roger Clemens

He put guys like me on his cereal for breakfast.

TOM PACIOREK, on Goose Gossage

The Hitters

[Rogers] Hornsby considered it a slump if he went 0 for 6.

DICK BARTELL

Lefty Gomez experimented with bifocals near the end of his career. He claimed he threw them away because they gave him too good a look at [Jimmie] Foxx's arms.

DICK BARTELL

If they'd had to pitch to him, they'd have voted for him.

CASEY STENGEL, on those
who didn't support Ted Williams's Hall of Fame induction

Very carefully.

GAYLORD PERRY, on how to pitch to Hank Aaron

Going over the hitters, it was decided that we should pitch Frank Robinson underground.

JIM BOUTON

To have his body, I'd trade him mine and my wife's. And throw in some cash besides.

PETE ROSE, on Mike Schmidt

Robin Yount in the first, Robin Yount in the fourth, and Robin Yount in the seventh.

ROGER CLEMENS, on "the three most dangerous hitters"
in the American League

Simply born to run.

Blogger **"67MARQUEZ,"** on all-time steals leader Rickey Henderson

The Head Game

I'm trying not to put too much pressure on myself, but I think I'm overcompensating. I'm putting too much pressure on myself to not put too much pressure on myself.

DANN BILARDELLO

I'm not Superman. I just think I am.

LONNIE SMITH

You've got to think you're better, then show them why you're better.

JIMMY ROLLINS

So much for the past. As for the present, I think I have a future.

CASEY STENGEL,
on being fired from the Dodgers

I don't worry about the past. The homers will take care of the future. And that will make the present OK.

KEN GRIFFEY, JR.

It's mind over matter. If you don't mind, it don't matter.

SATCHEL PAIGE

Ain't no sense worrying about things you got no control over, 'cause if you got no control over them, ain't no sense in worrying. And ain't no sense worrying about things you got control over, 'cause if you got control over them, ain't no sense worrying.

MICKEY RIVERS

Heading West

We figured we'd better let 'em win one or they'd leave town. And
they left town anyway.

The Yankees' **PHIL RIZZUTO**,
on the Brooklyn Dodgers' first World Series win in '55

Preliminary diagnosis indicates that the cause of death was an
acute case of greed, followed by severe political implications.

DICK YOUNG, on the Dodgers' demise

It was like having the girl you love tell you she's marrying another
guy because he has more money and a new house in San
Francisco.

VIC ZIEGEL, on the New York Giants' move west

The Heart of the Order

The game is played with a round bat and a round ball, the players
run around the bases, and what goes around comes around.

FRANK WILLS

Almost the only place in life where a sacrifice is really
appreciated.

MARK BELTAIRE

In baseball, you don't know nothin'.

YOGI BERRA

It's never predictable even though it never changes.

NED MARTIN

Hard-Core Hecklers

One of the old-time umpires was asked what he remembered most about the New York fans. After thinking about it for a minute, he said, "They had terrible aim."

KEN KAISER

They don't deserve a major league franchise. I don't mind getting hit by a regular bottle, but when they break off the tops before throwing them, that's just too much.

WHITEY LOCKMAN, on Philly fans

Heckler Comebacks

Hey, get on the mound!

TED WILLIAMS, to a bench jockey

You'd better check your wife—a ballplayer is missing!

Traditional player response to spectator hecklers

Hey, I don't get on you when you're picking up my garbage in the morning!

MITCH WILLIAMS

HECKLING BACK

When fans pay for their tickets, they also purchase the right to occasionally boo, heckle, and generally lash out at the players on the field.

Sometimes, baseball guys lash back.

Dodgers manager Tommy Lasorda, for one, knew how to inject some self-serving theater into hostile receptions. When L.A. would play road games against its San Francisco rivals, Tommy had this routine where he'd emerge from the visitors' clubhouse in right field and nonchalantly stroll down the foul line, pretending not to hear the loud chorus of boos and catcalls raining down on him from the grandstands. Then, suddenly, in theatrical fashion, Lasorda would start blowing kisses back at the crowd, tip his cap, and smile as the Giants crowd went to an even higher boil; a pro wrestling villain couldn't have hammed it up any better.

Others have been known to be a bit more, let's say, direct, about their feelings.

Hank Aaron, for instance, once hit a milestone home run into Wrigley Field's bleachers, only to have the Bleacher Bums toss the ball back at him when he came out to his outfield position at the top of the inning. Aaron decided to fire it right back at 'em, thereby becoming the first player to give away the same souvenir twice.

Ross Grimsley displayed some of the same kind of disdain in his heart in the mid-1970s, when he was being heckled while warming up in the Fenway Park bullpen. Grimsley decided to fire a ball at the offending fans on the other side of the fence, no doubt figuring that the protective netting would ensure that the Boston fans got nothing but a scare, but unfortunately for him, the ball somehow burst through the netting, hit the heckler, and resulted in a lawsuit.

The most passive-aggressive response of all probably came from the Twins' Torii Hunter. When rowdy fans would throw coins at him in the outfield, Hunter would often collect them and, at the end of the tax year, declare the spare change as income on his IRS returns.

The Quotable Rickey Henderson

All I'm asking for is what I want.

On his contract demands

Hey, man, where have you been? Haven't seen you in a while.

> To a newly arriving Billy Beane, who'd just returned after months in the minors

Who's he?

> After being told Tom Robson had just been fired
> (he'd been Henderson's hitting coach for the previous five months)

Richard Pryor.

> Rickey's hotel registration alias, used to avoid fans and the media
> (he also used "James Brown" and "Luther Vandross")

Rickey on Numbers

Ten years? Ricky's been playing at least 16, 17 years.

> After a teammate offered him a bus seat, explaining "You have tenure"

Well, Rickey's not one of them, so that's 49 percent right there.

> On Ken Caminiti's estimate that
> 50 percent of major leaguers were on steroids

Two-thirds of the fans will be there to see Rickey, two-thirds to see Billy [Martin], and two-thirds to see the Yankees.

> On the crowd for an upcoming Athletics-Yankees game

I was about how could I get on base 400 percent of the time.

> **HENDERSON**, who may have meant 40 percent

Rickey on Rickey

This is Rickey calling on behalf of Rickey.

> A message on a GM's answering machine

Do I talk to myself? No, I just remind myself of what I'm trying to do. You know, I never answer myself so how can I be talking to myself?

Listen, people are always saying, "Rickey says 'Rickey.'" But it's been blown way out of proportion. People might catch me, when

they know I'm ticked off, saying, "Rickey, what the heck are you doing, Rickey?" They say, "Darn, Rickey, what are you saying 'Rickey' for? Why don't you just say, 'I'?" But I never did. I always said, "Rickey."

Hitters

Just swingin'.

BABE RUTH, on his strategy

He could roll out of bed in the middle of winter and get a base hit.

BILL GILES, on Rusty Staub

He's the only guy I know who can drive in three runs with nobody on base.

MARK McLEMORE, on Juan Gonzalez

He's one of those hitters who could make contact on a pitchout.

BILL SIMMONS, on a '99-vintage Nomar Garciaparra

Hitters vs. Pitchers

Their arms are 20 years ahead of their brains.

BRANCH RICKEY, on pitchers

All pitchers are liars and crybabies.

YOGI BERRA

I hate hitters. I start the game mad and stay that way.

DON DRYSDALE

Two pitchers.

TED WILLIAMS, after asking "What's dumber than a pitcher?"

Home Run Trots

I'd rather hit home runs. You don't have to run as hard.

DAVE KINGMAN

Making it around the bases without falling down.

LEON WAGNER, on the hardest part of homering while hung over

Maybe he's afraid they're going to take it off the board.

VIN SCULLY, on Mickey Hatcher's sprint around the bases in the '88 World Series

Humility

Players

My dream as a kid was to get to the big leagues. I guess I wasn't specific enough. I should have said, "My dream was to get to the big leagues and be successful."

BRIAN KINGMAN, on going 8–20

This is just an easy park to hit in.

WILCY MOORE, on beating out an infield hit in Detroit
(He had a .102 career average)

I'd sure like to trade it for a great bat.

ELLIS VALENTINE, on his great arm

That just shows you how this league has gone to hell.

CHUCK FINLEY, on being named American League Player of the Week

Even before the start of spring training, Herzog had said, "If Rich Billings is the starting catcher again, we're in deep trouble." When that evaluation was passed along to Billings, he simply nodded and said, "Whitey, obviously, has seen me play."

MIKE SHROPSHIRE

I remember at my induction to the Canadian Hall of Fame, I was nervous to be speaking to all the people there. My father said, "John, you're Canadian and you're a baseball player—they won't be expecting much."

JOHN HILLER

Teams

We placed 9th in a 10-team league. With our talent, we should have been 11th.

STEVE HAMILTON

We're not as bad as people think, although that's not saying much.

BUDDY BELL

We're still working on grounders.

CASEY STENGEL, on the Mets' inability to field fly balls

Baseball is supposed to be a noncontact sport, but our hitters seem to be taking it literally.

LARRY DOUGHTY

WHY I DID IT

Baseball, it's said, is a game of humility. Every baseball player who's ever struck out, given up a long home run, committed an error, or otherwise flubbed a move knows that hard truth, but some truly take the feeling to heart.

Certain guys have a way of poking fun at themselves on and off the field. Dick Stuart's league-leading error totals at first base prompted him to order a license plate reading "E-3," for example, and Graig Nettles named his dog "Ohfer," as in "0 for 4 at the plate." Frank Lucchesi, who went through league-leading loss totals during his time as Phillies skipper, explained his managerial moves on a radio show he called *Why I Did It*.

Other players were equally up front about their dire situations. There was Billy Loes, for instance, who predicted that Brooklyn would lose the World Series in six games; this was a fairly remarkable prediction, considering that Loes played for Brooklyn. Fred Manrique was once asked what the Twins needed to improve. He replied, "A second baseman," which was somewhat unexpected, considering that he was the Twins' starting second baseman at the time.

But Tom Yawkey of the Red Sox may have outdone all of the above when it came to baseball humility.

Through his decades as Red Sox owner, Yawkey steadfastly refused to court attention through the media or garner any undue attention in the clubhouse. It's said that in the mid-1970s, Bernie Carbo saw a familiar but nondescript middle-aged man by his locker, assumed the guy was another team assistant, and ordered up a cheeseburger and fries. Tom Yawkey, the Yale-educated multimillionaire, said "Sure," then promptly retrieved Carbo's cheeseburger and fries.

I was such a dangerous hitter I even got intentional walks in batting practice.

CASEY STENGEL

My only regret is that I can't sit in the stands and watch myself pitch.

BO BELINSKY

The only way he's gonna catch me is if he plays winter ball.

REGGIE JACKSON, on John Mayberry's challenge to the American League homer title

I can hit .400, .350, .300, or .200. I can do it all.

JUNIOR ORTIZ

I could sit on the bench and score three runs.

RICKEY HENDERSON

Injuries

I walked into our clubhouse and saw four doctors, three therapists, and five trainers. Back when I broke in, we had one trainer with a bottle of rubbing alcohol, and by the seventh inning we had drunk it all.

TOMMY LASORDA

My bad shoulder feels good, but my good shoulder feels bad.

ROBERTO CLEMENTE

It was a serious situation. I pray for his buttocks and his family.

JIM BOWDEN on a player's backside surgery

DEEPEST SYMPATHY

Ballplayers know they may have to deal with injuries on a daily basis. Very often, they learn to deal with them through laughter.

Take Casey Stengel, for instance. Well after his playing days, while serving as the Boston Braves' manager in 1943, Casey was struck by an errant taxi in Kenmore Square.

Hilarity ensued.

One of Boston's more notorious, attack-minded columnists nominated the offending cabbie as "sportsman of the year," and Casey's many friends were only slightly less rough in their kidding. After hearing that the overcrowded Massachusetts General Hospital had assigned Casey a bed in the maternity ward, for instance, several friends sent him Mother's Day cards. Another sent him a more conventional note but addressed it care of the psychiatric ward.

Frankie Frisch, Casey's oldest friend in the game, also sent a telegram. It read: "Your attempt at suicide fully understood. Deepest sympathy you didn't succeed."

Unfortunately, the injury was also memorable in the fact that it never fully healed. Decades afterward, Case still limped around with a misset shin bone, and when newcomers noticed, the Ol' Perfesser "explained" that the doctors had sewn his leg back on backward.

Intangibles

Don't get me wrong—there are certain qualities players must possess to be successful in Major League Baseball that are not reflected in the box score, but if [a young] Chipper Jones's willingness to lay out a high school player is more important than his career .400 OBP, then I've got some teenagers to punch.

J. C. BRADBURY

The International Pastime

Baseball is very different in Japan. For example, if you're at third base, before coming home, you have to take off your shoes.

BILL MAHER

I love the Dominican Republic—great meringue, no Starbucks—but, geez, how are they generating 98 major leaguers from one island? Is everyone in Santo Domingo walking around with a Louisville Slugger and a *Bill James Abstract*?

NORMAN CHAD

Ah, how could he lose a ball in the sun?! He's from Mexico!

HARRY CARAY, on Jorge Orta

The real Big Red Machine.

BILL LEE, on Communist China

The Internet

While it might be foolish to suggest that fantasy leaguers played a leading role in establishing the viability of the World Wide Web, one thing is indisputable—their eagerness to embrace the medium was surpassed only by those who wanted to look at pictures of naked women.

SAM WALKER

If you think about it, [baseball sites] help office productivity. What are the top two reasons workers leave their office? Starbucks and cigarettes. Caffeine and nicotine, two things that are bad for you. We cut that and substitute baseball. How many times have people said, "I better not smoke that cigarette—I've got to watch the Yankees on MLB.TV?"

BOB BOWMAN, CEO of MLB.com

Mickey Rivers on IQ

Out of what? A thousand?

RIVERS, on Reggie Jackson's claim that he had an IQ of 160

Well, you better stop readin' and writin' and start hittin'.

RIVERS, after a struggling Reggie Jackson said, "I must be crazy. I've got an IQ of 160 and I'm arguing with a man who can't even read or write"

MICKEY RIVERS: I'll bet you a hundred bucks I have a higher IQ than you.

LEE MAY: Man, you don't even know how to spell IQ.

Reggie Jackson vs. Billy Martin

Those two couldn't pass a salt shaker across the table without finding something to argue about.

LEONARD KOPPETT

It was a strange and wonderful relationship—he was strange and I was wonderful.

REGGIE JACKSON, on Billy Martin

Just write, "Jackson smiled for the first time all year."

JACKSON, on rumors of Martin's firing

Job Security

If you don't win, you're going to be fired. If you do win, you'll put off the day you're going to be fired.

LEO DUROCHER

All managers are interim managers.

MIKE FLANAGAN

Always rent.

CHUCK TANNER'S advice to new managers

Jay Johnstone

That's some title. I'm not sure about the "temporary" part.

TOMMY LASORDA, on Johnstone's autobiography, *Temporary Insanity*

Don't blame me for Johnstone—he was crazy before I met him.

JIMMY PIERSALL

Michael Jordan, Ballplayer

ERR JORDAN

SPORTS ILLUSTRATED HEADLINE on Jordan's minor league career

Couldn't hit a curveball with an ironing board.

BOB FELLER

Baskets don't curve.

KEN KAISER, on why Jordan succeeded only in hoops

I'm hoping Michael Jordan keeps playing in the NBA for a long, long time, because the longer he plays basketball, the less likely it is he'll try to play baseball.

MICHAEL VENTRE

Character Profile: RABBIT MARANVILLE

Walter "Rabbit" Maranville had a great sense of humor. And boy did he need it.

At barely over 5'5" and 150 pounds, Rabbit was among the smallest shortstops of the twentieth century, the one who always seemed to attract opponent intimidation tactics such as bean-balls, take-out slides, and hard tags. In the early, extremely rough era stretching from the 1910s to the 1930s, each and every ball game was liable to bring him bumps and bruises, stiffness and soreness, spasms and sprains, and tweaks and tenderness, all livened up by the occasional small tear and crack.

For all that, though, nothing could keep Rabbit down. He not only survived but thrived, lasting a record 23 years at short while crafting a Hall of Fame career. The runt everyone tried to knock off ended up among the most resilient and winning ballplayers of his era.

Lightning-fast reflexes, quick feet, and hard work could account for a lot of Rabbit Maranville's longevity but, beyond that, the little guy had far too much fun to quit. It turned out that, as much as he needed some comic relief, he could come up with plenty of it.

The most public part of Maranville's daring was in his any-thing-goes attitude toward the game. When he was on base, he had a habit of, quite literally, dancing off the bases, breaking into little step routines that worked to both distract the opposing pitcher and entertain the fans. Once, after he took a questionable umpire's call on a low strike, he set himself on his knees for the next pitch. Another time, after a long rain delay, Rabbit took the field in rubber boots and, while slumping, went up to "bat" with a tennis racket in his hands. After forcing out a sliding runner at second base, he'd sometimes sit atop the poor opponent for a couple of seconds.

Without a doubt, Maranville's signature antic was the "vest catch." He would camp under an easy pop-up, arms fast by his side, and the ball would hit him on the shoulder, then gently roll down his chest and plop into his waist-level glove.* Not exactly

---

* The vest catch spawned a legion of imitators, of course, but few could avoid having the ball bounce off their heads. If that also happened to Maranville from time to time, it would explain a lot.

textbook fielding, of course, but Rabbit never failed to get a huge round of applause from the grandstands.

After Rabbit Maranville played his way through a tough day on the field, he felt perfectly free to do anything and everything necessary to liven things up during the downtime after hours. His off-field enthusiasms may have been too creative and bold to fall into the category of mere pranks. On at least one occasion, following his customary drink or five, he dived into a hotel fountain, emerged with a goldfish between his teeth, then swallowed the little fellow with a theatrical flourish. Another time, he soaped up Al Simmons's bat before batting practice, then watched as the hard-hitting, obscenity-spewing slugger tried to figure out why he was fouling off pitch after pitch after pitch. Working with a teammate/accomplice, he once filled manager Bill McKechnie's hotel closet with live pigeons, then feigned sleep in their darkened room until the startled skipper opened the door and a furious flock winged past him.

That's not to mention a certain umm, eventful, photo op with his sidekick, Charlie Grimm, described on page 322.

At certain points, Rabbit's slapstick went so far that some even questioned his sanity. He was known to walk on the ledges of hotels, for instance, far enough up that the slightest slip would lead to a deadly fall. In 1925, his days-old tenure as a Cubs player-manager came to an abrupt end when he decided to run through the club's railroad cars, splashing cold water upon his napping players while hollering that "nobody falls asleep under Maranville management!" During a 1931 overseas trip to Japan, the unusual suspect somehow got his hands on an imperial soldier's uniform, then solemnly marched along in a lockstep military parade, at least until he was arrested by angry Tokyo policemen.

At age 42, in spring training, Maranville suffered a career-ending injury during a collision at home plate and, even as he was being carted off the field with a broken leg, asked the umpire if he was safe on the play. (He was.)

When will we ever again see the like? It's rare enough to see a single performer displaying Hall of Fame–quality toughness or Charlie Chaplin–quality comedy; it seems too much to ask a man to provide both nowadays. Almost no one's ever worked as hard as he's played.

Well, almost no one.

Knuckleballs

A butterfly with hiccups.

WILLIE STARGELL'S description of the pitch

For Christ's sake, if the hitter can't hit 'em, how do you expect me to catch 'em?

GUS TRIANDOS

Use a big glove and a pair of rosary beads.

JOE TORRE

You don't want a knuckleballer pitching for you. Or against you.

TOMMY LASORDA

Knuckleheads

You never want to win 20 because then they'll expect you to do it every year.

BILLY LOES

He refused to bunt no matter what the situation and seemed to endorse any product that would pay him 50 bucks. He never stopped talking during his entire career and carried on feuds with almost everyone but the ushers.

BRENDAN C. BOYD and **FRED C. HARRIS**, on Dick Stuart

He's turned his life around. He used to be depressed and miserable, now he's miserable and depressed.

HARRY KALAS, on Garry Maddox

I tell him something, it goes in one ear, hits something hard, and bounces back out.

LOU PINIELLA, on Rob Dibble

When he drank, which was all the time, he was a ruthless SOB. But you know, he wasn't all that nice when he didn't drink.

ANONYMOUS PLAYER, on "Sudden" Sam McDowell

Dock [Ellis] had two skills: He could pitch and he could get into trouble.

PETER GOLENBOCK

Ron [Blomberg] didn't care about fielding. To him, it was something you did while waiting to hit.

STEVE KLINE

Run till you're out.

STEVE LYONS, on his baserunning philosophy

DEION SANDERS: I'll do anything possible to help the team—steal, walk, bunt, anything.
SPORTSWRITER: Get hit by a pitch?
SANDERS: No.

DR. STRANGEGLOVE, OR HOW I LEARNED TO STOP WORRYING . . .

How bad a fielder was Dick Stuart? Well, he led the league in errors in seven of his first nine years at first base. In 1963, he set a still-standing record of 29 errors at the position. During his time with the Red Sox, he once dropped an easy pop fly, collided with a fielder on another pop fly, and failed to cover his base . . . on three consecutive plays. He was bad.

The thing that really set Stuart apart as "Dr. Strangeglove" was that the knucklehead didn't particularly worry about his fielding. Or lack thereof. No, with his mind set solely on hitting, Stuart felt free to have some fun on the field.

Once, a pitcher's throw to first base bounced in the dirt in front of him, so Stuart started scrambling around for the ball, took one quick look at the nearby umpire, and said, "Don't just stand there—help me find the SOB!" Another time, when a pitcher was firing pickoff pitches to him at first base, Stuart asked, in all seriousness, for softer throws, since the better, quicker tosses were stinging his hand. Stuart once picked up a hot dog wrapper that had blown onto the field, heard the Fenway crowd give him a sarcastic round of applause, and took a little bow in return.

What's the expression—better to laugh than to cry? Well, at least once, Dick Stuart's manager did.

It seems that one day, when Stuart was still playing for the Pirates, the public address announcer made a customary announcement: "Anyone who interferes with a ball in play will be ejected from the ballpark." Displaying a deadpan sense of humor, Pittsburgh manager Danny Murtaugh said, "I hope Stuart doesn't think that means him."

Knuckleheads: Joe Pepitone Division

Joe [Pepitone] played for the semipro Nathan's Famous Hot Dog team (a club which some Yankee teammates might have thought was named after him).

WILLIAM RYCZEK

All I know is 20 guys are on top of me and one guy keeps pulling my hair. That pissed me off more than anything.

JOE PEPITONE, on a 1967 brawl

He was very fast and graceful in the outfield—when he wanted to be. He didn't want to be very often.

MAURY ALLEN

Sandy Koufax

Either he throws the fastest ball I've ever seen or I'm going blind.

RICHIE ASHBURN

I see how Koufax won 25 games. What I don't see is how he lost five.

YOGI BERRA

On the nights when he pitched, he was the last to board the team bus. Nobody minded. The Dodgers weren't going anywhere without him.

JANE LEAVY

When Sandy Koufax retired.

WILLIE STARGELL, on his biggest thrill in baseball

The Language Barrier

I never got any endorsements or commercials. I never understood why. I have an accent, but so does Ricardo Montalban.

CESAR CEDENO

They don't speak English and neither does he.

ANONYMOUS MONTREAL FAN,
on French-Canadians' love for Bill Lee

YO LA TENGO

For its modern appeal that stretches to several continents, what used to be called the national pastime should, more appropriately, be called the international pastime. While it's always been a wonder to see the various nationalities playing together, it's sometimes been a headache to get them talking to one another.

On at least one occasion, the language barrier led to a serious outfield collision. It happened on the infamous '62 Mets, when center fielder Richie Ashburn called off teammates on a shallow fly ball; "I've got it!" he shouted, but shortstop Elio Chacon, who didn't know much English, still plowed into Ashburn. When Ashburn, ever the adaptable one, subsequently decided to switch his call-off to "*Yo la tengo!*" he did manage to avoid Chacon . . . but collided into Frank Thomas, who, as it turned out, didn't know much Spanish.

On most other occasions, the language barrier was more of an inconvenience than an emergency. For instance, Masanori Murakami, the first Japanese player to come to the big leagues, struggled to learn English, at least until his American teammates taught him a "welcome" phrase for their Giants manager; that's the reason Murakami once greeted Herman Franks with the words "Take a hike, Herman."

Finally, umpire Ron Luciano used to do a lot of talking to Tony Oliva of the Twins, who always nodded and replied, "Pretty good,

Ronnie." It was some years later that Rod Carew pulled Luciano aside and confided that Oliva hardly understood a word out of the ump's mouth; Oliva smiled and said "Pretty good" to just about anything.

Lawyers

Life is full of trials, which is a good thing for lawyers.

HUGHIE JENNINGS, law school graduate / Hall of Fame manager

He passed the bar exam and there were times when I hardly passed a bar.

JIM LEYLAND, on Tony La Russa

We're going to charge them double, bill them by the third of an inning, and generally berate them.

MIKE VEECK, on his "Lawyers' Night" promotion

Life Advice

People need to lie back now and then and listen to the grass grow.

DICK WAKEFIELD

The trick is to grow up without growing old.

CASEY STENGEL

Don't look back. Something might be gaining on you.

SATCHEL PAIGE

Don't look at the hole in the donut. Look at the whole donut.

GABE PAUL

Progress always involves risks. You can't steal second base and keep your foot on first.

FREDERICK WILCOX

Caution is the easy way out.

BILL VEECK

Don't give up. Tomorrow is just another day.

CASEY STENGEL

Live your life like every day is Opening Day.

YOGI BERRA

I was in Vietnam. A big payroll doesn't always win.

SANDY ALDERSON

He's listed as day-to-day . . . aren't we all?

VIN SCULLY

Somebody once said to me, "Sure, you and Ernie [Banks] want to play two because you know you're gonna get two or three hits. No wonder you guys are so jolly." And I said, "Maybe that attitude is why we're getting the hits."

BILLY WILLIAMS

I'm 0 for 26. I'm surprised I'm not batting 12th.

PRESTON WILSON, on being dropped to 8th in the order

What do you think I am, a groundskeeper?

Player **BILLY MARTIN**, on batting 8th

AND INTRODUCING . . .

Sometime during the 1970s someone came up with the bright idea of introducing major league players' at-bats with individual theme songs. Ballpark music directors have been thinking up inventive lineup introductions ever since.

Every so often, road players will be introduced through a tune somehow acknowledging their home origins, which is why Fergie Jenkins used to come in to the tune of Andy Williams's "Canadian Sunset," Al "The Mad Hungarian" Hrabosky came in with Liszt's "Hungarian Rhapsody," and Sid Fernandez had the theme from *Hawaii Five-0*.

Other music programmers tried to put a little twist on the player's name itself. Notable performer-performance matches included:

TOM GORDON: Theme to *Flash Gordon*
CRISTIAN GUZMAN: Night Ranger's "Sister Christian"
MICKEY HATCHER: Theme to *The Mickey Mouse Club*
VANCE LAW: Theme to *Dragnet*
JAMES LONEY: Theme to *The Lone Ranger*
MIKE SCHOOLER: Alice Cooper's "School's Out"

More inventive musical accompaniments tend to link the player to some kind of off-field reference.

For instance, when Bobby Bonilla jilted the small-market Pirates for a fat free agent contract elsewhere, his next appearance in Pittsburgh was cued to Steve Miller's "Take the Money and Run." After headlines reported that the Athletics' Bert Campaneris was hit by a paternity suit, an Anaheim organist played "Yes, Sir, That's My Baby," and shortly after Adrian Beltre returned from a severe injury caused by a blow to his groin area, the Safeco Field organist played the theme from *The Nutcracker Suite.*

Grady Little

Too Little, too late.

STEPHEN KING, on Little's tardy replacement of Pedro Martinez
in the '03 American League Championship Series

I guess Grady was saving his bullpen for Game Eight.

Red Sox fan **"STEVE M."**

Long Balls

Ruth could hit the ball so far nobody could field it.

CASEY STENGEL

The homers he hit against us would be homers in any park, including Yellowstone.

PAUL RICHARDS, on Harmon Killebrew

When he hits a home run, there's no souvenir.

WILLIE STARGELL, on Dick Allen's
hitting balls out of the park

It was an insurance homer—that's why I hit it halfway to the Prudential Building.

REGGIE JACKSON

I'd like to warn the airplanes not to fly too low.

GEORGE FOSTER, on hitting at Shea Stadium

Sooner or later, that home run Jose Reyes hit off Roger Clemens is going to land.

WILL LEITCH

Anything that goes that far in the air ought to have a stewardess on it.

PAUL SPLITTORFF

Not to put too fine a point on it, but [John J.] McGraw looked like a leprechaun without a conscience.

FRANK DEFORD

Had the look of a man who'd been through extra innings.

JONATHAN EIG, on Miller Huggins

He has the kind of face that even Dale Carnegie would want to punch.

BILL VEECK, on Walter O'Malley

I'd rather have made the All-Star team.

JIMMY PIERSALL, on being named one of *Sport* magazine's "Ten Most Handsome Men in Baseball"

I hope Carmen doesn't find out about this.

YOGI BERRA, on being named one of the most "stimulating" men in America

He's a hard-nosed, big-nosed kind of player.

CASEY STENGEL, on Billy Martin

Looked like everybody's brother-in-law and played like him, too.

BRENDAN C. BOYD and **FRED C. HARRIS**, on Harry Chiti

Funny, he doesn't look a day over 60.

BILL JAMES, on Phil Niekro at age 46

Now I have a mustache.

BILLY MARTIN, on how he's changed over the years

Looks 18, throws 98.

TOM VERDUCCI, on Tim Lincecum

Looks like a ninth grader who snuck onto the team only because he was related to the manager.

BILL SIMMONS, on Dustin Pedroia

My wife says, "Gosh, how do these people still know you?" Well, that's probably because I have the same hair.

JOE PEPITONE, on his long-lasting fame (and toupee)

Looks: Yogi Berra Division

An ugly duckling who made it big in a world of swans.

BILL VEECK

He looks like the bottom man on an unemployed acrobatic team.

LARRY MacPHAIL

I think you look like Tyrone Power.

CASEY STENGEL

Los Angeles

In L.A. and San Francisco, it was "Let's beat 'em." Back in New York, it was "Let's kill 'em."

JACKIE BRANDT, on the Dodgers / Giants transition to California

As part of the $20 million renovation, the Dodgers are planning to replace every seat in the park. So fans won't be inconvenienced, the work won't begin until the bottom of the sixth.

BILL SCHEFT

They took off in 25 different cabs. And, in Southern California, there were 25 different freeways to get them to 25 different beaches.

DON BAYLOR, on the late-1970s Angels

Watching baseball is different in L.A. Before I came out here, I'd never seen a game canceled due to bad vibes.

BILLY CRYSTAL

Los Angeles of . . . Something

"Orange County American League Baseball Representative"

BOB RYAN'S reference
for the "Los Angeles Angels of Anaheim"

"Los Anahangeles."

KING KAUFMAN

"Los Angeles Angels of Anaheim Near Fullerton"

RICK CHANDLER

This year, the loser had to take legal custody of the name Anaheim.

BILL SCHEFT, on the Dodgers-Angels interleague series

It was a come-from-ahead loss.

MIKE LITTWIN

Wouldn't that be nice?

CHARLIE BROWN, after Lucy says "Sometimes you win, sometimes you lose"

Peter Bavasi resigned last winter as general manager of the Blue Jays with the incredible parting comment that the thrill was gone and therefore it was time to move on to new challenges. Well, yes, Peter, I can understand how the thrill would go out of losing 105 games a year for about five years. I know that first 57–105 season has to be a rush, but after a while it gets to be routine, like anything else.

BILL JAMES

Love of the Game

The Fans

It's what gets inside you. It's what lights you up.

LOWELL GANZ and **BABALOO MANDEL**, in *A League of Their Own*

There are only two seasons—winter and baseball.

BILL VEECK

Isn't it annoying, the way life keeps intruding on baseball?

STEPHEN KING

They say you've got to be realistic, but I prefer baseball.

DIEGO MUSILLI

My three favorite sports are baseball, baseball, and baseball.

MIKE LUPICA

Baseball, you had me at "Play ball."

JIM CAPLE

Now, you tell me, if I have a day off during the baseball season, where do you think I'd spend it? The ballpark.

HARRY CARAY, on why he didn't vacation

BASEBALL ISN'T BORING. YOU ARE.

Fan banner

Baseball, like pizza or sex, will never go out of style. Count on it.

DIEGO MUSILLI

The Players

No. I only got old.

COOL PAPA BELL, on whether he ever got tired of baseball

Everything.

GREG MADDUX, on the best thing about baseball

The trouble with baseball is that it is not played year-round.

GAYLORD PERRY

Playing baseball for a living is like having a license to steal.

PETE ROSE

This is like a fraternity—a fraternity where you don't have to go to school and everyone has a hell of a lot of money.

CURT SCHILLING, on the '04 Red Sox

I would have paid the Yankees $7,000 to let me play. They pay $3,500 for a few days at fantasy camp. A whole season would be worth at least $7,000.

DOOLEY WOMACK

Sex

Almost as much fun as baseball.

TED WILLIAMS, on sex

The Other National Pastime.

DAVID H. NATHAN

Baseball is so associated with sex: "He's playing the field," "Hoo, he scored," "Oh, he didn't get to first base." "I struck out"/"Why?"/"She wanted a diamond." It's always about base-ball. Always baseball.

JERRY SEINFELD

I'm the most loyal player money can buy.

DON SUTTON

Loyalty is what you keep pets for.

WADE BOGGS, on leaving the Red Sox for the Yankees

They say he's unlucky, but if he keeps swinging like that, he's gonna be unlucky his entire career.

CASEY STENGEL

It's not easy to hit .215—you have to be going terrible and have bad luck, too.

STEVE KEMP

Angry as hell, I stormed back to my office, punched the door and broke my hand. It was our only break that day.

BILL GILES, on the Phillies' loss in the '77 National League Championship Series

Managers and Managing

He knew baseball like Einstein knew algebra.

TOM DALY, on George Stallings

He knew almost everything and suspected the rest.

CASEY STENGEL, on Wilbert Robinson

He's the kind of guy who can eat a quarter and spit out three dimes.

CLINT HURDLE, on Davey Johnson

You've seen the drawing of two buzzards on a limb, and one of them says, "Patience, my ass. I say let's kill something." That's [Whitey] Herzog. He didn't believe in waiting around.

BILL JAMES

Good players.

YOGI BERRA, on what makes a good manager

I don't trip my players on the way to the dugout.

CASEY STENGEL, on the secret to managing

Managing isn't that difficult. You just have to score more runs than the other guy.

Braves owner **TED TURNER**, who once named himself manager

All I do is write their names on the lineup card and let them play. It's not a tough job. I haven't misspelled one name yet.

HARVEY KUENN

It's like raising kids who fall out of trees.

TOM TREBELHORN

Brilliant managerial thinking and dumb Irish luck.

DANNY MURTAUGH,
on the secrets of his success

Managerial Advice

Trust your gut, don't cover your butt.

PAUL RICHARDS

Stay away from firearms and don't room higher than the
second floor.

FRANKIE FRISCH'S advice to young managers

Have a strong stomach and a long contract.

DICK HOWSER

Managerial Communication

Once, when Shirley Povich of the *Washington Post* grew impa-
tient after an hour waiting for a specific answer to his question,
[Casey] Stengel snapped, "Don't rush me."

STEVEN GOLDMAN

Beating around the bush takes work and I'm lazy.

BOB LEMON

Yelling is just a way of communicating loudly.

EARL WEAVER

I had no trouble communicating. The players just didn't like what I
had to say.

FRANK ROBINSON

Managerial Communication:
Dusty Baker Division

People ask me how I'm going to deal with the egos of today's players. They forget that in L.A., we had some major egos, too. I was one of them.

He doesn't have to march to the same drummer, just as long as he's in the same band.

BAKER, on Barry Bonds

Managerial Philosophy

I'm not the manager because I'm always right. I'm always right because I'm the manager.

GENE MAUCH

If they could hit like Ted Williams, I would.

TED WILLIAMS, on whether he'd allow his players the star treatment

Better Living Through Confrontation.

MIKE SHROPSHIRE, on Billy Martin's credo

Managerial Stress

Most nights, I slept like a baby. That is, I woke up every two hours crying.

DICK WILLIAMS

People may think it's easy, but it isn't. Managing is a lonely, difficult job. It's not fun. It's a nighmare. But I enjoy it.

MAURY WILLS

It's bases on balls, doc. Those damned bases on balls.

GEORGE STALLINGS, on his heart condition

If everyone in this country had to manage a major league team, there would be no need for Social Security—the job takes 10 to 15 years off your life.

RICH DONNELLY

Mickey Mantle

With tears in my eyes.

FRANK SULLIVAN, on how he pitched to Mickey Mantle

Son, nobody is half as good as Mickey Mantle.

AL KALINE, after a fan said he "wasn't half as good as Mantle"

Marriage

She wanted a big diamond.

MOOKIE WILSON, on why he was married at home plate

One team, one wife.

STEVE BLASS, on the secret to success

Yeah, but I love you more than football and basketball.

TOMMY LASORDA, after his wife said that he didn't love her as much as baseball

WE INTERRUPT THIS MARRIAGE TO BRING YOU THE BASEBALL SEASON.

Plaque on the wall of Tony La Russa's home

Billy Martin

He's the only guy I know who could hear a guy give him the finger from the back of the barroom.

MICKEY MANTLE

Some people have a chip on their shoulder. Billy has a whole lumberyard.

JIM MURRAY

Playing for Yogi was like playing for your father. Playing for Billy is like playing for your father-in-law.

DON BAYLOR

If you approach Billy just right, he's okay. I avoid him altogether.

RON GUIDRY

Billy Brawls

It's not that Billy [Martin] drinks a lot. It's just that he fights a lot when he drinks a little.

DICK YOUNG

I don't throw the first punch. I throw the second four punches.

MARTIN

[Rangers traveling secretary Burt] Hawkins suggested to Billy that he might go f—k himself, at which point Martin offered to heave Burt out of the airplane. "If you think you're big enough, Billy Boy, then give it a try," Burt responded. Thus challenged, Martin got up and smacked a 65-year-old man with a heart condition. Other than that, it was a quiet flight to Kansas City.

MIKE SHROPSHIRE

Today is Opening Day in baseball. Out in Yankee Stadium, Billy Martin just threw out the first punch.

JOHNNY CARSON

Pepper Martin

A chunky, unshaven hobo who ran bases like a berserk locomotive, slept in the raw, and swore at pitchers in his sleep.

BOB CHIEGER

He will spend all day trying to beat you and then stay up all night trying to make you well.

BRANCH RICKEY

Don Mattingly

One hundred percent ballplayer, 0 percent bulls—t.

BILL JAMES

All line drives and silence.

PAUL SOLOTAROFF

I like being closer to the bats.

MATTINGLY'S stated reason for moving his locker

Willie Mays

I don't compare 'em, I just catch 'em.

MAYS, on his greatest catch

Catching Willie Mays in a rundown is like trying to assassinate a squirrel with a lawn mower.

BILL JAMES

There have been two geniuses: Willie Mays and Willie Shakespeare.

TALLULAH BANKHEAD

Neither could you!

Indians rookie **TOMMY HINZO**, after Bobby Bonds screamed, "You couldn't hold Willie Mays's jock!"

Mickey McDermott

Eleven other managers tried that, and they ain't managing.

CASEY STENGEL, on why he wasn't pitching the much-traveled McDermott

W-0, L-0, SV-0, G-4, IP-6, H-14, BB-10, SO-3, ERA-13.50. I led the league in nothing but stolen towels.

McDERMOTT, on his record in Kansas City

I was a very clean pitcher. I took a lot of early showers.

McDERMOTT

Media Relations

You have to watch out for those reporters. They ask you questions, they write down your answers, and then they put 'em in the paper.

BILL FISCHER

I try to have respect for people in general, whether it's ballplayers or lowlifes like the media.

JIM RIGGLEMAN

If you ask me a question I don't know, I'm not going to answer.

YOGI BERRA

The more you hear what Steve [Carlton] has been saying lately, the more you realize how fortunate America was that he refused to speak to the media all those years.

JOHN STEIGERWALD

REPORTER: What are your thoughts on [Jays manager] Jimy [Williams] getting fired?
GEORGE BELL: If you want to ask me a question like that, ask me loud enough, in front of the whole team.
REPORTER [loudly]: What are your thoughts on Jimy getting fired?
BELL: No comment.

Superstar apologizing to writers—in baseball, this occurs as often as a quadruple play.

SCOTT OSTLER

The '62 Mets

They say we're going to get players out of a grab bag. From what I see, it's going to be a garbage bag.

ROGERS HORNSBY, on the '62 Mets

The Mets is a very good thing. They give everybody a job. Just like the WPA.

CASEY STENGEL

The Mets have only three weaknesses: pitching, batting, and fielding.

ROBERT LIPSYTE

The Mets can't fight, either.

JACK MANN, on one of their brawls

It was a team effort.

CASEY STENGEL, on losing 120 games

New York wanted National League baseball back in the worst way, and got just that.

JOHN HELYAR

CANZERONI, CANZONARRI, CANZONARRIA . . .

Casey Stengel had an odd, career-long habit of addressing strangers as "Doctor" in much the same way that less imaginative sorts would call others "dude" or "buddy." The Ol' Perfesser simply didn't care to properly memorize names and no one knew why, exactly. Maybe he had more important things to think about, or maybe he consciously tried to play up his "colorful" reputation or deemphasize players' individuality.

For whatever reason, Stengel had honed his habit by the time he was managing the woeful Mets of the early 1960s. Here's a sampling of the era's players and their "Stengelese" translations:

TIM HARKNESS: "Harshness," "Harshman"
ROD KANEHL: "Canoe"
CHARLIE NEAL: "O'Neal"
JOE PIGNATANO: "Pignatelli"
MARV THRONEBERRY: "Thornberry"
RON SWOBODA: "Saboda"
CARL WILLEY: "Smalley"

Chris Cannizzaro, otherwise known to history as "a defensive catcher who can't catch," also had Casey names varying from "Canzeroni" to "Canzonarri" and "Canzonarria."

Others were given more far-ranging "Stengelese" tags. Casey referred to Galen Cisco ("Ohio State") and Ken Mackenzie ("My Yale Man") through their alumni associations and Charley Smith ("Davis") and Tracy Stallard ("Larsen") were, apparently, linked with similar players from years past. The erudite Jay Hook was "Professor." Reliever Bob Miller was "Nelson" while broadcaster Lindsey Nelson was "Miller."

Needless to say, most young players didn't realize that the old boy was messing around with his name games, but whenever one of them pointed out his "mistakes," Casey Stengel would only give a knowing look and ask, "Do I make my checks out right for you?"

The '62 Mets: Attendance

Never has so much misery loved so much company.

JIMMY BRESLIN, on the '62 Mets'
lowly standings and high attendance

Never before have so many seen so few perform so badly.

MAURY ALLEN

Hey, if we can make losing popular, I'm all for it.

CASEY STENGEL

We had deep depth.

YOGI BERRA, on the '69 Mets' bench

They came slow but fast.

CASEY STENGEL,
on the team's late-season comeback

We were overwhelming underdogs.

BERRA, on the World Series

Mets vs. Yanks

The best things about New York were playing for the Yankees and leaving the Mets.

ELLIOTT MADDOX

According to a recent survey of New Yorkers, 51 percent said they would root for the Yankees in a Subway Series and 35 percent said the Mets. That's 86 percent. Which means the other 14 percent answered, "What are you, a cop?"

BILL SCHEFT

MET FANS BELIEVE.

T-shirt seen at the 2000 World Series

YANKEE FANS KNOW.

T-shirt seen at the same series

Milwaukee

A Drinking Town with a Baseball Problem

RICK REILLY'S suggested motto

I opened my eyes to see if I was in heaven or if I was in Milwaukee.

KEVIN SEITZER, on being hit by a pitch

The Minors

The longest 12 miles in America.

BOBBY BROWN, on the distance between Triple-A Newark and Yankee Stadium

This is kind of like purgatory. You're in between heaven and hell, heaven being the big leagues and hell being anything other than baseball.

VON HAYES, on managing in the minors

Mismatches

The people who came to see us play the Orioles were the same kind who went to see the lions eat Christians.

JIM BOUTON

Charlie Gehringer could hit me in a tunnel at midnight with the lights out.

LEFTY GOMEZ

In 12 years I struck him out once, and I think the umpire blew the call.

WHITEY FORD, on Nellie Fox

Character Profile: BILL VEECK

Today's major league franchise operations seem to have all the spunk and spontaneity of Fortune 500 board meetings.

It's no wonder, really. The game's always been a business, and that's never been truer than it is today. Every year, the major leagues generate billions in revenue, franchises plow through nine-figure budgets, and its stars pull down the kind of annual contracts that make lottery winners look like lottery losers. With that much on the line, it's to be expected that some of the most important "uniforms" are three-piece suits, that some of the most influential pinstripes are worn by bankers, and debt-to-equity ratios get more attention than strikeout-to-walk numbers.

The corporate, big-money mode of baseball has dominated for so long, in fact, that it's possible to forget that, at one time, the game was different. Once, it was possible for an owner to be more of a fan than a financier, more of a showman than a businessman.

Once, there was a Bill Veeck.

Veeck always stood out among team honchos because he literally grew up within the game of baseball.

While other team leaders either bought or inherited their power, the teenage Bill used his father's onetime position as the Cubs' general manager to finagle his way into jobs in Wrigley Field's groundskeeping, marketing, and fan outreach departments in the 1930s. Before he was drafted into military service in World War II, he was largely responsible for introducing the outfield ivy and picturesque center field scoreboard that define the Friendly Confines to this day.

It may have been that up-from-the-bottom, do-it-yourself background, but Veeck's climb into team ownership, first in the minor leagues and then in the majors, were always marked by inventiveness. He either introduced or popularized a laundry list of fan-friendly innovations, including ethnic theme nights, gimmick giveaways (free beer, free ladies' stockings), and players' names on the back of their uniforms, not to mention postgame shows that included clowns, minicar races, fireworks, and the acrobat Jackie Price (see page 80 for more on that character).

Most of all, Veeck's inventive nature led to a belief that ingenious, humor-based events could always goose attendance. From an early age, he had a knack for springing cheerful surprises, then turning them into fan-pleasing moments.

In order to increase attendance to his Indians and Browns games in the late 1940s and early 1950s, for instance, he gave fans the ability to call the team's moves on the field ("Grandstand Manager's Day"). He sent the midget Eddie Gaedel up for an official major league at-bat (see page 82). He once had the conductor of the Chicago Symphony Orchestra lead a full house, equipped with free kazoos, in playing the world's largest rendition of "Take Me Out to the Ballgame" and, for Opening Day 1976, Veeck joined in on a bicentennial-themed "Spirit of '76" parade. Anything for a laugh, anything to bring more smiles from the faces in the crowd.

The gags varied, but the irreverent spirit behind them didn't; as Veeck always explained, ball club owners couldn't guarantee a win, but you could always guarantee fun. "Every fan a king," he once said, paraphrasing another rabble-rouser, and he lived the words, spending virtually every day of the season rubbing elbows on his ballpark concourses, then devoting virtually every day of the off-season to giving speeches before any group that would have him.

"Sportshirt Bill" was so interested in making new friends that, in St. Louis, he took an "open-door policy" to a new extreme, making a point of literally removing his office door from its hinges, then inviting in all customers interested in trading a story, sharing a laugh, or downing a drink. When fans revolted against the rumor that Lou Boudreau would be traded, Bill made the rounds of Cleveland sports bars, personally assuring the Tribe diehards that he would do no such thing.

If there was a downside to Veeck's good sense of humor, it was that his stunts and comments tended to draw ready criticism from the less imaginative and more stodgy, which was virtually everyone else with a steady job in the major leagues' front offices. Most often the powers-that-be said that, multiple attendance records aside, Veeck was still "making a mockery of the game."

What a joke.

Veeck knew that a winning ball club is the greatest fan attraction of them all, and he also knew how to build those winning ball clubs. Veeck built a championship team with the 1948 Indians, a pennant winner with the 1959 White Sox, and a shocking, well-remembered runner-up with the 1977 White Sox; historic accomplishments all. The ability to repeatedly convert shoestring budgets into winning teams probably would have earned him his place in the Hall of Fame even if he had been born without a sense of humor.

Veeck is often remembered as a great showman, not because he lacked substance, but because of his influential style. In his own, inimitable way, he managed to do for baseball what P. T. Barnum did for circuses and Cecil B. DeMille did for the movies: He was decades ahead of his time in making the attraction a mass entertainment; a show capable of bringing surprise and delight to millions of new converts. There were more than a few financial successes along the way, of course, and if any team owner ever laughed all the way to the bank, Bill Veeck laughed all the way to the bank.

Monetary Incentives

Yeah, I played for the love of the game, but the more money I got, the more I loved the game.

KEN BOYER

$4,024.86.

LARRY GARDNER, on how much his World Series sacrifice fly meant to him

The Money

My father looked at the check and told the scout, "Throw in another hundred and you can take the rest of the family."

JOE DUGAN, on his signing bonus

As a former player, I have mixed feelings about free agency. It's like coed housing in college. We're shocked and confused and why didn't it happen 20 years ago?

BOB UECKER

With the money I'm making, I should be playing two positions.

PETE ROSE

Hey, I'm just happy to be making an obscene amount of money.

A ballplayer from a *New Yorker* cartoon by Harry Bliss

Yaz, you're my idol. I want my son to be just like you—rich.

JOE FOY, to Carl Yastrzemski

The bad thing about big league baseball is all the travel—all you can do in these big cities is shop. The good thing is that you can afford it.

BOBBY GRICH

He must have tried to lift his wallet with one hand.

PHIL RIZZUTO, on Frank Crosetti's sore arm

Money Problems

I kind of expected a cut, but that's what you'd call an amputation.

BABE RUTH, on the Yankees' salary offer

"The big leagues—I'd play there for nothing," I thought to myself. The Giants must have been reading my mind.

GAYLORD PERRY, on his team's $4,500 salary offer

This year I can't buy a hit and that means that with the contract I'll get next year, I won't be able to buy a pack of cigarettes.

RICH BILLINGS

Two things nobody grows up dreaming about are being broke and being an umpire. Thanks to baseball, I got to be both.

KEN KAISER

People think we make $3 million and $4 million a year. They don't realize that most of us only make $500,000.

PETE INCAVIGLIA

Morality

The immoral Babe Ruth.

JOHNNY LOGAN, on the greatest player ever

Morality isn't a factor.

DANNY OZARK, on his team's morale

Stan Musial

He could've hit .300 with a fountain pen.

JOE GARAGIOLA

He was never colorful, never much of an interview. He makes a better statue.

BILL JAMES

Mustaches

Go shave before someone throws a ball at it and kills you.

CASEY STENGEL, to Frenchy Bordagaray

How can I intimidate batters if I look like a damn golf pro?

AL HRABOSKY,
after being ordered to shave his Fu Manchu

The Name Game

Players

That ball went from bat to Wertz.

DIZZY DEAN, on a line drive to center fielder Vic Wertz

A living testimonial to the fact that naming your child after a famous celebrity does not necessarily help.

BRENDAN C. BOYD and **FRED C. HARRIS**, on Jesus McFarlane

He had the physique, beard, and last name of a guy who could have been playing left field in a South Side beer league.

RICHARD ROEPER, on Greg Luzinski

He was traded for a player to be named better.

BUD GERACIE, on the Indians' trading away Stubby Clapp

JOSH ALMIGHTY

Fan banner during Josh Beckett's dominating performance in the '07 American League Championship Series

After [Twins pitcher Kevin] Slowey stomped the Royals, their only hope is to face a pitcher called "Clyde Hangingcurvey."

JOE POSNANSKI

That's Mark with a "K," Reynolds with an "E."

KEVIN KERR, on Mark Reynolds' leading the National League in both strikeouts and errors

I'VE GOT A NAME . . .

On the back of most major league uniforms is stitching bearing the players' last names and their numbers. Couldn't be more simple. Name and number. Simple.

Well, not quite so simple.

Even something as seemingly straightforward as jersey names have had some twists and turns over the years. For instance, there was a brief time in the late 1960s and 1970s when MLB's regulations didn't necessarily require the use of surnames, so enterprising sorts such as Tony Conigliaro (TONY C.) and Vida Blue (VIDA) decided to use first names instead. It wasn't too long before nicknames were used by guys such as Ralph Garr (ROADRUNNER) and Ken Harrelson (HAWK).

The practice eventually died out, of course, to the point where only one player uses something other than a surname; the exceptional Ichiro Suzuki took to using his first name when he played on a Japanese team that featured a couple other players named Suzuki, then chose to continue the Ichiro habit even after reaching the majors.

On a couple other occasions, it wasn't the name but the spelling that drew attention.

When Bill Veeck signed Ted Kluszewski to his White Sox in 1960 he devised a publicity stunt that had an intentional misspelling of Big Klu's big surname. The club grabbed some headlines, but the last-place Nationals drew even more attention in 2009, when they played a game with jerseys reading NATINALS. That year, even their uniform makers were making errors.

Teams

The name "Giants" is right for my team. Who could stand in awe of a team named the Cubs? Cubs are cute. Or the Dodgers? I never dodged anything in my life. Cincinnati? Too many Republicans. Pittsburgh always depresses me. What I like best about St. Louis is the zoo. And the beer is fine in Milwaukee. But the Giants are a name to look up to, you might say.

TALLULAH BANKHEAD

I was glad I was traded to the Cubs. Some of my relatives thought a Texas Ranger was a cop.

MITCH WILLIAMS

Now I know why they call them the Angels—no matter what the pitcher throws, they never hit back.

DON RILEY

The ex-'Pos

RYAN FINLEY, on the former Expos/new Nationals

GM Matt Silverman recently said of the name change, "We're no longer the bottom feeding fish. . . . We're much more about the energy of the sun." That's right. The team that plays in a dome now has sunshine for a mascot.

CORK GAINES, on Tampa Bay's change
from the "Devil Rays" to the "Rays"

LOST AT SEA

Fan banner seen during the '08 Mariners' 101-loss season

The National Anthem

The only thing that's certain is that they'll play the national anthem before every game.

RICK MONDAY

Every time they play this song, I have a bad day.

JEFF KING

Once the national anthem plays, I get chills. I even know the words to it now.

PETE ROSE

The land of the free and the home of the . . . BRAVES!

Atlanta fans' finale flourish

New York State of Mind

New York is a home run town.

MILLER HUGGINS

It's a tough town not to have fun in.

MICKEY MANTLE

New York City is to baseball championships what Rome is to crucifixes.

JEFF PEARLMAN

All manner of New Yorkers, from Mayor Michael Bloomberg to Chris Rock to Jerry Seinfeld, proclaimed their city as the greatest place in the history of places. It was all very understated, as per the local custom.

RICH HOFMANN, on Johan Santana's intro press conference

Nostalgia

I ain't what I used to be, but who the hell is?

DIZZY DEAN

Basically, baseball has always been not as good as it used to be.

RON LUCIANO

There sure is a lot of bulls—t going on in here today. The older they get, the better they were when they were younger.

JOHNNY SAIN, on Old Timers' Day

"I used to play for the Big Red Machine." "Tony Perez was awesome." "There aren't as many good teams or players these days." "I had a career postseason batting average of .182." One of these four is something that you don't hear old Joe Morgan mention too often.

JASON MAJOR

You want to clear up a pitcher's memory, just ask him about his no-hitter.

TED LYONS

Numbers

TIM MCCARVER: Well in New York if you are gonna take a number, seven is an excellent choice. A lot of baseball history and home runs goes along with it.
RALPH KINER: Old Eddie Kranepool.
MCCARVER: I was referring to Mickey Mantle.
KINER: He was pretty good, too.

It's Bo Derek's number and she's perfect, too.

RICK CERONE,
on the Yankees' assigning him number 10

Because, on a scale of one to ten, I'm a 15.

DENNIS LAMP, on wearing number 15

He wore number 43, and that's what he would do. It was 4-3, 4-3, all day long. He made 821 outs to second base in his career.

JOE POSNANSKI, on Rick Manning

People are saying it was a great mass. As a matter of fact, afterward the Yankees retired Roman numeral XVI.

DAVID LETTERMAN, on the pope's visit to Yankee Stadium

Oakland

Oakland is the luckiest city since Hiroshima.

STUART SYMINGTON,
when the A's moved from Kansas City

The Charlie Finley era was not embraced by the Bay Area. On the plus side, if I had a ticket and knew I was going to be late, I could always call ahead and they'd hold the game up for me.

KEN LEVINE

There's nothing in Oakland I'd want.

San Francisco mayor **ART AGNOS**, on why he refused to make the customary wager before the '89 World Series

Anemic Offense

We're going so bad that back-to-back home runs means one today and one tomorrow.

EARL WEAVER

They made a pennant out of a base on balls, a ball of string, a Band-Aid, and a letter from their pastor.

JIM MURRAY, on the '65 Dodgers

It was unbelievable. You had to pitch a shutout to tie.

GOOSE GOSSAGE,
on the mid-1970s White Sox

One of a Kind

Crowds were to [Babe] Ruth what water was to a fish.

RED SMITH

[Jimmie Wilson] tried to take [Dizzy] Dean under his wing, which was kind of like trying to keep a rhinoceros in your bathroom; Dean would make Nook LaLoosh look like a Republican senator.

BILL JAMES

Legend has it that the owners hired the judge off the federal bench. Don't you believe it. They got him out of Dickens.

LEO DUROCHER

An intellectual roughneck who knew the difference between Richard Wagner and Honus Wagner.

BOB BROEG, on Frankie Frisch

The most unsilenceable man who ever lived.

LEO DUROCHER, on Larry MacPhail

Part philosopher, part preacher, part outfielder.

RED SMITH, on Reggie Jackson

[Thurman] Munson's not moody, he's just mean. When you're moody, you're nice sometimes.

SPARKY LYLE

He had no real goals in life other than to have a good time and hit pinch-hit home runs in the World Series.

BILL LEE, on Bernie Carbo

He could strut before he could walk.

LLOYD MOSEBY, on Rickey Henderson

A teddy bear off the field and a grizzly in the batter's box.

TONY MASSAROTTI,
on David Ortiz

One of a Kind: Bill Lee Division

America's paragon of left-handedness.

CURRY KIRKPATRICK

He lobbied against sugar but he's the only one in his family who takes his coffee sweet.

CURRY KIRKPATRICK

Headlines from the Onion

- Joe Buck Can't Resist Urge to Join "Go Cards!" Chant
- Magglio Ordóñez, Placido Polanco Stay Up All Night Talking About Favorite Hitting Situations
- PNC Park Threatens to Leave Pittsburgh Unless Better Team Is Built
- Rookie Tragically Misinterprets Suicide-Squeeze Sign
- Mets Earmark $53 Million for Pitching Relief
- Mothers Lose 10th Annual MLB Mother's Day Game 24–2
- Curt Schilling to Start Liveblogging from Mound
- Manny Ramirez Asks Red Sox If He Can Work from Home
- Report: Another Baseball Team Almost Does Something As Interesting As Yankees, Red Sox
- Mets Fans Perplexed by New Stadium's Prominent Tim Teufel Statue
- Dodgers' Playoff Hopes Dashed Following Acquisition of Belly Itcher

Owners

It's a thin line between genius and insanity, and in Larry's case it was sometimes so thin you could see him drifting back and forth.

LEO DUROCHER,
on Dodgers owner Larry MacPhail

Not as long as I'm alive.

PAUL RICHARDS, when told that
the Astros' Roy Hofheinz was "his own worst enemy'

If he came into power during the Revolutionary War, we'd all be drinking warm beer and singing "God Save the Queen."

BUD SHAW, on the White Sox's Jerry Reinsdorf

More errors than hits.

BASEBALL WEEKLY, on Tom Werner's tenure in San Diego

Owners: Big Spenders Division

There's three things you can't buy: love, happiness, and the American League pennant.

Baseball adage

That's like Al Capone speaking out for gun control.

BLACKIE SHERROD,
on Ted Turner's criticizing high player salaries

The guy who paid Alex Rodriguez the record $252 million contract wants a salary cap, and I'm thinking, "Apparently, it's to replace the dunce cap."

STEVE ROSENBLOOM, on Tom Hicks

Satchel Paige

He was, without any doubt, the greatest pitcher I've ever seen, and I've been looking in the mirror for a long, long time.

DIZZY DEAN, on Satchel Paige

Satch doesn't hold conversations, he holds court.

BILL VEECK

Half of them are lies, but I don't know which half.

HANK AARON, on Paige's stories

The Perfect Game

So far.

CASEY STENGEL, when asked if Don Larsen's perfect game was the best he'd ever seen

Tell Len I'm very proud of him. I hope he does even better next time.

TOKIE LOCKHART, grandmother of Len Barker, on his '81 perfecto

The Phillies

There were no good years. I cheered in bad and worse.

JAMES MICHENER,
on growing up with the old Phils

Cursed would have been an improvement. This franchise was doomed.

FRANK FITZPATRICK

All spring the Phillies kept calling themselves "the team to beat." So far, the Nats are taking them up on their offer.

CRAIG CALCATERRA

THE CITY OF BROTHERLY LOVE

In 1682, William Penn founded a small settlement on the banks of the Delaware River and dubbed it "Philadelphia," "the city of brotherly love."

If he ever met a Philly sports fan, he probably would've reconsidered the name.

The town features a fan base that's never been known for being either brotherly nor lovely. They have been known to toss batteries and various other illegal objects, taunt seriously injured players as they were carted off the field, and generally gripe about everything short of an annual championship parade. Everybody's heard how, during a football game, Philadelphia fans actually booed Santa Claus. (They also threw snowballs at him.)

In other incidents, positive intentions have gone slightly awry.

In the 1930s, for example, the old Baker Bowl featured a sign reading THE PHILLIES USE LIFEBUOY SOAP; right after it, someone scribbled "And they still stink." Decades later, in the 1980s, the Phils acknowledged one of their fan favorites by giving away Larry Andersen masks; the masks were used in store muggings for years afterward. It's also hard to forget a "Fan Appreciation Day" from the early 1990s, when the gussied-up conductor of the local symphony orchestra showed up for a 7th-inning rendition of "Take Me Out to the Ball Game"; One of those appreciated fans stole the maestro's special baton.

This is not to say that Philly guys are always negative, though.

There was, indeed, one occasion, in 2003, when a group of Philadelphia fans gathered together, smiled, linked hands, and cheered. Now, they were witnessing the demolition of old Veterans Stadium at the time . . . but still, they cheered.

Baseball Philosophers

The best thing about baseball is that you can do something about yesterday tomorrow.

MANNY TRILLO

This game is like an Etch A Sketch—you need to shake it and start over again.

NICK SWISHER

If I am remembered by anyone, I would want it to be as a guy who cared about the planet and the welfare of his fellow man. And who would take you out at second if the game was on the line.

BILL LEE

Pinstripes

The [Yankee] pinstripes have a slimming effect. Except on David Wells.

JOEL STEIN

I hope the school colors are pinstripes.

Hillsborough, Florida, school board member **SUSAN VALDES**, on the newly named Steinbrenner High School

The Pirates

If rooting for the Yankees was like rooting for U.S. Steel what was it like cheering for the Pirates? Cheering for a plumbing and heating company? A hardware store? An all-night diner?

JIM REISLER

Time stood still, money grew on trees, and Santa Claus arrived three months early.

PITTSBURGH PRESS EDITORIAL,
on the Pirates' '60 pennant

The Pirates need David Copperfield, not [GM David] Littlefield, because somebody has to make four horrendous contracts disappear.

BOB SMIZIK

Bad Pitches

The pitch was a cross between a changeup and a screwball. It was a screwup.

BOB PATTERSON

We tried to set up the double play. But the shortstop doesn't play in the bullpen.

LOU PINIELLA, after an intentional walk set up a grand slam

You bet they did. One of them moved right out of the park.

FRANK ROBINSON, when asked if
Gary Lavelle's pitches had movement

AND HERE'S THE PITCH . . .

Football doesn't have symbolic first passes. Basketball doesn't have ceremonial first dunks. Only baseball has ceremonial first pitches, and occasionally fun ones, at that.

In the 1965 debut of the Astrodome, for instance, Houston had 24 of its hometown astronauts toss out "first pitches" to all 24 players on the club roster. About a decade later, the last-place Indians had none other than Bozo the Clown toss a first pitch. Wonder if club execs knew exactly how appropriate that one looked?

Teams have also been known to salute some lesser-known stars.

When the Royals switched from artificial turf to all-natural grass for the 1995 season, for instance, they had head groundskeeper George Toma toss out Opening Day's first pitch. Just to signify Toma's newfound importance, they had him decked out in a white tuxedo and then driven off in a chauffeured pink luxury car; the bright colors must have really stood out against that new green grass.

The Dodgers once honored a longtime peanut vendor named Roger Owens, who was famed for his expert bag tosses. Owens threw out the ceremonial first pitch of the 1977 season from the second deck of Chavez Ravine, and in 1995, the Dodgers had him on the mound, and this time he tossed a bag of peanuts from behind his back. The veteran vendor later said he was the only "pitcher" in the major leagues making less than $1 million per year.

More often, though, former players are asked to do the duties, in order to recall some fondly remembered glory. Negro League great Luis Tiant, Sr., was invited to throw a first pitch for his son's Red Sox in 1975. The proud papa went into his elaborate full windup and threw several hard strikes, then assured the Sox he was ready to go four or five innings if needed, just like the old days.

Bygone days may have also been on the mind of Nolan Ryan when he threw out a first pitch in 2007. The Hall of Famer offered his trademark pitch, a fastball, at 85 miles per hour; just as he'd once been the fastest 20-, 30-, and 40-year-old on record, Ryan proved himself the fastest 60-year-old ever to take the mound.

Good Pitches

Didn't that last one sound low?

LEFTY GOMEZ, on Bob Feller's fastball

To hit it, you have to start your swing on the on-deck circle.

KEN KAISER,
on Nolan Ryan's fastball

Too good to take, not good enough to hit.

BOB SKINNER, on Randy Jones's changeup

Oh, about $4 million.

ELROY FACE, on the difference between a
split-finger fastball and a forkball

Player-Managers

Baseball's been good to me since I quit trying to play it.

WHITEY HERZOG

Earl [Weaver] wouldn't take himself out of a ballgame. He'd play hurt. Then again, since he was a lousy ballplayer, it wouldn't have made a difference.

JIM PALMER

REPORTER: So with all that clean living, why do you look so old?
DANNY MURTAUGH: Have you ever looked up my batting average?

Playing a Game

The umpire says "play ball," not "work ball."

WILLIE STARGELL

I ain't ever had a job. I always played baseball.

SATCHEL PAIGE

Playoff Pressure

Thirty-two pounds per square inch at sea level.

BILL LEE, on the definition of playoff pressure

Nah. I'm too dumb to get scared.

JIM "CATFISH" HUNTER, on whether he felt playoff pressure

There's no tomorrow if we don't win tomorrow.

TONY GWYNN, on being down 0–2
in the '84 National League Championship Series

Playoff Race

By looking up.

FRANK ROBINSON, on how the Giants viewed the playoff race

The Rangers are 17 games out of first. Their magic number is negative 14.

MICHAEL SCHUR

Politics

I try to take a national view of the American League and an American view of the National League.

Vice President **HUBERT HUMPHREY**

Dick Cheney threw out the first pitch at the Reds' opener. Cincinnati catcher Jason LaRue said the ball had nice movement but undisclosed location.

BILL SCHEFT

People just don't know what to make of a left-wing conservative.

PETE VUCKOVICH, on his politics

Practice, Practice, Practice

They'll be two buses leaving for the ballpark tomorrow. The two o'clock bus will be for those who need a little work. The empty bus will leave at five o'clock.

DAVE BRISTOL

The workout is optional—whoever doesn't work out gets optioned.

BOBBY VALENTINE

Presidential Presence

To show you how Walter [Johnson] stands in comparison to the president in Washington, at the opening game there, Calvin [Coolidge] will throw out the first ball and Walter will throw all the rest.

WILL ROGERS

Can you play first base?

FRANK ROBINSON, when President Reagan asked
if he could help the struggling Orioles

I've been out of work for six months. Maybe there's a future here.

RONALD REAGAN, on his '89 stint
as a guest broadcaster with Vin Scully

I think my average was about .240 or .250. I think if I were playing today in the bigs, I'd probably get about $8 million a year for that.

GEORGE H. W. BUSH, on being a "good glove/no hit" player at Yale

If you think you're a big shot in politics and want a lesson in humility, campaign with Ted Williams at a fishing show in Manchester, New Hampshire.

GEORGE H. W. BUSH

Born on third base; thinks he hit a triple.

ANN RICHARDS, on George W. Bush

He's a great president.

OZZIE GUILLEN, when asked about Barack Obama's first-pitch-throwing ability

You know, nobody thought I was going to win, either.

BARACK OBAMA, at a White House ceremony
for the world-champion Phillies

Presidential Presence: JFK Division

The worst news for the Republicans this week was that Casey Stengel has been fired—it must show that experience does not count.

KENNEDY, who became the youngest man elected president in 1960

A couple of years ago they told me I was too young to be president and you were too old to be playing baseball, but we fooled them.

to Stan Musial

Well, I've left you in first place.

after a Senators win on Opening Day

THE FAN IN CHIEF

The president of the United States of America is known as the leader of the free world. In the baseball nation, he's often set apart as a ceremonial fan in chief.

John F. Kennedy sat through all 27 innings of his three Opening Days and threw first-pitch fastballs that Al Lopez described as "sneaky fast." Ronald Reagan, who started his public career as a Cubs broadcaster, became a lifelong member of the team's fan club, and when George H. W. Bush served in office, he had his old first baseman's mitt stashed in a desk drawer in the Oval Office. Whenever the commander in chief was having a bad day, he'd pull it out and give the glove a couple quick punches with his fist.

Harry Truman used to joke that he would have become a ballplayer, if not for the fact that his eyesight was only good enough for umpiring. Dwight Eisenhower once said that, when he was growing up, he wanted to be a major leaguer while a friend wanted to be president . . . so neither of them ended up living their dreams. In

1969, Richard Nixon mused that if he had to do it all over again he would've become a sportswriter.

(One observer was heard to mutter, "I wish you had become a sportswriter.")

And then there was Barack Obama. Once, while campaigning, the die-hard White Sox fan was asked to sign memorabilia from the crosstown Cubs. Well, as you'd expect, the future president found a compromise; The Cubs gear got both an autograph and a "Go Sox!" inscription.

The Prices

The game never changes, but the prices do.

BUCK O'NEIL

There's a restaurant here in New York City, in a hotel called the Parker Meridian, and they're selling a $1,000 omelet. And I'm thinking, "Well, if I want to spend $1,000 on a meal, I'll go to Yankee Stadium."

DAVID LETTERMAN

I assume that includes lawn service and a lap dance.

NORMAN CHAD,
on ticket prices at the new Yankee Stadium

Prospects and Suspects

Ask him if he wouldn't mind posing with me.

Hall of Famer **DAZZY VANCE**, when asked to pose
for a picture with phenom Herb Score

I guess your fellas don't need gloves when you pitch.

CASEY STENGEL, on a young strikeout artist's tryout

Stick with baseball and someday you'll be wearing silk underwear.

> Youth coach **OLIN SAYLORS**, to a young Jim Rice

He shouldn't have gone to high school—it took three years off his pension.

> **WALT WEISS**, on Ken Griffey, Jr.

[Rookie Mark] Prior's job is simply to show promise, blaze one fastball, maybe save one game. Also, to save the manager's job, the general manager's job, save the season, win the pennant, boost morale, and lower our handicap, straighten out our kids, and maybe find us a parking spot.

> **GREG COUCH**

Looks like Tarzan, runs like Jane.

> **ANONYMOUS SCOUT**, on Rich Diana

He should be good, but he ain't.

> **CASEY STENGEL**, on the perpetually promising/disappointing Don Larsen

According to the publicity release he could hit like Johnny Mize and field like Dick Sisler. As it turned out he hit like Casey Wise and fielded like Dick Stuart.

> **BRENDAN C. BOYD** and **FRED C. HARRIS**, on Frank Leja

The Royals protected David Howard in the expansion draft over Jeff Conine because, in their words, without him they wouldn't have a shortstop. Well, Howard would go on to prove that even with him they didn't have a shortstop.

> **RANY JAZAYERLI**

Strikes.

> **TIPPY MARTINEZ**, on Danny Ainge's weakness

I got this kid who's 19, and in 10 years he has a chance to be 29.

CASEY STENGEL, on rookie Jim Gosger

In assessing his 1968 breakout, [Roger] Repoz gave much of the credit to his use of an Exer-Genie, an exercise machine developed by NASA for astronauts. If only the Angels had played their games in outer space.

BRUCE MARKUSEN

Had lots of tools. He might be a carpenter now.

JOE POSNANSKI, on Alexis Gomez

If he's that good of a hitter, why doesn't he hit better?

BILLY BEANE

Albert Pujols

This year in the National League, [Albert] Pujols was practically the best team, never mind the best player.

KING KAUFMAN

Superman plays for the Cardinals.

CRAIG CALCATERRA

Character Profile: BILL LEE

Over the years, many words have been associated with the inimitable Bill Lee: "radical," "revolutionary," "raucous." Sometimes the word "ridiculous" came to mind. It's possible that no other pitcher has been so often held up as the epitome of that stock baseball character, the flaky left-hander, but here's another word for the Lee résumé: "conservative."

That's right, conservative.

Lee was straitlaced virtually from the start. The son of a Republican businessman and a stay-at home mom, William Lee III enjoyed what he later described as a *Leave It to Beaver*–type existence in the Southern California of the 1950s and early 1960s. He started throwing expert curveballs at age eight and was studious enough to get into the University of Southern California on an academic scholarship. If baseball didn't work out, he planned to get a job as a forest ranger.

Even when he made it up to the Red Sox in 1969, Lee remained, in many important respects, a button-down traditionalist.

Between the white lines, he was pure business, as focused and competitive as any starter on the Boston staff, which helps explain how he won 51 games from 1973 to 1975. Lee paid his respects to elder statesmen such as Johnny Pesky and Bobby Doerr, idolized Teddy Ballgame, studied opponents, took extra batting practice, and never turned down an autograph request. Long after he'd retired as an active major leaguer, he barnstormed across the country and around the world, often speaking out against newfangled innovations such as the designated hitter rule, night games, player agents, and artificial turf. In all those ways, he was stuck in 1959.

Lee must have poured a lifetime's worth of straight-arrow attitude into his love for the game, actually, because, as it turned out, he just couldn't help being rebellious in just about every other way.

Lee's relationship with long-accepted baseball customs, for instance, resembled the dealings between a runaway bull and a china shop. Old-time jocks were meat-and-potatoes types; Lee was a health-nut vegetarian. The old-timers drank stiff drinks; he sprinkled marijuana on his pancakes. They read the *Sporting News* and comic books; he favored Vonnegut and Steinbeck. They kept their (mostly conservative) political views to themselves; he supported left-wing movements such as environmentalism and the nuclear freeze, once declaring that "the only law I believe in is the law of gravity."

In Boston circles more often dominated by blue bloods and machine politicians, there's no doubt that Bill Lee adopted the acts and attitude of another town fixture: the college activist. Who else would have had the nerve to show up for a road game in an astronaut suit? Or don off-field headgear ranging from propeller caps to pith helmets? Or rehab a bad shoulder by straphanging on MBTA trains?

The targets of Lee's rebelliousness, not surprisingly, included his bosses in the Sox organization. Ever have that daydream where you finally tell off your boss? Well, Bill Lee often lived that one out, and in the newspapers.

He charged that several of his managers, being former hitters, subconsciously hated pitchers, so they couldn't handle a staff rotation or bullpen. He openly questioned some of the front office's moves, then said that the difference between the Sox's traveling secretary and vice president came down to the fact that "Jack Rogers does a nice job and Haywood Sullivan has a nice job." When his buddy Bernie Carbo was shipped off the team, Lee walked off the job for a day, explaining, "They keep saying we're all supposed to be family here. If you're family, you don't send your children to Cleveland."

The man simply didn't know how to press a "mute" button. He provided a steady stream of quotes and stunts that almost wrote the script for what a glib, boat-rocking ballplayer could be. As a matter of fact, years later, that's exactly what happened: The real Bill Lee was the inspiration for the fictional Sam Malone on the *Cheers* sitcom.

Now, was it all sunshine and giggles in the Spaceman's orbit? No, not always. Actually, there were several times when the Red Sox's bad boy probably should have been a bit less radical and a bit more Republican.

Lee's confidence could be inspiring, for example, but not when it prompted him to toss the lollipop curve that Tony Perez took deep in Game Seven of the '75 World Series. Mouthing off to hated Yankees Graig Nettles and Billy Martin made for exciting headlines, but it also touched off a vicious brawl that led to his season-ending shoulder injury in '76. A raging feud with manager Don Zimmer may have been interesting, too, but the ball club hardly needed the distraction during the Sox's '78 playoff run.

At his best, though, Bill Lee showed just how much freedom and fun there was to be had within baseball. For years, the Spaceman found a way to play the game on the field and play by his own rules off the field. We should all be so lucky.

Put-Downs

He had precious little power, nor did he have any speed, and he was entirely ungraceful. . . . [Ron] Hunt displayed all the elegance of a rusty box of nails slid across an oil-stained garage floor.

STEVE TREDER

FRANK ROBINSON: Bring on Ron Gaspar!
MARV RETTENMUND: Not "Ron." It's "Rod," stupid.
ROBINSON: OK, bring on Rod Stupid!

WASHINGTON SLEPT HERE.

Fan banner, on Claudell Washington

He had Reggie Jackson's ego and Ron Jackson's talent.

JIM CAPLE, on Deion Sanders

If it's true we learn by our mistakes, then Jim Frey will be the best manager ever.

RON LUCIANO

Darryl Strawberry is not a dog. A dog is loyal and runs hard after balls.

TOMMY LASORDA

Recently Leyritz proclaimed that "I will forever be a Yankee. No matter what I do, I will be tied to this organization." I know what Jim was trying to get at, but he should understand—when a guy's hitting .218, that kind of statement comes off as a threat.

DIEGO MUSILLI

Put-Downs: Hall of Fame Division

Anyone who thinks Roger Maris is in a class with Ruth and Gehrig probably thinks Tony Orlando was in a class with Beethoven and Mozart.

BILL JAMES

An up-and-coming Ruben Sierra disliked how the media used to constantly compare him to Roberto Clemente. I doubt Clemente would've been too thrilled, either.

DIEGO MUSILLI

Aaron Rowand, whose first name is the only reason he'll ever be compared to a Hall of Famer . . .

CRAIG CALCATERRA

Rose-colored headline of the week: KNOBLAUCH GETS FIRST CRACK AT HALL. The judges would have also accepted "last crack."

CRAIG CALCATERRA

Put-Downs: Fielding Division

The first big-league catcher to wear glasses on the field, [Clint] Courtney struggled with pop-ups, circling the ball and squinting through Coke bottle lenses. The media likened the sight to a waiter serving pizza on roller skates.

MIKE KLINGAMAN

His quickest motion was bending over and rubbing his ankle when a line drive bounced off it.

DICK BARTELL, on Ike Boone

As a hitter, he's in a class with Albert Pujols, Manny Ramirez, and Albert Belle. As a third baseman he's in a class with guys who really need to work on playing third base.

BILL JAMES, on Miguel Cabrera

TOMMY LASORDA: It's close and late and there's a man on second. What are you thinking?

PEDRO GUERRERO: Don't hit it to me.

LASORDA: Yeah, yeah. But what else are you thinking?

GUERRERO: Don't hit it to [Steve] Sax, either.

The $500 was for his fielding.

JOE TRIMBLE, on Nick Etten's $17,500 contract

He'll never take me out alive.

KEN SINGLETON, after Carlos Lopez collided with two Oriole outfielders

Put-Downs: Hitting Division

He could speak 11 languages but couldn't hit in any of them.

ANONYMOUS REPORTER, on Moe Berg

Everybody's seen players have off games and off years. If you ever saw Bobby Meacham, you saw an off career.

DIEGO MUSILLI

Well, he's a .300 hitter: He hits .150 right-handed and .150 left-handed.

DICK WILLIAMS, on Allan Lewis

You know, on a lot of teams you would send a pinch hitter for Manny Trillo.

HARRY CARAY,
on Trillo's pinch-hitting appearance

Put-Downs: Pitching Division

I read you got four pitches. You sure do. You got a singles pitch, a doubles pitch, a triples pitch, and a home run pitch.

ANONYMOUS FAN, to Lindy McDaniel

They say a starter has to be consistent, and Jose Lima is consistent, all right, but mostly when it comes to giving up home runs, which should really lead the club to consider a more inconsistent starter in the very near future.

DIEGO MUSILLI

Chan Ho Park decided to forgo his chance at being obliterated by opposing hitters in Los Angeles in order to play for the Korean Olympic team. That sound you hear is several million Dodgers fans exhaling with relief. In other news, the Korean Olympic team is now in deep, deep trouble.

CRAIG CALCARETTA

For more than a century, ballplayers have lent their names and likenesses to just about any product produced. Since at least the days of Honus Wagner and Christy Mathewson, they've endorsed household items ranging from clocks to locks and socks and everything in between.

None made quite the same splash as Reggie Jackson.

Jackson signed as a Yankees free agent in 1977 partly because of the endorsement opportunities to be found in New York City, including the sweet kinds; Jax mused that he, like Babe Ruth, might have his own candy bar in the Big Apple. One World Series MVP award later, in 1978, Reggie's dream came true in the form of a chocolate-caramel-and-nut concoction that was dubbed the "Reggie!" bar.

The Reggie! made its big debut in the Yankees' '78 home opener, when it was given away as a free fan promotion. Jackson, true to his dramatic reputation, hit a big home run, and the crowd went wild. Before you knew it, Reggie! bars rained onto the field.

It was an instant PR bonanza.

As the grounds crew scrambled to clear the chocolatey obstructions, television cameras zeroed in on the on-deck hitter, Lou Piniella, who used some of the complimentary candy for his practice swings. Others weren't quite so playful; Yankees coach Yogi Berra, citing his favorite endorsed product, noted that fans wouldn't have thrown Yoo-hoo like that, and Bob Lemon, the opposing manager, bemoaned the waste, saying, "People are starving all over the world and 30 billion calories are laying out on the field." It was up to Billy Martin, the Yankees skipper, to chip in a defense of the Reggie! incident—he noted that Boston fans occasionally threw metal objects out to the field, so the mass candy tossing "proves that we have sweet fans."

Apart from being aerodynamic, how was the Reggie! bar itself? Most believed that, like its outspoken namesake, the candy had some good substance and even better marketing; Catfish Hunter once said that he unwrapped one and it told him how good it was.

Put-Downs: Running Division

He started off as an outfielder, but his shadow covered more ground than he did.

DICK BARTELL,
on Shanty Hogan

[Ernie] Lombardi was probably not born to be a catcher, but that was the position that required the least mobility. He would have made a great designated hitter. He would have made a terrific wall.

STEVEN GOLDMAN

Ran as if suitcases had been tied to his shoes.

SCOTT SIMON, on Hank Sauer

If he raced his pregnant wife he'd finish third.

TOMMY LASORDA, on Mike Scioscia

Believe me, he wasn't going anywhere unless there was a steak sandwich at second base.

KEN KAISER, on Kent Hrbek

I've been working on my jump for nine years.

CECIL FIELDER, explaining
his first stolen base in 1,096 games

I asked one baseball insider what it would take for [David] DeJesus to steal more bases, and he said, "Move the bases closer together."

JOE POSNANSKI

Put-Downs: Throwing Division

Couldn't out-throw Mickey Rooney.

CHARLES MAHER, on Mickey Rivers

Absolutely the worst fielder I had ever seen. . . . One of his tosses almost killed a peanut vendor in the 26th row.

BILL LEE, on Juan Beniquez

The Quotable Dan Quisenberry

No homework.

On his favorite thing about baseball

The batter still hits a grounder. But in this case the first bounce is 360 feet away.

On a bad sinker pitch

I don't miss the cheers. I just go to the ballpark, sit in the stands, and pretend they're cheering for me.

On retirement

Manny Ramirez

Boston police arrested a disoriented individual loitering in Fenway Park's outfield during a game last Thursday, but charges were quickly dropped when the man identified himself as Manny Ramirez, the Red Sox's left fielder. A check against his driver's license and $160 million contract confirmed the information.

DIEGO MUSILLI

I'm just glad he came back.

TERRY FRANCONA, on Manny's taking a break during a pitching change

I don't believe in curses. I believe you make your own destination.

RAMIREZ,
after the '04 World Series

Red Ink

I'm going to write a book: *How to Make a Small Fortune in Baseball.* First, start with a large fortune . . .

RULY CARPENTER

Doctors are still wondering what caused the Yankees owner's fainting spell. They've narrowed it down to low blood sugar, poor circulation, or the phrase "$48.8 million in revenue sharing."

BILL SCHEFT

The '78 Red Sox

Fenway Park was like St. Petersburg in the last days of the czar.

PETER GAMMONS,
on the "Boston Massacre" of '78

A perfect day for a funeral.

ANONYMOUS BOSTON WRITER, on the Red Sox's '78 divisional playoff

Bury me at home plate, right next to the team's pennant chances.

RAY FITZGERALD,
on the end of the Red Sox's '78 season

Our pain isn't as bad as you might think. Dead people don't suffer.

BILL LEE

Red Sox Fans

You know what they say about the Red Sox—it's not life and death. It's more serious than that.

KEN MAGRATH

Intense, nasty, and they can ride you like cheap underwear.

GOOSE GOSSAGE, on Boston fans

Game Seven of the ['03] ALCS drew a 73 share in Boston. That means 73 percent of the televisions in use were watching the game. I know what you're thinking but, technically, a TV being thrown out a window during Aaron Boone's home run trot is still "in use."

BILL SCHEFT

Now you can spend eternity in the loving embrace of the Sox, which is more than Manny ever did.

RICK CHANDLER, on the newly introduced "Red Sox funeral caskets"

Red Sox Optimists

I can't wait for spring training to start.

CARL YASTRZEMSKI, on losing the '75 World Series

Hurrying along Storrow Drive the morning after the World Series ended, a taxi-cab passed beneath a gigantic banner suspended from an overpass: WILMINGTON FORD CONGRATULATES THE BOSTON RED SOX 1975 WORLD CHAMPIONS. The driver glanced up and mumbled to himself, "1976, dammit, 1976."

RON FIMRITE

That's history, pal.

DENNIS ECKERSLEY, on the Red Sox's pre-2004 title drought

Why pitch nine innings when you can get just as famous pitching two?

SPARKY LYLE

I want to thank all the pitchers who couldn't go nine.

DAN QUISENBERRY, on his "Reliever of the Year" award

I, too, used to be a Cardinal.

DUCKY MEDWICK, upon being introduced to the pope

Take your bat with you.

EARL WEAVER, to players on their way to chapel services

Pete Rose is beloved in Cincinnati. You run him [out of a game] in Cincy and it's like throwing the pope out of St. Peter's.

ERIC GREGG

Possibly the only preacher with a great knockdown pitch.

EDDIE GOLD and **ART AHRENS**, on Lindy McDaniel

Now we're 24 morons and a Mormon.

JOHN KRUK, after the '90 Phillies added Dale Murphy

HOLY COW!

Back when he was catching in the Negro Leagues, Double Duty Radcliffe wore a chest protector inscribed with the words "Thou Shalt Not Steal." Frank Torre, a devout Catholic, would sometimes attend morning mass while dressed in his uniform and spikes, just so he could head straight from the church to the ballpark. When the pious Vernon Law was asked to retaliate against a rival pitcher's inside pitching, Law did brush him back, later stating that "he who lives by the sword dies by the sword."

Religion and baseball have always been intertwined, though they've never been completely compatible. In the 1978 pennant race, a nun sent the Red Sox's Bob Stanley a telegram reading "Get in there and kick some ass. God be with you." Hmmm. Are ass-kicking and God compatible? (To judge from the '78 Red Sox's fate, the answer is "no").

Lou Piniella once told George Steinbrenner that he shouldn't be forced into a team-mandated haircut, since even Jesus Christ had long hair, thereby raising the question: What would Jesus' style be? No one can be completely sure, but since Piniella couldn't walk on water, Steinbrenner forced his outfielder to get a haircut.

The Ring

I kid him all the time: "You look like Liberace, with all those rings."

DEREK JETER,
on ten-time champ Yogi Berra

REPORTER: What could the Mets do to improve their look?
MODEL JACQUELINE MIRANNE: A World Series ring. In fashion, jewelry always complements an outfit.

Retired Numbers

Well, this is a real honor. I'm glad I'm not dead.

LARRY DIERKER, on the Astros' plans
to retire his number 49

What took them so long? Did they have to get written permission from Mike Gallego?

BILL SCHEFT, on the Athletics' waiting 17 years
to retire Reggie Jackson's number

They're going to retire my uniform. With me still in it.

STEVE HOVLEY

As a group, their potential was in their past.

STEVEN GOLDMAN, on the '34 Dodgers

I was throwing as hard as I ever did. The ball just wasn't getting there as fast.

LEFTY GOMEZ

In 1968, I retired as a player. It was a popular decision.

BOB UECKER

I'm too lazy to work and too scared to steal.

TOM BOLTON, on why he was putting off retirement

I was standing in the on-deck circle in 1985 when some leather-lunged guy in the stands screams, "Kuiper! Go to the booth—now!" I remember thinking, "I'm going to accept this as a compliment." A year later, I was broadcasting.

DUANE KUIPER

When your dentist's kid starts hitting you, it's time.

TOMMY JOHN (his former dentist's son was Mark McGwire)

He lost bat speed overnight the way you and I lose a BlackBerry.

BILL SIMMONS, on Jim Rice

Branch Rickey

He could recognize a great player from the window of a moving train.

JIM MURRAY

A man opposed to Sunday baseball except when the gate receipts exceeded $5,000.

JOHN LARDNER

If President Truman would sic Rickey on Russia, Joe Stalin would wake up one morning to discover that all he had left was Siberia plus a couple of southpaw pitchers who wouldn't report.

JOHN CARMICHAEL

Branch Rickey on Negotiation

I got $100,000 worth of advice and a very small raise.

EDDIE STANKY

Rickey has both money and players. He just didn't like to see the two of them meet.

CHUCK CONNORS

He was always going to the vault for a nickel's change.

ENOS "COUNTRY" SLAUGHTER

Rivalries

Apart from 1955, the old Brooklyn Dodgers vs. the Yankees Subway Series went down like Charlie Brown vs. the football.

DIEGO MUSILLI

SHOE SHINE, 10 CENTS. GIANT FANS, 15 CENTS.

—Sign seen at Ebbets Field

I saw 99 fights and two games, all in the same day.

ANONYMOUS REPORTER, on a Giants-Dodgers doubleheader in the 1930s

L.A. HAS THE ACTORS, S.F. THE STARS.

Giants fan banner

Obviously they can't handle a winner, but I don't think they're going to have to worry about that for much longer.

Dodger **REGGIE SMITH**, on rowdy Giants fans

Well, I don't think there's good blood.

BILLY MARTIN, when asked about bad blood between the '77 Yankees and Royals

I hope they lose for another 100 years. At least by then, I'll be dead.

ANONYMOUS CARDINALS FAN, on the Cubs

Rivalries: Red Sox vs. Yankees Division

The train to New York.

Yankees fan **JIMMY WALKER**, on "the best thing in Boston"

The best general manager the Yankees ever had.

HENRY D. FETTER, on the Red Sox's Harry Frazee

I SUPPORT TWO TEAMS: THE RED SOX AND WHOEVER BEATS THE YANKEES.

Fan banner

Those guys were really stupid. Must have been Red Sox fans.

PHIL RIZZUTO, on break-in burglars' failure to steal his '50 MVP plaque

When the Red Sox come to New York, the average IQ level in Yankee Stadium goes up by about ten points.

GEORGE VECSEY

It was real hatred. Fisk hated Munson. Munson hated Fisk. Everyone hated Bill Lee.

DON ZIMMER, on the
Sox-Yanks rivalry of the '70s

RED SOX: 2, METS: 0, YANKEES: NO GAME TODAY.

Fan banner seen before
Game Three of the '86 World Series

I haven't had a lot of good experiences with Red Sox fans. Most of them are obnoxious, ugly, and, frankly, could use a shave. Their boyfriends are, if anything, even worse.

DIEGO MUSILLI

Beating them was like beating the IRS.

DAN SHAUGHNESSY, on the Sox defeating the Yankees
in the '04 American League Championship Series

Even if you filled the inside of the Grand Canyon with a gigantic 20-story shopping mall and a 50-story luxury hotel, it wouldn't be a worse idea than new Yankee Stadium. . . . But congratulations and best of luck with it.

BILL SIMMONS

Whenever they're ready to get rid of this place, let me push the button.

DAVID WELLS, on Fenway Park

Road Games

On the road, when you go downstairs for coffee in your underwear, they throw you out of the kitchen.

ANDY VAN SLYKE, on the difference
between home and away

It's great being on the East Coast. You get to eat three hours sooner.

KEN LEVINE, on leaving L.A.

Brooks Robinson

He plays third base like he came down from a higher league.

ED RUNGE

Other stars had fans. Brooks had friends.

TOM BOSWELL

Brooks never asked anyone to name a candy bar after him. In Baltimore, people named their children after him.

GORDON BEARD

Frank Robinson, Manager

He's mellowed considerably over the years and if you stand up to him, he'll respect you for it and back off. Either that or he'll cut out your heart and mail it to your mother.

KEN LEVINE

Robinson and I only had one disagreement—he wanted every call to go his way, and I had to call them fairly. That disagreement lasted my entire career.

KEN KAISER

John Rocker

Rocker reportedly claimed that in the last six years he has suffered more abuse than Hank Aaron or Jackie Robinson. Please. What, was he ever turned away from a lunch counter because they refused to serve idiots?

BILL SCHEFT

New York police are also already preparing for Monday's Braves-Mets game, which marks the return of controversial Atlanta Braves pitcher John Rocker. Police are particularly nervous because this Monday is Homo Day at Shea Stadium.

JIMMY FALLON

Role Models

He was one of baseball's few college men and its finest role model. He lived cleanly and spoke eloquently. Only his pitches were nasty.

JONATHAN EIG, on Christy Mathewson

Babe Ruth without the bad habits.

JONATHAN EIG, on Lou Gehrig

Here's hoping he did enough to inspire the next generation of nerdy, unassuming white guys that never get into trouble.

JOSH ZERKLE, on Greg Maddux's retirement

Rules

I believe in rules. Sure I do. If there weren't any rules, how could you break them?

LEO DUROCHER

It's against baseball's unwritten rules to try to steal a base with a big lead, the answer to which is "I'll stop playing hard when you do, Mr. Losing Team." It's a second-cousin to "How dare you bunt when I've got a no-hitter going," the reply to which is "Shut up." The judges will also accept "Bite me."

KING KAUFMAN

The Running Game

My feet were harder than his head.

KID ELBERFELD, on why he spiked runners
going for headfirst slides

You better look in your lockers and make sure he didn't steal your jockstraps.

CASEY STENGEL to his team,
after Jackie Robinson stole multiple bases on them

RIDING IN STYLE

When ballplayers go from here to there, they don't always run. Or walk. Or trot, for that matter. Sometimes they ride.

It was sometime in the 1950s when some sharp-minded promoters started using automobiles to bring relievers from the outfield bullpen areas to the mound. The White Sox probably started it off with their use of station wagons, but the dynastic Yankees refused the new transportation, jokingly explaining that they rode only in Cadillacs. (The Sox replied by enlisting black Cadillac hearses for the bullpens, but the New Yorkers still refused.)

As the years followed, different teams put different spins on bullpen cars. The Brewers acknowledged their blue-collar fans by bringing relievers in on Harley-Davidson motorcycles, Philadelphia brought their "firemen" into ball games on mini-firetrucks, and the 1970s-era Yankees decided to finally introduce their own ride, a flashy, pinstriped Datsun. To this day, in Japan, that leading car exporter, they still have relievers come in on cars, new models advertising both their team ties and their green fuel efficiency.

Of course, not all bullpen cars have been as welcomed as others. In the mid-1970s the Indians used fans' donated cars, but the team's pitchers were embarrassed by the clunkers—the relievers took to jogging beside them during their trips to the mound. A few years later, the Mariners front office began using a gimmicky tugboat/car, but gave up on it after one disgusted pitcher stole the contraption's ignition keys.

Career 2.28 ERA and threw 29⅔ consecutive scoreless innings in World Series. Could also hit.

JOE POSNANSKI

You have your choice—one base on four balls, or four bases on one ball.

WAITE HOYT, on the Babe's walks and homers

I've already bought a ticket for the right fielder to sit in the stands.

JOHN J. McGRAW, on positioning his fielders against Ruth

The Ruth is mighty and shall prevail.

GRANTLAND RICE, on the '23 World Series

Buddy boy, I'll take Babe Ruth, and you can have the next three.

BURT HAWKINS, on the best ballplayer he'd ever seen

Nolan Ryan

A good night tonight is 0 for 4 and don't get hit in the head.

OSCAR GAMBLE

Everybody would like each other and no one would get a hit.

RANCE MULLINIKS, on a world full of Nolan Ryans

Hell, if he hasn't struck you out, you ain't nobody.

RICKEY HENDERSON, on being victimized
for Ryan's 5,000th career strikeout

Marge Schott

You know how women are. At Christmas they buy things and charge it.

On buying the Reds

All they ever do is watch baseball games.

On why she didn't want to hire scouts

First it snows on Opening Day and now this.

On the on-field death of umpire John McSherry

Her only two concerns are her dog and money. We're hoping she buys the kennel and sells the team.

Anonymous Reds player

RED MENACE

Sports Illustrated cover

Scouts

When I was 21, I could throw a baseball 92 miles an hour. This led to a strange courtship between my left arm and a series of pencil-mustached, overweight, middle-aged men.

MATT MCCARTHY, on being scouted

Scouts can serve a very unique role. I'll share with you a story that I always do with questions like this. Back a few years ago, I was at a low minors game featuring some hotshot phenoms with all kinds of big numbers and superstar bodies. Afterward, a scout told me to forget all that, that the best player on the field was this slap-hitter with a serious weight problem. Not only was he the best player, he said, but he was the best hitter the scout had seen in years. That player's name? Joe Shlabotnik. My point is, scouts suck.

DIEGO MUSILLI

Good Seats

In 20 years of moving around a ballpark, I've discovered that the knowledge of the game is usually in inverse proportion to the price of the seats.

BILL VEECK

I hate those big-time luxury boxes up there, all that fancy ballpark real estate. They're stuffy, elitist, wimpy, and why won't somebody invite me up please?

DIEGO MUSILLI

Tom Seaver

He exuded confidence without opening his mouth. One look at him told you that he had a future of big cigars and long limousines.

BILL LEE

Kid, I know who you are, and before your career is over, I guarantee you everyone else will, too.

HANK AARON, after a
21-year-old Seaver introduced himself

I drove him to Shea Stadium in my old Corvette. It had a T-top that leaked in the rainstorm. Water dripped on Tom's forehead. He looked up and said, "Why don't you buy a Porsche?" I said, "Because I'm not Tom Seaver." He laughed and said, "That's a fact."

PAT JORDAN

Second Guessing

Listen, if you start worrying about the people in the stands, before too long you're up in the stands with them.

TOMMY LASORDA

You make a deal based on your best judgment at the time. If it works, fine; if it doesn't, you can't kick yourself. The writers and the fans will do that for you.

WHITEY HERZOG

I didn't need a replay to feel bad. I could just look at my paycheck for that.

KEN KAISER

The '70s

In the '70s I threw in the 90s. In the '90s I threw in the 70s.

FRANK TANANA,
on his career trajectory

There are some things that are still exactly the same as they were in 1970. Vin Scully's still around. No one likes Pete Rose. Jim Edmonds was fragile and Royce Clayton couldn't hit, although in 1970, that was because they were infants. Julio Franco is contemplating retirement. It's really the same game.

CRAIG CALCATERRA

Short Series

They say anything can happen in a short series. I just didn't expect it to be that short.

AL LOPEZ, on the '54 World Series

Ralph Waldo Emerson once said that "life is a series of surprises, and would not be worth taking or keeping if it were not." In related news, Baltimore is 5–1.

CRAIG CALCATERRA

[The sportswriters] based their ideas that something was wrong with A-Rod on his performance in a very, very small number of games in October, which is like basing John Gielgud's acting career on *Arthur 2: On the Rocks.*

MICHAEL SCHUR

Is any other area of American life filled with the kind of absurd, overinflated self-importance that's found in baseball?

Just think about it—as cherished and glorious as the national pastime may be, it's still, well, a . . . game. A diversion, an entertainment. It comes down to a glorified exercise in pitch the ball / hit the ball / catch the ball—a bunch of guys running around with a little white sphere, a stick, and some gloves. With all due respect, it's kids' stuff.

And, yet, in our time, baseball has become so respectable, so beloved—nay, revered!—that the media treats it as far, far more than a game. Its stars are now under the kind of 24/7 spotlight that would make a U.S. senator run for cover. Its statistics are given more scrutiny than the numbers that rule the federal government's trillion-dollar budgets. Its greatest performers are called icons and legends, and its ballparks are treated like shrines.

Everybody knows this.

Well, almost everybody.

Manny Ramirez never got the memo.

On one level, Manuel Aristides Ramirez has always been deadly serious about baseball. While growing up in the Dominican-American neighborhoods of Washington Heights in Manhattan, Manny brought a first-generation immigrant's work ethic to his favorite activity. By the time he was a senior in high school, his coach was telling the *New York Times* that Manny was the hardest-working player he'd ever seen. Hitting was, and is, his life. The inner-city kid who once showed up seven hours before a varsity high school game was, 20 years later, the superstar who put in team-leading amounts of video study, conditioning, and batting practice for the Red Sox. No less than Don Mattingly called him the most prepared player he'd ever been around. Don't go by appearances—just below that pine tar–encrusted batting helmet, do-rag, and baggy uniform are a mind and body as thoroughly prepared as any in the majors.

Apart from a lifelong dedication to mastering his craft, though, Manny's never seemed to buy into the supposition that baseball carries a cosmic significance approximately equal to issues of life and death. As committed as he might be to top-flight offensive performance, that's about all he cares about.

Certainly, Manny Ramirez never had a senatorial concern for all the pomp and circumstance swirling around the grand old game. For example, we all know that ballplayers are supposed to go along with every stiff preorchestrated media conference, but when Manny was ordered to one just before the 2001 All-Star Game, he begged off, explaining that his grandma was sick. ("They've got to change her blood, stuff like that. She's like 90 years old.") Also, ballplayers are expected to treat rival teams like blood enemies, but when a close friend, the Yankees' Enrique Wilson, showed up for a Boston road trip in the summer of 2003, Manny had an off-day drink with the guy. Then, when columnists started treating the incident like they'd just uncovered federal treason, Manny shrugged and said he wouldn't mind playing for the Yankees himself one day.

In other words, he laughed it off.

Oh, and the tiny "small ball"–type fundamentals that purists lovingly chronicle? Never meant that much to him. Like Ted Williams, Manny displays a less-than-fanatical commitment to outfield defense and baserunning. He's been known to throw to the wrong base, miss the cutoff man, and not quite hustle on a sure double. At times he forgets the number of outs in an inning or sits out the occasional game or two with nagging injuries. Apparently, somewhere along the line, he nodded, grinned, and decided that his customary 40+ home runs and 130 RBIs per year can make up for a whole lot. You know what? He is right. His version of big ball is worth all the small ball in the world.

And when it comes to on-field decorum, he's always been a heretic in the church of baseball.

During pitching switches, for instance, outfielders are supposed to do . . . umm, something or other. Kneel in prayer. Contemplate Cooperstown's immortality. Calculate their own slugging percentages. Something like that. Manny doesn't. When pitchers are getting pulled, he takes it easy, often listening to tunes on his custom MP3-playing sunglasses or taking a swig from his back-pocket water bottle. One time, he took a cell phone call; another time, he headed off to chat with the scorekeeper ensconced within the Green Monster, barely making it back in time to catch a line drive. On the day he became a naturalized American citizen in May 2004, he ran out to Fenway's left field waving a miniature red-white-and-blue flag.

The media has long grown accustomed to using these incidents to peg Manny as a clueless man-child, emphasis on the "child" part. An idiot savant, maybe, emphasis on "idiot." But just how off-base is Ramirez, really? When it comes down to it, all of the headline-grabbing "controversies" amount to not much. A lame excuse, a carefree drink, some goofing off, a couple of harmless gestures. In a realm where the game was treated as less than a sacred epitome of Americana—say, if these kinds of things had happened in an earlier, more freewheeling era in the game— they'd be written off as local color. Manny, almost alone, has the presence of mind to treat them as such. Though it's often lost amid all the hyperventilating media reports, when it comes down to the most important part of baseball—winning—Ramirez has always been the straight and sober one.

Think about it: Manny's established himself as a Hall of Fame– quality slugger, keyed more than a decade of winning teams, and has done it while being paid a king's ransom. With that in mind, his "eccentric" viewpoint begins to look like something completely different—an affable approach to a hyperserious business, an idiosyncratic refusal to buy into stifling conformity, a throwback ballplayer's scoffing at the assumption that he has to act like some kind of buttoned-down company man. No matter how strange the expectations are around him, Manny's always insisted on being Manny.

Sign Stealing

A Hypothetical Conversation Between the Commissioner and a Team Stealing Signs

COMMISSIONER: I understand you're stealing signs.

TEAM: Uhhh, no I'm not.

COMMISSIONER: That's not what the other team told me. They said your mascot hangs out in center field and uses those giant novelty pennants to signal the hitter in semaphore.

TEAM: Those tattletales! They stole signs first! They've got a guy who sneaks into the hot dog sign in left field and wiggles the bun if it's a fastball.

COMMISSIONER: I understand you're upset, and we're going to investigate the other team, too, but you have to stop this.

TEAM: You can't make me!

COMMISSIONER: Now, don't be like that. You and I both know I can, but I don't want to do that.

TEAM: Oooookay.

COMMISSIONER: Go and give your mascot the week off, and when he comes back, I don't want to see him anywhere near the bleachers. Do you understand?

TEAM: Fine. And I didn't want to steal signs anyway.

DEREK ZUMSTEG

A CALL TO THE BULLPEN

The five most memorable bullpen-call incidents of all time:

1. Connie Mack, who started out in the game of baseball before telephones were invented, never used a phone to retrieve relievers in from the outfield bullpen, preferring to use hand signals instead. In the late 1940s, he had a special system for his three primary relievers: Mack would wave way above his head if he wanted 6'4" Lou Brissie, he'd give a medium wave for 6' Alex Kellner, and for 5'6" reliever Bobby Shantz, Mack would wave down low.

2. During Satchel Paige's major league tenure as a relief pitcher, the noted ladies' man reportedly spent most of his in-game bullpen time calling his various girlfriends around the country. Satch gave up on the reach-out-and-touch-someone only after his employers objected to the long-distance charges.

3. During their infamous '62 season, the Mets had two equally lackluster bullpen pitchers named Bob Miller; as the famous story goes, Casey Stengel once called for "Miller" to come into the game, was asked which one he meant, said "Surprise me," and hung up.

4. While serving as Yankees manager in '85, Billy Martin was hospitalized with a minor injury but tuned in on his team's game on TV, then telephoned his tactical instructions through the Yankees' dugout phone. The arrangement was against MLB rules, of course, so when umpire Ken Kaiser got wind of the goings-on, he grabbed the receiver, yelled, "You're disconnected, Billy!" and ripped the cord out.

5. Not long after that one, Martin, still hospitalized, called in to the dugout once again. After Cleveland newspapers reported the story, fans somehow snooped out the number of the Yankees bench, then called in with their own suggestions, most of which were illegal, physically impossible, or both.

It was a relay race with bats.

JOHN HOLWAY, on a 23–22 contest

This is one of those nights where batting practice just continues into the game.

KEN SINGLETON, on the nine homers in a Yankees-Orioles contest

I sort of started off in a slump and went downhill from there.

GARY WASLEWSKI

I could go into a slump and raise my average.

BILLY GRABARKEWITZ

I could spit farther than I was hitting.

TED WILLIAMS

I'm going through a stretch right now where I look out from the plate and see one big glove.

DOUG MIENTKIEWICZ

We went five weeks into the season with five guys not hitting their weight, and none of them were fat guys.

PETE ROSE

We've all been lousy. Now, let's all be good.

CASEY STENGEL'S advice on breaking a team slump

Every season has its peaks and valleys. What you have to try to do is eliminate the Grand Canyon.

ANDY VAN SLYKE

Not-So-Smarts

That eliminates 19 of us right away.

ANONYMOUS RED SOX PLAYER, after a reporter quoted a "veteran, intelligent" source

Hard-throwing, light-thinking.

JACK LANG, on Dick Selma

A strong arm and a weak mind.

DIZZY DEAN, on the secret of his success

Frenchy [Bordagaray]'s speed would have helped them if he'd run in the right direction.

TOMMY HOLMES

Marv [Throneberry] never made the same mistake twice. He made different ones.

RALPH KINER

He used to give the sign, then look down to see what it was.

ROGER CRAIG, on Choo-Choo Coleman

I don't know why the sinker works when it does work. So I sure as hell don't know why it doesn't work when it doesn't work.

GREG MINTON

I'm in the best shape of my life and that includes my brain.

LENNY DYKSTRA

After a certain point, you just can't ask an inherently undisciplined hitter to suddenly master the strike zone. It would be like expecting Paris Hilton to stop being stupid. People are who they are.

DIEGO MUSILLI

They used to say he didn't spit on the ball—he blew his breath on it and the ball would come up drunk.

RUBE MARQUARD, on Bugs Raymond

You didn't know whether to bring a bat or an umbrella to the plate.

HANK BAUER, on Lew Burdette's spitballs

Too much spit on it.

BILLY LOES, on his dropping a ball in mid-windup

[John] Wyatt has so much Vaseline on him that if he slid into second base he would keep right on going until he hit the outfield fence.

JOE PEPITONE

The entire pitching staff of the Angels was throwing spitballs. If KY Jelly went out of business, they all would have been pitching in Double-A.

BILL LEE

When you lose velocity on your fastball, of course, you have to come up with command of another major pitch. Throw the sinker. Throw the change. Or, as Whitey Ford suggested, learn to load 'em up. Not the bases. The balls.

MICKEY McDERMOTT

Do I look like a doctor?

JOE NIEKRO, on whether he doctored balls

Spitters: Gaylord Perry Division

[American League president Joe] Cronin came out for legalization of the spitter; the National League president, Warren Giles, came out against it. "We don't catch all the murderers, but we don't legalize murder because of that," said Giles. I don't think it was very nice of Mr. Giles to compare me and my fellow spitballers to murderers. We were more like con men.

Do I still wet them? I sure know how. But that doesn't mean I do it—or even that I ever did it. Maybe I'm just kidding. Maybe I got 'em out on sheer talent.

REPORTER: What's your name, honey?

ALLISON, AGE FIVE: Allison Perry.

REPORTER: Are you here rooting for your daddy?

ALLISON: Yes, sir.

REPORTER: You're daddy's quite a pitcher, isn't he?

ALLISON: Mommy says so.

REPORTER: Your daddy has quite a reputation for throwing a funny pitch. They say he uses grease, but nobody knows where he keeps it. Do you, Allison?

ALLISON: At home, in the garage.

REPORTER: Isn't that cute? Does your daddy throw a grease ball, honey?

ALLISON: It's a hard slider.

I guess he can pick out the dry side.

—On how Rod Carew could hit his spitters

Since Perry smells like a pharmacopoeia, Billy Martin once brought a bloodhound to the park to sniff through the ball bag for evidence. What happened? "The dog died of a heart attack," says

Martin. On another occasion, Martin asked umpire Bill Kunkel to "just smell the ball, please." Kunkel told him, "Billy, I have allergies and a deviated septum." "Jesus," roared Martin, "I've got an umpire who can't see or smell!."

TOM BOSWELL

300 WINS IS NOTHING TO SPIT AT.

GAYLORD PERRY'S favorite T-shirt inscription

THE SPITTER AND HIM

All through history, baseball competitors have done it. They've corked bats, stolen signals, and tried all sorts of illegal tricks to get an upper hand. They've cheated.

Gaylord Perry cheated, too, but with one crucial difference— he had a lot of fun with it. Like many others before and after, Perry applied Vaseline, KY Jelly, Crisco, spit, and various other illegal substances on his baseballs, but no other player did it with such panache.

Often, Perry would smile as he made brushing gestures against his belt, cap, jersey, and pants before he wound up for the pitch— even when he wasn't reaching for something!— and he did the routine on purpose, just to get in the hitters' heads. When enraged opponents would, predictably, request that the umpire check Perry for the slippery stuff, the righty would oblige by sticking both his hands up in the air, as if he was being accosted by a stick-up mugger on the mound. Soon enough, as the umpire would be walking away without any telltale evidence, Perry would be giving the hitter a little wink and a nod, then go right back to his "hard slider" routine.

Maybe that Perry playfulness came from a security that he wouldn't get caught and, if it did, that confidence was pretty well-founded. The hurler wasn't cited for spitballing until 1982, about 21 years (and 740 games) into his Hall of Fame career, and until that point, he felt free to come just short of admitting his extracurricular moisture.

Perry wrote a 1974 autobiography entitled *The Spitter and Me*, for example, and rode around in a car with license plates reading SPITTER. He also offered to do commercials for Vaseline, but that was a step too far; the product makers told Perry that they "soothe babies' backsides, not baseballs."

Sportswriters

If writers knew any goddamn thing, they'd be managers.

BILLY MARTIN

The only reason you're a sportswriter is because you're too damn stupid to operate a forklift.

DAVE NELSON

Sportswriters: Ted Williams Division

You pour water on a sportswriter.

TED WILLIAMS, on "the recipe for instant horses—t"

First I'd like to find a gold mine. Then I'd buy a major league club. Then I'd bar all writers from the park.

TED WILLIAMS, on his postretirement plans

Sportswriters on Sportswriters

Don't write to us complaining about how we have maligned your favorite ballplayer, belittled baseball, befouled the very air you breathe. We know only too well that we could not have played baseball half as well as even the most inept players mentioned herein. We know that much better than you, in fact. We tried.

BRENDAN BOYD and **FRED C. HARRIS**

It's easy to second-guess managers and that's why I do it.

MAX KELLERMAN

Can we please, finally, pry the ballot out of the hands of the Baseball Writers' Association of America and hand it to somebody less self-important, like the College of Cardinals?

CHARLES P. PIERCE

One less than you think, Jimmy.

JACK LANG, when Jimmy Cannon asked
how many great sportswriters there were in the game

One sportswriter says to another, "Every actor wants to be a baseball player and every baseball player wants to be an actor." "What do writers want to be?" says the other sportswriter. "Rich," he answers.

PAT JORDAN

Thin Staffs

I can think of two: Jeremy Bonderman and Jeremy Bonderman.

RON SHANDLER,
on the best pitchers on the Detroit staff

I feel the same way about the four-man rotation as I do about Nicole Kidman.

JERRY NARRON

They both show a lot, but not everything.

TOBY HARRAH, on statistics and bikinis

Tell your statistics to shut up.

CHARLIE BROWN, in a *Peanuts* comic by Charles Schulz

Another thing that hasn't changed about baseball—you're still just as smart as your earned run average.

JIM BOUTON

Stat Inflation

SPORTS ANCHOR: Roger, the last time you faced the Mariners, you struck out 30.
ROGER CLEMENS: It was 20.
ANCHOR: Well, maybe next time.

Soon there'll be more people in the 500-homer club than there are in the Kiwanis Club.

JOE POSNANSKI

When somebody gets real hot in sports, say hits a lot of home runs early, I've never been one to say, "That guy is on a pace to hit 200 home runs" or whatever. But I will say this—if Jennifer Lopez keeps getting married at this rate, she's got a chance to put up some pretty big numbers.

MIKE LUPICA

Statistical Interpretation

Figures are notorious liars, which is why accountants have more fun than people think.

JIMMY BRESLIN

I make out they're a misprint and turn to the financial section.

> **CASEY STENGEL**, on
> the early Mets' batting averages

REPORTER: Last year, you hit two homers and this year you already have seven. What's the difference?
ALEX JOHNSON: Five.

I was so sick I thought I was going to die, but how can you die with 19 wins?

> **JIM BOUTON**, on winning his 20th game despite the flu

Keep quiet about it. I don't want anyone to know I'm doing so well pitching so badly.

> **SPARKY LYLE**, on having a 5–1 record despite a lousy ERA

This puts me on a pace to hit six.

> **MIKE GALLEGO**, on hitting five home runs in one week

Statistical Interpretation: Creative Division

Ninety percent of this game is half-mental.

> **JIM WOHLFORD** (not Yogi Berra)

[Manny Ramirez] told me he puts 70 percent of his weight on his back foot and 40 percent on his front foot. I thought for a second, "I've got to try that."

> **RUSSELL BRANYAN**

Steinbrenner on Steinbrenner

Breathing first, winning next.

> On his priorities

I didn't invent the system, but I use it.

On free agency

Get it immediately, if not sooner.

To his secretary

You're the manager—you do the managing. I'm the owner—I'll do the second-guessing.

I guess I am a sonofabitch to work for. I don't know if I'd want to work for me.

Working for the Boss

He's the kind of owner who likes a 163-game lead with 162 games left.

LOU PINIELLA

The phone would ring in the middle of the night and you knew it was either Mr. Steinbrenner or a death in the family. After a while, you started to root for a death in the family.

HARVEY GREENE, on the "Bronx Zoo"–era Yanks

His favorite line is, "I will never have a heart attack. I give them."

BOB WATSON

It was peanut butter and jelly.

STEINBRENNER, on rumors he fired a secretary for late delivery of a tuna sandwich

There's nothing quite so limited as being a limited partner of George Steinbrenner's.

JOHN MCMULLEN

He's a man of his word. You just have to get it in writing.

CATFISH HUNTER

George is an overbearing, arbitrary, arrogant SOB, there's no denying that. But I just love him.

C. L. SMYTHE

Talking Back to the Boss

I'll take one. Just as long as you take one, too.

LOU PINIELLA, after Steinbrenner demanded his players take lie-detector tests

GEORGE STEINBRENNER: Where are you?
JOE TORRE: I'm playing golf.
STEINBRENNER: Well, while you were out in the g——d woods having fun, we're trying to figure this damned thing out for tomorrow.
TORRE: How did you know my ball is in the woods?

Well, two things he knows nothing about are weight control and baseball.

GRAIG NETTLES, on Steinbrenner saying Nettles was "definitely fat and probably finished"

Talking Back to the Boss: Goose Gossage Division

Tell Goose I've lost 11 pounds since June.

GEORGE STEINBRENNER, on Gossage's calling him "the fat man"

If Doyle needs a physical, George needs a mental.

GOSSAGE, on Steinbrenner's ordering a struggling Doyle Alexander to get a medical exam

Goose should do more pitching and less quacking.

STEINBRENNER'S response

Casey Stengel

One hundred percent pure ballplayer, emphasis on play.

GLENN STOUT, on a young Casey Stengel

Dumb like a fox.

CHUCK HILLER

Casey was not like anybody.

YOGI BERRA

YOU COULD LOOK IT UP.

Caption on the Casey Stengel portrait
hanging at the entrance to the Hall of Fame library

Stengelese

They brought me up to the Brooklyn Dodgers, which at that time
were in Brooklyn.

The pitching isn't as bad as it appears; it only seems that way.

I at once commenced not thinking of retirement.

On being hired to manage the Yankees at age 59

Nobody knows this yet, but one of us has been sold to Kansas City.

To Bob Cerv (Stengel and Cerv were alone at the time)

Old Timers' weekends and airplane landings are alike—if you
can walk away from them, they're successful.

My health is good enough above the shoulders.

I'll tell you something. They examined all my organs. Some of
them are quite remarkable, and others are not so good. A lot of
museums are bidding for them.

There comes a time in every man's life, and I've had plenty of them.

The St. Louis Blues

First in booze, first in shoes, last in the major leagues.

Common description of the old St. Louis Browns

Streaks

The secret to winning streaks is to maximize the victories while at the same time minimizing the defeats.

JOHN LOWENSTEIN

Gas is up and so am I.

MANNY RAMIREZ, on his hot streak

Strike!

The summer vacation I'd always wanted.

LOU PINIELLA, on the '81 labor strike

A recent poll revealed that, because of the [1994] strike, men are having more sex. But the sex doesn't last very long because there's no baseball to think about.

CONAN O'BRIEN

Superstitions

Count their money.

KEN KAISER, on what ballplayers do for good luck

I'm not superstitious, but I do think it's bad luck to bet against the Yankees.

RING LARDNER

I have one superstition—whenever I hit a home run, I make certain to touch all four bases.

BABE RUTH

If it comes true, it's not a superstition.

YOGI BERRA

Surgeries

You can tell my brother is a baseball person—he waited to the off-day to have surgery.

JOE TORRE, on Frank Torre

Think an extra-inning game, plus a couple of rain delays.

BOBBY MURCER, on his five-hour surgery

Team Togetherness

I didn't ever think it would be any big deal and I was right.

DON WILSON, on teaming with Tommy Davis

Listen, we voted on the playoff shares. You owe us 25 cents.

RICO PETROCELLI, to a recently retired Tony Conigliaro

First time Straw ever hit the cutoff man.

Blogger **"METSFAN,"** after Darryl Strawberry
punched teammate Keith Hernandez

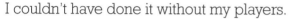

Teamwork

Clean living and a fast outfield.

LEFTY GOMEZ, on the secret to his success

A fellow has to have faith in God above and Rollie Fingers in the bullpen.

ALVIN DARK

I couldn't have done it without my players.

CASEY STENGEL, on the Yankees' World Series titles

Your teammates heal all wounds. Though not as much as ibuprofen and ice.

JIM CAPLE

High Tech

The A's are going to let you use your mobile phone as an e-ticket. When the old man at the gate rips your phone in two, don't say I didn't warn you.

CRAIG CALCATERRA

Twice in the last few days, a prominent New York typist has written a column grumbling about the decline of the complete game. The complete game! Heavens, next thing you know, rotary-dial phones will be a thing of the past.

KING KAUFMAN

Luis Tiant

Believe me, it's easier to get a plumber on Sunday than it was to time a [Luis] Tiant pitch. He'd go into his windup, and into his windup, and continue his windup—hey, let's go, we're getting older back here—and continue his windup and then, continue his windup, and finally throw the ball.

KEN KAISER

When I was a boy growing up in Cuba, Luis Tiant was a national hero. Now I'm 36 and he's 37.

TONY PEREZ

Tossed

"You're the vernacular for a sexual function liar," says [umpire Al] Salerno. "And you are the practitioner of an unnatural sexual act," [manager Dick] Williams says. Salerno throws him out of the game.

LEN SCHECTER, paraphrasing an on-field exchange

I feel greatly honored to have a ballpark named after me, especially after I've been thrown out of so many.

CASEY STENGEL, at the ribbon-cutting for Huggins-Stengel Field

I just found out I'm married to a four-year old.

MRS. LOU PINIELLA, on her husband's
latest temper tantrum/ejection

I still miss being on the field on a gorgeous June night. Occasionally I'll get to yell at one of my two kids, but it's not the same thing. My kids have gone off on their own, so I can't even eject them from the house.

Umpire **KEN KAISER**

Traded

Acrimonious trades get the "ugly divorce" tag, but anyone would rather be traded than divorced—a trade stings for a while, then you realize you lucked into a clean slate somewhere else. It's like remarrying without going on a single date. An actual divorce is considerably more painful, and there's no standing ovation waiting in a new city.

BILL SIMMONS

Being traded is like celebrating your 100th birthday. It might not be the happiest occasion in the world, but consider the alternatives.

JOE GARAGIOLA

Getting traded was like being sent to a different family on Christmas morning.

ED LYNCH

I'll tell you what—I'm getting good at packing.

BRUCE CHEN, on his multiple trades

People ask me where I live and I tell them "in escrow."

MIKE KRUKOW, on his changes of address

It was like coming home from school and finding my mother dressed in combat fatigues.

BRENDAN C. BOYD and **FRED C. HARRIS**,
on Hank Bauer in an A's uniform

Trade Scenarios

I don't think he'll ever live that down.

DENNIS BENNETT, on his even-up trade for Dick Stuart

Every five years a man has to change his Sox.

STEVE LYONS, on going from the Red Sox to the White Sox in 1986 and then back to the Red Sox in 1991

He went from Cy Young to Sayonara.

GRAIG NETTLES on Sparky Lyle, who went from a 1977 award winner to 1978 trade-bait

Who needs a potential home run hitter when you have a proven home run pitcher?

D. J. GALLO, on the Pirates' turning down a Ryan Howard–for–Kip Wells trade

Our two biggest expenses were housing and going-away parties.

BOB QUINN, on the "Bronx Zoo"–era Yankees

Trade Scenarios: Don Zimmer Division

We played him; now we can't trade him.

BUZZIE BAVASI, on Don Zimmer's "play me or trade me" demand

We gotta trade him while he's hot.

CASEY STENGEL, after Zimmer broke a 0 for 34 slump with a couple of hits (Zimmer was traded a few days later)

He had more stints in Washington than most congressmen.

DICK BARTELL, on five-time Senators player Bobo Newsom

Have arm, will travel.

MIKE MORGAN, on his 13-team, 22-year career

Tradition

The Red Sox have been playing in Boston since 1901. If you didn't know better you might have thought Paul Revere had once played second base.

BILL REYNOLDS

This much, you have to give the Cubs— they know how to do tradition.

JOHN DONOVAN, after an '07 playoff loss

Tradition took it on the chin again the other day when concession stands at Yankee Stadium began serving Crunch 'n Munch instead of Cracker Jacks. Meanwhile, Gary Sheffield hit the cutoff man on back-to-back throws.

JIM ARMSTRONG

TV

Well, if you've got to go, at least it's on national television.

REGGIE JACKSON, on a teammate's receiving death threats before the '72 World Series

[Tommy] Lasorda was the best. He'd come out to argue "C'mon, you missed that." I'd say, "Tommy, it wasn't even close." He'd say to me, "Are we on national TV?," I'd say no, and he'd say, "See you later."

Umpire **ERIC GREGG**

Baseball games aren't played on paper but inside TV sets.

STEPHEN KING

It's amazing how loud you have to yell at the TV so the players can hear you.

STEWART O'NAN

Ump Eyesight

You cross-eyed old ump
You're as blind as a stump.
Made me look like a chump
You horse's rump!

CHARLES GHIGNA

I never missed one in my heart.

BILL KLEM

They never miss one in their heart. But they use their eyes.

CASEY STENGEL

I never questioned the integrity of an umpire. Their eyesight, yes.

LEO DUROCHER

The sun is 93 million miles away, and I can see that.

BRUCE FROEMMING, on his eyesight

EARL WEAVER: I'm going to check the rule book on that!
UMPIRE: Here, use mine.
WEAVER: That's no good—I can't read Braille.

Umpire/Human Relations

If I did, I didn't bump him hard enough, because he was still standing.

DON BAYLOR, on whether he'd bumped an ump

You're still the second best umpire in the league.

DICK GROAT'S customary line to an unfavorable ump
(he quickly noted "Everyone else is tied for first")

Umpire-Human Relations: Billy Martin Division

I hope you and your family have a wonderful holiday season
Because you sure had a horses—t summer.

BILLY MARTIN'S Christmas card
to umpire Jim Evans

Will Rogers never met a man he didn't like, but he never met
Billy Martin.

DALE FORD

Umpiring

For anyone who enjoys being screamed and cursed at and occasionally threatened, and having things thrown at them, while living
out of a suitcase six or seven months a year for almost no money
and absolutely no praise, this is the perfect job.

RON LUCIANO

We're supposed to be perfect our first day on the job and then
show constant improvement.

ED VARGO

When I'm right, no one remembers. When I'm wrong, no one
forgets.

DOUG HARVEY

An umpire is like a woman—makes quick decisions, never
reverses them, and doesn't think you're safe when you're out.

LARRY GOETZ

Ken Kaiser on Umpiring

There are only a few things in life that prepare a person to be an umpire. Certainly a military career. Definitely Catholic school. And marriage. Places where people get right in your face and scream at you as loudly as they can.

Believe me, if Gandhi had been an umpire, he would have had to reconsider his belief in passive resistance.

As an umpire you can't have any favorites. You have to despise every player and manager equally.

It was a toss-up who despised the other one more. I like to think I won, but I had the advantage—he was real easy to dislike.

On Eddie Murray

Ugly Uniforms

Unfortunately, the Padres played like their uniforms looked.

DON ZIMMER, on the brown-and-yellow
San Diego teams of the early '70s

They look like Hawaiian softball uniforms, don't they?

CHARLIE HOUGH, on the Astros' mid-'70s "rainbows"

The secret here is they underrate us. They don't think we're ball-players, they think we're bananas.

ANONYMOUS A'S PLAYER, on the
team's gold-colored uniforms

It would have been hard not to improve on those ugly, dark green uni's of old. But I think they pulled it off.

KING KAUFMAN, on the new-look '08 Rays

UNIFORM CONDITIONS

When minor league prospects come up to the majors, they're told to have a due appreciation for their sport and all it stands for. They're told to respect the uniform.

Some players take the advice more seriously than others.

On the reverent side, there have always been guys such as Joe DiMaggio and Ted Williams, who loved their uniforms so much that they had them custom-tailored to fit just right. When Pete Rose played in Phillie pinstripes, he carefully aligned the stripes on his pants to the ones on his upper jersey. Roger Clemens, playing in Houston, hated the look of a sweaty jersey so much that he'd change into a clean one following every inning; when the Rocket pitched a complete game, he'd go through nine tops in one day.

Dick Stuart believed that a good-looking, well-cut uniform could add 20 points to his batting average, and Jose Cardenal evidently agreed, since he protested loose-fitting pants by sitting out a few exhibition games.

That reverent attitude wasn't unanimous, of course. The rebellious Bill Lee once wore his Red Sox uni while dancing in a Greek opera, of all things. Lou Whitaker was once victimized by a shipping mix-up shortly before an All-Star Game, so he decided to play the midsummer classic in a Tigers uniform purchased at a souvenir stand. Dizzy Dean once protested the Cardinals' low-ball salary offers by tearing his home uniform to pieces and, when reporters complained about the lack of pictures to the impromptu event, Dean decided to tear up his road uniform for the cameras.

One of the more unusual uniform stories involved the everaccommodating Brooks Robinson. When a little girl asked her favorite Oriole to borrow his game-used uniform for Halloween, Brooks received the front office's grudging permission, then duly handed over the threads. That's why, on October 31, 1975, when 11-year-old Stephanie Vardavas went out trick-or-treating as "Brooks Robinson," she really went out as Brooks Robinson.

Character Profile: LUIS TIANT

If any great player of the 1970s knew about the hard sacrifices and long struggles needed to succeed in the major leagues, it was Luis Tiant. Were the University of Adversity ever to hand out PhDs, he probably would have been first in line for a doctorate.

It started from Tiant's earliest days. When he was growing up amid the grinding poverty of rural Cuba in the 1940s and 1950s, baseball represented a lottery ticket, a desperate chance to escape into a world of big league fame and fortune through endless day-to-night workouts, practices, and performances. The pressure couldn't have been greater, especially since he faced the added expectation in living up to the reputation of his father, Luis Sr., a longtime star for the Negro Leagues.

The young Luis managed to push through despite the odds, eventually rising far enough to travel throughout the country as a teenager, then following that up with a climb up through semi-pro traveling teams throughout Mexico and the Caribbean. After years of paying dues in dusty towns in half a dozen countries, he finally made it up to Las Grandes Ligas in 1964.

Even then, at the highest level in baseball, Tiant had still more obstacles to overcome. After winning 20 games for the Indians in 1968, Tiant slid into a 20-loss season just a year later, then developed the kind of career-threatening arm problems that led three organizations to give up on him within two years. By the time he was 31, in 1971, Tiant was barely hanging on as a fifth starter for the Red Sox, going 1–7 with an atrocious ERA.

But none of it—not the poverty or the pressure or the problems or the pain—could stop him for long.

Tiant battled back to become a Red Sox go-to starter from 1972 to 1978, averaging more than 17 wins per season while always coming up with stopper victories during the playoffs, most memorably in the epic battles of the '75 World Series. In the last week of the 1978 regular season, when the team absolutely had to win or go home, Tiant demanded the ball and said he'd be facedown on the mound before he'd let them lose. The Red Sox Nation knows that the team lived to fight another day.

How did Tiant manage to battle back enough times to fashion a borderline Hall of Fame career? Well, there is a lot to be said for a good old-fashioned work ethic, talent, and a bit of luck, but, apart from those staples, Tiant knew how to come back because he knew how to react to situations with smiles rather than scowls.

Tiant was simply blessed with one of those ultrarare dispositions that can only be described as happy-go-lucky. Win or lose, streaking or slumping, he could be found in the clubhouse, grinning behind one of his trademark Cuban cigars, fracturing English to comic effect, snapping towels, inventing jokey nicknames for teammates. "El Tiante" skated around the ballpark concourses on off-days and could frequently be found preening before a mirror and pronouncing his balding, pot-bellied self "one good-lookin' sonafabeech." After a loss, he'd keep quiet for a few minutes, then loudly exclaim, "What's this, a morgue?" then turn up the radio and say, "We'll get 'em tomorrow!" Whenever the team plane was taking off, he'd holler out, "Get up! Get up!"

Peter Gammons and several former teammates called him the funniest man they'd ever known. Tiant had a talent for impersonations, and no one, from the clubhouse attendants up to Carl Yastrzemski, was safe from the needling. The guy was so gritty and good-hearted that everyone had no choice but to go along. In the early '70s, for example, he had a habit of visiting the toilet, flushing, then saying, "Bye, Bye, Tommy Harper!" Coming from anyone else, the dig would've been infuriating to the high-strung Harper, but with Tiant, he could only laugh along.

A player with Tiant's legendary toughness and playful humor was particularly welcomed in the Red Sox clubhouse of the 1970s. It was just after the infamous "25 players, 25 cabs" era, when cliques divided the team by everything from nationality to color to personality, and Boston society was divided by recessions, strikes, and social crises.

None of that mattered, though, at least not where Tiant was concerned. Everyone was included in the razzing, whether they were American or foreign-born, black or white, young or old, as plainspoken as Carlton Fisk or as outspoken as Bill Lee. No one on the Sox roster wanted to slack off, because that would mean letting down a teammate who was giving 100 percent effort 100 percent of the time. The good cheer was infectious. Everyone wanted to get on Tiant's good side because that meant a spot next to the life of the party, the one guy everyone liked.

Red Sox exec Dick O'Connell called Luis Tiant "the gutsiest player I ever saw." Yastrzemski called him "the heart and soul" of his teams. I'd call Luis Tiant the epitome of fun with a purpose; the more he laughed, the more he led.

The 9th

Mo Vaughn

A true triple threat—he killed his teams through low batting averages, whiff-o-riffic strikeout totals, and "fielding" that had to be witnessed to be believed.

DIEGO MUSILLI

Fatter than a porpoise, colder than a snowdrift.

SAM WALKER, on the late-career Vaughn

"The Mo Vaughn."

Informal TV producer slang for a superslow replay

Vegas

Around here when you say "World Series," people think poker.

JOE POSNANSKI, on Las Vegas

The Cubs are always extremely popular with bettors in Vegas, which is one of the many reasons why the casinos never lose money.

RICHARD ROEPER

I don't think Warren Spahn will ever get into the Hall of Fame. He'll never stop pitching.

STAN MUSIAL

This is one you can tell your grandchildren about—tomorrow.

RICKY HORTON, after
39-year-old Jerry Reuss won his 200th game

I could be wrong, but I'm pretty sure I saw him pitch for the Pittsburgh Crawfords in a 1936 Negro League game vs. the Homestead Grays.

KIRK MINIHANE, on 43-year-old Tim Wakefield

The only thing that burns inside me is Szechuan food.

TOMMY JOHN, age 44

These days, you walk into the Florida clubhouse, the speakers are blasting Perry Como.

BILL SCHEFT, on the Marlins'
hiring 72-year-old Jack McKeon

The San Francisco Giants have chosen 67-year-old Felipe Alou to be their new manager. He's the oldest manager in the major leagues. He's so old that when the players take the field, he yells, "Get off my lawn!"

CONAN O'BRIEN

Veteran Influence

I never saw him. Not late at night, not first thing in the morning, never. I was providing veteran influence to a suitcase.

DICK WILLIAMS,
on rooming with Tony Conigliaro

The Giants constantly talk about free agents' "star power" and "veteran influence," but if that's what they really need, they should go all the way and sign Willie Mays. Star power? He's in the Hall of Fame, for goodness' sake. Veteran influence? At 75 years old, he's veteran enough to influence his grandkids. Since Willie's been retired for more than 30 years, he's well-rested. I'm pretty sure he can still out-hit Pedro Feliz, too.

DIEGO MUSILLI

I'd rather you walk with the bases loaded.

EARL WEAVER, after Pat Kelly said "I'm going to walk with the Lord"

The leadoff walk will always come around to score unless it doesn't. I challenge anyone to prove me wrong.

KEN LEVINE

It's a nice day for baseball if it doesn't rain.

RALPH KINER

Mookie [Wilson] treated every day as if it were 75 degrees and sunny.

JEFF PEARLMAN

Now, there's three things you can do in a baseball game—you can win, you can lose, or it can rain.

CASEY STENGEL

The good thing about cold weather is that you can ice your arm while you're pitching.

JEFF PARRETT

Earl Weaver, the Man

Earl wouldn't be happy unless he wasn't happy. He was the only person I knew who could end happy hour just by showing up.

KEN KAISER

The first time [manager] Joe [Altobelli] said hello to some of the guys, he broke Earl Weaver's career record.

JIM PALMER

When the bastard dies, they'll have to hire pallbearers.

BILL HALLER

Billy [Martin] had a Jekyll and Hyde personality, as opposed to Earl, who had more like a Hyde and Hyde.

KEN KAISER

Earl Weaver, the Manager

Actually, I prefer four-run homers.

WEAVER, on three-run homers

I've got nothing against the bunt—in its place. But most of the time, that place is in the bottom of a long-forgotten closet.

If you think you're going to hit into a double play, do the right thing and strike out.

The guy who says "I love the challenge of managing" is one step from being out of a job. I don't welcome any challenge. I'd rather have nine guys named Robinson.

THE EARL OF BALTIMORE

Billy Martin may have displayed more rage. It's possible that Lou Piniella provided more volume. Doesn't matter.

No manager truly topped Earl Weaver when it came to umpire ejections. No one in major league history has inspired quite so many flamboyant exits from quite so many ball games.

Sure, Martin was known to wave his arms around and kick some dirt on the men in blue, but did he ever bring the rule book out to argue a call? Only Weaver did that, and more; when the umpire ordered him off the diamond, Earl started tearing up the rule book pages and tossing them in the air, confetti-style.

Sure, Piniella was known to throw a tantrum or a dozen when stalking out to argue, but did he ever unmoor a base, get tossed, and take the bag with him on the way out? No. The "stolen base" move could've only been pulled off by one man.

Weaver's, um, energetic and emphatic disputation style became so notorious that umpires gave him the thumb on nearly unheard-of occasions. Weaver was once forced to bid farewell to a spring training game. From a World Series game. From both games of a double-header. He was ejected during pregame ceremonies, and there was one ball game when Ron Luciano, Weaver's longtime nemesis, ejected "The Little General" before he even cleared the first step of the dugout.

Now there were some who suspected that Earl Weaver's nearly 100 career ejections were partly for show, that he did it to rally his ball clubs or fire up his home crowds. Well, maybe so, but the Earl of Baltimore definitely wasn't an easygoing fellow, in or out of the ball-park: he once found himself in church with umpire Marty Springstead and, by the end of the services, right there, in the house of the Lord, the two of them were arguing.

Earl Weaver vs. Jim Palmer

Weaver thought that Palmer was an arrogant know-it-all, while Palmer believed that his manager desperately needed a few tips on the fine art of pitching. I think they were both right.

DIEGO MUSILLI

The only thing he knows about pitching is that he couldn't hit it.

PALMER, on Weaver

PALMER: We all know why you never made the last out, Earl.
WEAVER: Why?
PALMER: Because they always pinch-hit for you.

Weighty Issues

Baseball is so taxing that sometimes guys can get in only 18 holes before a game. Put it this way—nobody's surprised that guys like Charlie Kerfeld, Mickey Lolich, and Terry Forster played baseball. What's surprising is that Dom DeLuise never did.

RICK REILLY

Only two things will keep Boog Powell from greatness—a knife and a fork.

FRANK LANE

There's one guy who spends all his meal money.

BOBBY VALENTINE, on Barry Foote

[Cecil] Fielder acknowledges a weight of 261, leaving unanswered the question of what he might weigh if he put his other foot on the scale.

BILL JAMES

600 pounds of fastballs.

BILL SIMMONS, on Rich Garces and Carlos Castillo

You know those TV shots where the pitcher and catcher are on the mound and they both cover their mouths with their gloves so no one can read their lips? Whenever I see Bartolo Colon do that, I expect him to start eating his mitt.

T. J. SIMERS

I honestly don't think he's lost a step. Although he doesn't bounce quite as high as he used to.

BILL LEE, on 72-year-old
Don Zimmer's shoving match against Pedro Martinez

He's not in classic baseball shape, unless that refers specifically to the shape of a baseball.

HOWARD MEGDAL, on C. C. Sabathia

Weighty Issues: Boomer Scott Division

Once when we were playing the Angels, [Scott] borrowed 20 bucks from Haywood Sullivan to go sightseeing. I didn't realize that you could sightsee in grocery stores, but when Scott returned several hours later, he'd gained seven pounds.

DICK WILLIAMS

He'd celebrated that winter by eating a Christmas dinner every night of the week.

WILLIAMS on Scott's 1967–68 offseason

Weighty Issues: John Kruk Division

I ain't an athlete, lady, I'm a ballplayer.

KRUK

Don't worry. I can always put the weight back on.

On his slimming down during spring training

If you'd haul ass, you'd have to make two trips!

From a heckler

That's our book on you—pitch under the belt, where you can't see it.

CHARLIE O'BRIEN

Weighty Issues: Umpire Division

I cover a considerable amount of ground when I'm standing still.

KEN KAISER, on why he rarely runs during plays in the field

I'm an umpire. I only have to call the bases. I don't have to steal them.

ERIC GREGG, on his weight problem

I'm going to play with harder nonchalance this year.

JACKIE BRANDT

It's permanent. For now.

ROBERTO KELLY, on changing his name to "Bobby" (he later changed it back)

They've got a lot of guys you fear the most.

DAVEY JOHNSON, on the Braves lineup

His limitations are limitless.

DANNY OZARK, on prospect Mike Anderson

VISITORS CLUBHOUSE: NO VISITORS ALLOWED.

Tiger Stadium sign

Pitching, hitting, defense. You just name it. I think that's one of the reasons we're in last place.

OZZIE GUILLEN

I don't think either team is capable of winning.

WARREN BROWN, on the 1945 World Series

The game was closer than the score indicated.

DIZZY DEAN, on a 1–0 game

David Cone is in a class by himself with three or four other players.

GEORGE STEINBRENNER

I can still run. I can still hit. I can still make errors.

LONNIE SMITH

I'm an English literature major. When we say "I saw the Patriots win the World Series," it doesn't necessarily mean we were there.

MITT ROMNEY

It feels straight to me.

C. C. SABATHIA, on why he wears his cap cocked

Good pitching will stop good hitting. And vice versa.

BOB VEALE

What? Mickey Rivers Division

He was lost out there. He was the lost Mohegan.

My goals are to hit .300, score 100 runs, and stay injury-prone.

I'm only working on the things I'm good at. Don't do no good to work on the things I'm not good at.

Me and George [Steinbrenner] and Billy [Martin] are two of a kind.

That felt good. I hadn't hit off a lefty in two months.

On doubling off Bob Stanley (who was right-handed)

Dick Williams

He treats everybody the same—like s—t.

GARY BELL

We have nine managers and one dietician in this league.

JIM FREGOSI, on Williams's enforcing strict weight limits

I don't think there was a player on the team who liked me. But I noticed that nobody sent back their World Series check.

DICK WILLIAMS, on the 1967 Red Sox

Williams is the best manager I've ever played for and as soon as he gets out of baseball I'm going to run him over with my car.

TIM FLANNERY

Tim and I laugh about that now, but I still know the make and model of his car.

WILLIAMS, on Flannery's comment

Mitch Williams

Walked more people than a seeing-eye dog.

FRANK LUKSA

More dangerous than smoking.

EARL WEAVER

If you're going to shoot yourself, do it in your room, not here [in the clubhouse]. You might miss and hurt someone.

JOHN KRUK'S advice to Williams

Ted Williams, the Hitter

I hit like Ted Williams.

WILLIAMS, on his style

Arthur had his Excalibur and Ted Williams has his bat.

HAROLD KAESE

Always, it was "Hitting! More hitting!" To Ted, a perfect game was 20–18.

CURT GOWDY

Now Boston knows how England felt when it lost India.

ED LINN, on Williams's retirement

Ted Williams, the Personality

He was sometimes tough to be with. Like any other great artist.

TED LEPCIO

Williams was the best player of what is known as baseball's golden age while still finding time to fly combat missions in two wars. If he had played tenor sax, he'd be three Ken Burns documentaries in one.

CRAIG CALCATERRA

I always thought that John Wayne did a great act of impersonating Ted Williams.

BILL LEE

I don't think I'd swap lives with anyone. Not Nolan Ryan, not Warren Spahn, not Tom Seaver. Well, maybe Ted Williams.

MICKEY McDERMOTT

A genius and a great guy.

DWIGHT EVANS

The grass is greener, the sun's not as hot, and the dirt isn't as dirty.

BOBBY DEWS, on winning

Champagne and lobster!

YOGI BERRA, on winning the World Series

While many were called, few were called up.

WILLIAM RYCZEK

Do unto others as they do unto you. And do it in the early innings.

PAUL DICKSON, on the "golden rule of the diamond"

Sit there and take it like a fan.

RUSSELL BAKER, on losing

'Twas better to have led and lost than never led at all.

TOMMY RICE, on the Dodgers' fade in the '24 pennant race

I fought the wall and the wall won.

DMITRI YOUNG, on his outfield collision

The child is the father of the fan.

DIEGO MUSILLI, on youth marketing

Like they say, "It ain't over 'til the fat guy swings."

DARREN DAULTON

When life give you lemons, smash 'em.

DAVID ORTIZ

It's not whether you won or lost but how many paid to see the game.

PETER BAVASI

You're rusting on your laurels.

TOMMY LASORDA, to the '79 Dodgers

We'll let bye-byes be bye-byes.

RICKEY HENDERSON, on his feud with Lou Piniella

To paraphrase Ben Franklin, a run saved is a run earned.

DICK BARTELL

They died with their boots.

DAVE ANDERSON, on an error-filled Dodgers loss

That was taken out of content.

ROGER CLEMENS

Wives

Sure I heard it. I'm one of 'em. That's why I wanna marry her.

> **DIZZY DEAN**, on the rumor that his fiancée had "screwed half the men in town"

Mary Frances Veeck and Friend

> Title of **BILL VEECK'S** weekly TV show

We may have to call off Family Day.

> **LEE MacPHAIL**, after Fritz Peterson and Mike Kekich swapped wives in 1973

I first met her in a New York bar. We had a lot in common. We were both from California and we were both drunk.

> **TUG McGRAW**, on his future wife

That [Ray] Knight's a lucky guy—he has a wife who makes a million dollars a year. Mine spends that.

> **PETE ROSE**, on "Mr. Nancy Lopez"

I'm a four-wheel-drive-pickup type of guy. So is my wife.

> **MIKE GREENWELL**

THE EX FILES

It happens to the best of ballplayers—eventually, the dream dies. Where they were once members of a cherished team, players sometimes reach the point where they're released, cut, kicked to the curb.

Yes, player divorces can be pretty traumatic.

Jerry Grote knew all about it. The Met catcher once retired in order to spend time with his family but, unfortunately, split with his wife, then failed in a highly publicized spring training comeback attempt. David Justice had a similarly public falling-out after his divorce from actress Halle Berry; a few years after they split, she won an Oscar, then thanked "my ex-hubby, who taught me to reach into my inner soul to search for the despair of this character."

The perpetually focused Pete Rose went 5 for 5 on the day his first wife filed for divorce, but Steve Garvey had a more typically negative experience when his marriage broke up; his ex-wife constantly called Garvey's manager, Dick Williams, to try to enlist him on her side of the case. Williams sympathized but told the former Mrs. Garvey that he couldn't even force Garvey to bunt.

Jose Canseco's marital breakup was more of a good news/bad news situation. The good news was that his ex-wife made big money after the divorce, thereby reducing Canseco's heavy child support bills. The bad news? Jessica Canseco made the money by publishing *Juicy*, a tell-all memoir that described how lousy Jose was in bed.

World of Sports

You can't sit on a lead and run a few plays into the line and just kill the clock. You've got to throw the ball over the plate and give the other guy a chance. That's why baseball is the greatest game of all.

EARL WEAVER

The ball is too big and there's no chance of a rainout.

ERIC HILLMAN, on why he doesn't play basketball

He's proven so far that he couldn't play shortstop, second base, third base, or the outfield, hit left-handed, hit right-handed, hit a jump shot, or guard Andrew Toney.

BILL JAMES,
on major league bust/struggling NBA player Danny Ainge

I'm bowling 300 but hitting .221.

YOGI BERRA, on his off-field hobby / on-field slump

When I hit a ball, I want somebody else to chase it.

ROGERS HORNSBY, on why he doesn't golf

The World Series

Last Thursday, the Philadelphia Phillies defeated the Tampa Bay Rays 4–3 in the World Series, a contest to see which team's home city is going to be set on fire by drunks.

SETH MEYERS

World War II

Was it as scary as pitching to Jimmie Foxx? I'll say. That's for keeps, that racket. But anyway, Jimmie couldn't hit me with a paddle.

BOB FELLER, on World War II

The Yanks are now leading both leagues—the American and the Pacific.

BOB ADDIE, 1942

THIS IS WAR

For all the death and destruction it visited upon untold millions, World War II was the worst disaster in human history. And yet, as far as baseball was concerned, it wasn't without its lighter moments.

When the Japanese staged their sneak attack on Pearl Harbor, for instance, Lou Gehrig's widow decided to return the "friendship medals" that the empire had bestowed on Gehrig years before; after the tokens made their way to the U.S. Navy sailors strapped them to some of the first bombs dropped on Tokyo.

Babe Ruth, Gehrig's former teammate, learned that some Japanese troops shouted "F—k Babe Ruth" as they attacked the Americans, and he also had some revenge, sort of; the Babe expressed the sincere hope that every enemy who mentioned his name would get themselves shot, then supported the U.S. war effort through fund-raising drives.

As misguided as they may have been in their belligerence, the Japanese still loved baseball.

Enos "Country" Slaughter, the future Hall of Famer, was stationed on a northern Pacific island toward the end of the war. He remembered that when American soldiers played interservice ball games, some holdout enemy soldiers would emerge from their hiding places in the distance, watch the games from afar, and retreat to safety only after the last pitch. The Japanese literally risked their lives to catch some ball games. "Talk about real fans," mused Slaughter.

More often, though, the war was a deadly serious business, even in baseball terms.

During 1944's Battle of the Bulge, for instance, German agents attempted to infiltrate Allied battle lines by dressing as American GIs, but our troops soon learned how to spot the real "Yanks": They simply asked the strangers if they'd heard of the Brooklyn Dodgers and/or the winners of the '41 pennant. If they said yes, they got a pass. If they said no . . .

Phil Wrigley

Phil Wrigley owned two things people stepped on: chewing gum and the Cubs.

GERALD ESKENAZI

I don't know what Wrigley is likely to do in a given situation. Except that, whatever it is, it's probably wrong.

ROBERT MARKUS

Wrigley Field

The Peter Pan of ballparks; it's never grown up and it's never grown old.

E. M. SWIFT, on the Friendly Confines

If you don't like Wrigley, you might as well renounce your citizenship now.

JIM CAPLE

The Cubs are for everyone who ever said "no" to their boss.

BILL VEECK, on day games at Wrigley

It was a historic evening I won't soon forget. Although I'll try.

MIKE ROYKO, on the first official night game at Wrigley

The New York Yankees

Yankee Pride

Get a job with the Yankees.

WAITE HOYT, on the secret to success in pitching

It's when the Yankees score eight runs in the first inning and then slowly pull away.

JACOB RUPPERT, on the
perfect afternoon at Yankee Stadium

Watching the Yankees in operation, one gained the impression that even the groundskeeper could come off the bench, take a couple of pitches, then line a double to right.

NOEL HYND, on the late-'30s dynasty

The turning point came when the Yankees suited up for the first game.

JOE WILLIAMS, on the '38 World Series

Dynamite.

ANONYMOUS BEAT WRITER, on what would prevent the Yanks from repeating

The Lord had giveth, but the Yankees had taken away.

ALLEN BARRA, on the '51 Giants winning a miracle pennant (and losing the World Series)

We're so efficient it puts me to sleep.

CASEY STENGEL, on dozing off on the '50s-era Yankees' bench

They were the most intense team I've ever seen. It was like being in a bathtub with Jaws.

BILL LEE, on the '78 Yankees

Tales of Yankee Power

For the New York Yankees, every year is next year.

ROGER KAHN

Can you imagine if you were a Yankee player and you didn't like the taste of champagne?

STEVE LYONS

Rooting for the Yankees is like owning a yacht.

JIMMY CANNON

Comparing any American League team to the Yankees is like saying that Canada has the second-largest army in North America.

BILL BALLOU

There's only one team, and that's the New York Yankees.

ART STEWART

The Yankees are baseball.

GEORGE STEINBRENNER

Yankee Haters

I was a Yankee fan. I didn't know better at that point in my life.

JIM PALMER, on his childhood

Ostensibly the "premier franchise" in baseball's storied history, the New York Yankees have lost, or in many cases not even played, more than three-quarters of the World Series to date. The team is dead last alphabetically.

Blogger **"GONFALON BUBBLE"**

It's nothing that two out of three against the Yankees won't cure.

BILL RIGNEY, on his flu

It's fiction.

CASEY STENGEL, on *Damn Yankees*

Yankee Imperialism

Star Trek fans know all about the Borg, a collective organism that roams the universe, assimilating the species it considers useful while annihilating their individuality in the process. The Borg is virtually invincible; its credo is "Resistance is futile." I think the Yankees stole their business model.

CRAIG CALCATERRA

The Yankees know only one way: "Throw a wallet at a problem. If the problem persists, find another wallet."

JOEL SHERMAN

Yankee Stadium

Yankee Stadium was a mistake. Not mine, but the Giants.

Owner **JACOB RUPPERT**,
on the Yanks' move away from the Polo Grounds

It was the unforgettable, oversized, off-the-scale standard that changed everything—the Babe Ruth of ballparks.

GLENN STOUT, on Yankee Stadium

We like to say that St. Patrick's is the "Yankee Stadium of cathedrals."

Archbishop **TIMOTHY DOLAN**, on the "Cathedral of baseball"

Yogi

Ballplayers always say, "I'd rather be lucky than good." Yogi is both.

JOE GARAGIOLA

He could fall in a sewer and come up with a gold watch

CASEY STENGEL, on his perpetually "lucky" catcher

Maybe he can't say it too good, but he can do it.

STENGEL

YANKEES—NO, METS—SI, WELCOME, YOGI

Fan banner, seen soon after Yogi's 1964
Yankees firing / Mets hiring

Anybody who thinks Yogi is dumb just isn't a smart man.

RED PATTERSON

Yogi survived D-Day and George Steinbrenner.

IRA BERKOW, on the Yanks' World War II veteran / ex-manager

A Yankee who Met fans loved.

CARLO DEVITO

To know him more was to love him more.

Biographer **ALLEN BARRA**

They say Yogi Berra is funny. Well, he has a lovely wife and family, a beautiful home, money in the bank, and he plays golf with millionaires. What's funny about that?

CASEY STENGEL

Yogi-isms

Slump? I ain't in no slump. I just ain't hitting.

If people don't want to come out to the park, nobody's going to stop them.

Nobody goes to that restaurant anymore. It's too crowded.

It's tough to make predictions, especially about the future.

It gets late early out there.

You can observe a lot by watching.

It's déjà vu all over again.

The future ain't what it used to be.

He must've made that picture before he died.

I don't care what people say. That's for them to say.

I've got nothing to say and I'm only going to say it once.

When you see a fork in the road, take it.

It isn't too far, it just seems that way. When you get to the house, you'll see it.

I want to thank everyone for making this night necessary.

On Yogi Berra Night

We made too many wrong mistakes.

On the '60 World Series

I'd say he's done more than that.

When asked if a young Don Mattingly had exceeded expectations

You mean now?

When asked "What time is it?"

Sometimes.

When asked if he attended all Yankee home games

REPORTER: Yogi, have you made your mind up yet?
BERRA: Not that I know of.

If I had to do it all over again, I would do it over again.

Yogi-isms: Perfect Game Division

The best it ever got. How could you ever beat perfect?

On catching Don Larsen's perfect game in the '56 World Series

It's never happened in World Series competition, and it still hasn't. Everything.

On what he remembered best about it

Forever Young

Funny, he doesn't look like an old man. Especially when he plays baseball.

JIM BOUTON, on Willie Mays at age 38

Right now, he's throwing like two 22-year-olds.

JIM COLBORN, on Jesse Orosco at age 44

I think he wants to be the first one to cross home plate and collect his salary check, pension, and Social Security at the same time.

TERRY KENNEDY, on Rickey Henderson's playing to age 46

60 going on 21.

WILLIAM RYCZEK, on Phil Linz (b. 1939)

Character Profile: CASEY STENGEL

When Casey Stengel was hired as Yankees manager in 1949, Red Smith wrote of "a comedian" running the team, and one of the club's co-owners, Del Webb, was heard to mutter, "My God, we've hired a clown." It was the exact wrong impression, but Ol' Case may have said and done a few things to encourage it.

At the most immediate level, Charles Dillon Stengel was simply blessed with a God-given gift for fun and games. It was evident from his earliest days, when the teenage extrovert bypassed schools, churches, and business offices in favor of pool halls, bars, amusement parks, or any other place where he could do more than his fair share of drinking, dancing, and socializing. He never changed, either. Even in the mid-1960s, up until his retirement at age 75, Stengel was known to saddle up to the nearest bar and regale all comers with monologues that would last well into the early morning, hours after men half his age had dozed off. "If you liked baseball, you were his friend," said one observer.

Stengel was one of a kind.

Within a few years of coming up to the majors in 1912, he was linked to a couple of nutty pranks involving a hidden sparrow and an errant grapefruit (see pages 327 and 335 for more on those) and he never lost his fondness for those types of attention-grabbing gags. When he was in his 40s, after more than 20 years in the game, he once mocked an umpires' refusal to call a rain delay by carrying an umbrella out to the third base coach's box; another time he protested darkening skies by carrying a lit lantern on to the field. When he was pushing 70, he lit a sparkler and danced a little jig in front of Comiskey Park's new exploding scoreboard and, during a Mexico City exhibition, he wore a pregame sombrero and hammed it up with a mariachi band. When the guy was nearly *80* years old, he rode around Shea Stadium in a *Ben Hur*–style chariot, whip in hand.

The temptation, in his time and ours, was to read Stengel's tomfoolery as a lack of substance, an absence of a certain intellectual gravitas. It's understandable enough. The type of individual who would willingly wrestle a greased pig isn't necessarily the epitome of a deep thinker. That may be so, as a general rule, but in Stengel's case, there's every reason to believe the man was even more intelligent than funny.

As many contemporaries could attest, Stengel always displayed an absolutely astonishing, near-photographic recall of tens of thousands of at-bats he'd witnessed over the decades and, even more important, he could apply those memories to piece together the kind of highly unconventional lineups, skill-based platoons, pinch-hitting assignments, and rotation/bullpen roles that few other managers could ponder, much less execute. While the Yankee powerhouses of the '50s enjoyed an undeniable advantage in terms of on-field talent, they enjoyed just as big of an advantage in the way their leader combined rock-solid information with applied problem-solving. Long before number crunchers used massive databases to maximize their teams' competitive edges, Stengel was using his own supercomputer—the one between his ears. You could look it up.

And it was the combination of Stengel's outgoing nature and that acute intellect that produced so much of his humor. If a baseball man has both a fun-loving instinct for capers and the wit to conjure them up, well, yeah, he'll be more silly than the clever guys and more clever than the silly guys.

But there was something else that made Casey Stengel an especially gifted baseball humorist—call it a certain flinty wisdom, an innate insight into how the world of baseball worked. One way or the other, Casey never seemed to lose sight of the ways that what some might consider fluff could actually be used for very practical purposes. PR purposes, for instance.

When Stengel started off as a skipper for basement-dwelling ball clubs in Brooklyn and Boston throughout the 1930s and '40s, he was all too aware that the beat reporters and everyday fans around him weren't particularly interested in the dismal doings on the field, so he often chose to make himself the lead story. Whenever the public was tempted to completely ignore the Dodgers or Braves, there he was, tirelessly providing "my writers" with another stunt, crafting another beauty of a one-liner, mugging for the cameras, talking up a bevy of spectators, or popping up at sandlots to give kids an impromptu clinic on the finer points of the game. No matter how monotonous his other clubs were in their constant losing—or the Yankees were in their constant winning, even—Casey's promotional tactics never failed to make for lively press copy, at least.

At other times, Stengel's brand of comedy was more pointed. The Ol' Perfesser's jokes could keep everyone light and loose during a losing streak, but when the skipper saw mental errors, his remarks could also become so cutting and public that targets would've almost preferred he'd scream at them instead. Even the most off-the-cuff jokes had a serious message behind them.

Without a doubt, the very peak of Stengel's fusion of fun and purpose came in his invention of a mangled form of English dubbed "Stengelese," one that gained its fullest popularity when the Yankees were winning championship after championship in the 1950s. Most Yankees fans know it well; it was all about long, screwball responses with endless, word-tripping digressions that sounded interesting but could be interpreted any number of ways. Consider:

What Casey Said	**What Casey (Probably) Meant**
"It's possible a college education doesn't always help you if you can't hit a left-handed changeup as far as the shortstop, but I'm not bragging, you understand, as I don't have a clear notion about atomics or physics or a clear idea where China is in relation to Mobile."	"In my humble opinion, book smarts aren't the same as baseball smarts."
"They say you can never do that, but he is and it's a good idea, but sometimes it doesn't always work."	"That move might work, or it might not. Either way, I'm not going to answer your question."

What Casey Said	What Casey (Probably) Meant
"I'm outta baseball and I was in it for a long time and it don't have to be forever."	"I haven't decided whether I want to stay retired."
"Sometimes I get a little hard-of-speaking."	(Wink.)
"Everybody line up alphabetically by height."	(Nudge.)

Stengelese, like legalese, could be barely understood at times, but there was always a careful sense behind the nonsense. The Ol' Perfesser was more than capable of communicating in crystal-clear, succinct sentences, and he chose to do otherwise only when confronted with heavy topics—such as benchings, injuries, clubhouse feuds, losing streaks—that he didn't particularly want to discuss in crystal-clear, succinct terms. He knew that if he kept the beat reporters chuckling, he wouldn't have to tackle those issues. At minimum, the linguistic somersaults helped keep the media scrutiny off ballplayers who were feeling quite enough New York pressure already, so what seemed like crazy talk was more like crazy-like-a-fox talk.

The most memorable example of Stengel's humor-as-distraction probably occurred when he was called to testify before Congress in 1958; the issue was federal regulation over baseball, a popular policy that might have cost the dynastic Yankees dearly, but the canny Stengel diverted the panel's attention with an impossibly disjointed 45-minute ramble through the old-timer's life and times, from Shelbyville, Kentucky, to New York City, from night games to the minors, from pensions to payrolls. Stengel rollicked on and on, making just enough sense to string his listeners along but never quite enough to fully answer their queries. By the time their witness had finished his performance, the Senate Subcommittee on Antitrust and Monopoly was in stitches, having long forgotten their boring law thing—just as Casey had intended all along.

It was a moment that could have been authored by only one character. Casey Stengel was an overgrown boy graced by fully formed genius, a practitioner of serious fun, a kidder who truly mastered the game; he was one of the Yankees' greatest winners, in more ways than one. At Stengel's funeral, in 1975, Richie Ashburn bestowed an epitaph any of us would envy: "Casey loved life and he loved laughter. He loved people and above all he loved baseball. He was the happiest man I've ever seen."

NICKNAMES

(Bill) "Dizzy" Akers

Dick Bartell: "He had his own way of making a triple play on a ground ball—he would drop it, kick it, and then throw it away. One of his pitchers asked him which side he was playing for."

Dick "Crash" Allen

By the time Allen went through several off-field misadventures in the late 1960s, Phillie fans hated him enough to routinely pelt him with bolts, beer bottles, and batteries from the stands, so he played first base while wearing a batting helmet, which became a "crash helmet"; Crash was also the title of Allen's no-apologies autobiography.

Sandy "The Iron Pony" Alomar, Sr.

For his consecutive-game streak, the muscle-bound 6', 200-pound Lou Gehrig was famously known as "The Iron Horse." When the wee 150-pound Alomar played every game during the 1970 and 1971 seasons, teammates started calling him "The Iron Pony."

(George) "Sparky" Anderson

This one first came up during Anderson's time in the minors, when an announcer noted how he "always made the sparks fly" in umpire arguments; he tried introducing himself by his real name for years afterward, but after a while no one recognized it, so "George Anderson" became "Sparky Anderson."

Joaquin "One Tough Dominican" Andujar

A teammate once put fake snakes in Andujar's locker on three successive days and, on the fourth day, just when Andujar thought he had the gag figured out, he found a live snake; the "Tough Dominican" was so shaken up that he missed a scheduled start.

(Frank) "Home Run" Baker

Just how dead was the "dead-ball" era of the 1910s, you ask? Well, its version of a "power hitter," Baker, never had more than 12 homers per year and finished with a grand total of 96. That dead.

(Johnnie) "Dusty" Baker

Like "Muddy" Ruel, Baker got this tag because he was always getting dirty while playing ball as a kid; Rod Beck called the Giants' '97 playoff run "Dustiny," and, in 2003, Cub fans sported "In Dusty We Trusty" T-shirts.

Steve "Bye-Bye" Balboni

This one dates back to Balboni's early Yankee days, when he was frequently called up and down from the minors; he eventually had to say bye-byes for ten trades and releases in 11 years.

Ernie "Mr. Cub" Banks

He hit more than 500 homers, but Banks was so beloved that he probably would've been inducted into the Hall of Fame as a utility man; verbatim pregame chatter: "Isn't it a beautiful day? . . . The Cubs of Chicago versus the Phillies of Philadelphia in beautiful, historic Wrigley Field! Let's go, let's go! It's Sunday in America!"

Ed "Simon" Barrow

As Red Sox owner in the late 1910s, Harry Frazee took to calling his imperial GM "Simon," as in "Simon Legree," the merciless slave owner from *Uncle Tom's Cabin*; Frazee meant it as a compliment.

Dick "Rowdy Richard" Bartell

As a Giants infielder in the 1930s, Bartell led the league in both double plays and fistfights; "They hated him with a cold fury in Brooklyn," it was said. (Dick had several other nicknames, all of which are unprintable in a family book.)

(Emil) "Buzzie" Bavasi

He earned his nickname for the way he buzzed all over the place as a boy, but he wasn't nearly as successful as a young player; one time, Dodgers owner Larry MacPhail refused to sign a would-be pitching prospect because he found out that Bavasi had once gotten three hits off the kid.

Rod "Shooter" Beck

Beck was a closer who looked and acted like an Old West gun-slinger; he gave up more than his share of long balls, too, which is how his other nickname, "Upper Deck Beck," came into circulation.

Walter "Boom-Boom" Beck

They said the first "boom" came from opponents' bats, the second "boom" from the ball's landing at some point over in the distance; Beck allowed 63 homers, or 126 "booms," in his career.

Craig "Pigpen" Biggio

. . . used the exact same pine tar–encrusted, grimy helmet through more than 10,000 career at-bats. David Schoenfield wrote that "Craig Biggio's name has never been linked to perfor-mance-enhancing drugs, but I know two things he tested positive for: hustle and dirt."

Joe "New Newk" Black

When Don Newcombe was called away into military service dur-ing the '52 season, his replacement became the Dodgers' first African-American starter and Rookie of the Year since . . . Don Newcombe.

(Larvell) "Sugar Bear" Blanks

One was a cartoon character on '70s cereal boxes, the other a light-hitting flake on '70s infields; the connection between the two was never very clear, but "Sugar Bear" was definitely more catchy than "Larvell."

Ron "Designated Hebrew" Blomberg

When the highly touted Jewish slugger first came to New York City, scouts thought Blomberg might be another Greenberg, but nowadays he's mostly remembered as the very first designated hitter, aka the "DH"; Bloomie also called himself "The Yiddish Yankee."

(Stanley) "Frenchy" Bordagaray

Bordagaray played his ancestry up to the hilt; back in the 1930s, he once showed up to the Dodgers' spring training camp wearing a beret and sporting a neatly trimmed goatee.

Jim "Bulldog" Bouton

For his inability to get into games, high school teammates called Bouton "Warm Up." For his tenacious attitude as a Yankees starter, opponents called him "Bulldog." For advocating the early union movement, teammates called him "The Communist." For writing *Ball Four,* Pete Rose called him "Shakespeare."

(Dennis) "Oil Can" Boyd

Back home in Mississippi, "oil" was slang for beer; one opponent called Boyd "Trash Can," because he was always talking garbage.

"Downtown" Darrell Brown

A minors phenom turned majors flop with enough pop for only one homer in 591 career at bats. Billy Gardner said, "That must be an awfully small town."

Mordecai "Three Finger" Brown

One of the greatest curveballs of all time was produced by a right hand mangled by a childhood farming accident. Jack Buck used to say that Three Finger Brown always gave 60 percent.

(Walter) "Jumbo" Brown

When playing from 1925 to 1941, Brown was hefty enough to be compared to a famed circus elephant of the day. He weighed more than 300 pounds. The pitcher, not the elephant.

Don "Bootin'" Buddin

Guess which Red Sox shortstop led the American League in errors in both 1958 and 1959?

Rick "Rooster" Burleson

As a Red Sox shortstop in the 1970s, Burleson was said to be a bantam rooster of a competitor; according to Bill Lee, "Nobody liked to lose, but Rick got angry if the score was even tied."

"Sleepy" Bill Burns

Sportswriter Tom Shea: "He followed two simple rules—on days he didn't pitch, he slept through the game, and on days he pitched, he slept only between innings."

Jose "Mistake-o" Canseco

How stupid was "Mistake-o"? In 1993, a fly ball bounced off Canseco's empty head and over the fence for a home run; it costs his team the game. Six days later, he talked his way into a mop-up relief appearance and proceeded to blow out his rotator cuff; that stunt cost his team the season.

(Bill) "Rough" Carrigan

As a Red Sox catcher in the 1910s, he was the kind of take-no-prisoners character who didn't mind tagging Ty Cobb on the mouth during a hard slide at home plate, a move akin to poking a (real) tiger with a sharp stick.

Gary "Camera" Carter

A dedicated Christian and family man who grinned through his many TV interviews, Carter was an oddball among the assorted miscreants on the '86 Mets; teammates said that he had to ice down his cheeks after media hour.

Rico "The Beeeg Boy" Carty

Carty, who spoke with a thick Caribbean accent, loved referring to himself in the third person, as in "The Beeeg Boy, he can heeet"; after a while he called himself "The Beeeg Mon."

Sean "The Mayor" Casey

The tag came from his neverending chatter with baserunners at first base, his accessibility with the media, and the charity work he did in the community. "The Mayor" labeled his blog site "City Hall."

Orlando "Cha Cha" Cepeda

Cepeda was among the first to introduce clubhouse music and intro songs to the majors; "Cha Cha" insisted that his dancin' helped his swingin' (at the plate).

Ron "The Penguin" Cey

Cey was so short and bow-legged that he didn't run so much as waddle, but how many flightless little birds have made six All-Star teams while smacking 316 career home runs?

Frank "The Peerless Leader" Chance

In the first decade of the 1900s, the Cubs' player-manager was so admired that beat reporters dubbed him this, probably the single most flattering nickname of all time; the usage was so routine that newspapers eventually shortened it to "The PL."

Roger "Rocket" Clemens

Appropriately enough, Clemens' hometown (Houston) is also NASA's hometown.

Ty "The Georgia Peach" Cobb

Stan Musial chalked up exactly 1,815 career hits at home and another 1,815 on the road, but that isn't the greatest numerical coincidence in baseball history: It's the fact that the Georgia-born Cobb hit .366 and eventually punched out 366 people.

Mickey "Black Mike" Cochrane

Nicknamed for either his swarthy complexion or dark moods, take your pick; Cochrane's given name was "Gordon."

(Clarence) "Choo-Choo" Coleman

When Coleman was asked, "What's your wife's name and what's she like?" he replied "Her name is Mrs. Coleman and she likes me"; he claimed to have no clue how he got his nickname and, hey, maybe he didn't.

Vince "Vincent Van Go" Coleman

The speedy but none-too-swift Coleman once said he'd never heard of a baseball pioneer named Jackie Robinson, so it's unlikely he ever brushed up on an Impressionist painter named Vincent Van Gogh, either.

(Harry) "Rip" Collins

Due to his ripping fastballs to the outfield, right? Wrong. Back home in Texas, Collins was very fond of something called "Ripy" whiskey.

"Tony C." Conigliaro

Not the most original moniker, true, but the hotshot Red Sox bachelor once roomed with a Tony Athanas and a Bill Bates, forming a carousing after-hours trio popularly known as "Mr. A., Mr. B., and Mr. C."; they printed up calling cards and everything.

Clint "Scraps" Courtney

Because Courtney 1) was as tough as scrap iron, and 2) got into numerous fistfights ("scraps").

Harry "The Giant Killer" Coveleski

During the 1908 pennant run, the Phillies' ace beat the Giants three times in two weeks, eventually costing New York the pennant; after retiring to Shamokin, Pennsylvania, a few years later, Coveleski opened up a "Giant Killer" saloon.

Johnny "Jesus" Damon

In 2004, Damon's shoulder-length locks and beard earned him notice in *People* magazine's "Sexiest Man Alive" issue, but that didn't stop Red Sox fans from jeering his departure for the Bronx; one T-shirt read LOOKS LIKE JESUS. ACTS LIKE JUDAS. THROWS LIKE MARY.

Ron "Mr. Perfect" Darling

Darling refused to wear his Mets hat between starts because it messed up his just-so hairdo.

"Gentleman" Jake Daubert

Daubert was as meticulous and dapper a dresser as any major leaguer of the 1910s; when Brooklyn teammate Casey Stengel took extra batting practice in Daubert's place, Casey said it was because the team captain was having his nails manicured.

Willie "The Strange Ranger" Davis

While he played for Texas in 1975, Davis did yoga and roomed with a giant Doberman; either one, alone, might have been overlooked, but the combination?

Dominic "The Little Professor" DiMaggio

Joe's little brother looked and played like one of the most brainy fielders of his generation; Ted Williams used to joke that "We had perfect communication when I played left and he played center. He said, 'I've got it,' and I said 'You take it.' Worked all the time."

Joe "The Yankee Clipper" DiMaggio

Named after the most graceful, powerful nautical ship of its time—the Joe DiMaggio of the seas, in other words.

Atley "Swampy" Donald

As the Yankees' scout for his native Louisiana in the early '70s, he signed Ron Guidry, who, in 1978, broke Donald's own team record for consecutive wins; "Swampy" must have had mixed feelings on that one.

Brian "The Hulk" Downing

Back in the 1970s, Downing was among the first ballplayers to seriously commit to a conditioning routine that had him lifting something heavier than a beer mug; in today's game, the 5'10", 195-pound Downing would probably be known as "The Smurf."

"Dirty" Jack Doyle

This was either because Doyle was a dirty uniform–type gamer or because he bent and broke a few rules; maybe it was a little of both.

Don "Big D" Drysdale

"Big" as in height (6'6") and league-leading hit-by-pitch totals; when Drysdale got ticked off at batters, he used to fire at them twice, with the second brushback intended to let 'em know the first one was no accident.

"Jumpin'" Joe Dugan

Because Dugan leaped out of the way of barreling baserunners? Not quite. The nickname originated because he would go AWOL ("jump") from his ball clubs every so often.

Steve "Stunning" Dunning

Dunning started off as a handsome, highly touted Stanford grad, then slowly trailed off into obscurity; he once gave up a leadoff homer in three straight starts in the early 1970s, which was stunning, but not in a good way.

"Blind" Ryne Duren

For opposing hitters, the fact that Duren's glasses were as thick as Coke bottles probably wasn't as distressing as his drinking problem, mean streak, or the fact that his warm-up fastballs sometimes whistled through the batter's box.

Lenny "Dude" Dykstra

For his supposed toughness, fans called Dykstra "Nails"; reporters and teammates called him "Dude" because the word was at the beginning or the end of virtually every sentence out of his filthy mouth.

(Norman) "The Tabasco Kid" Elberfeld

In the first decade of the 1900s, Kid poured whiskey on bleeding spike wounds, spit tobacco juice into umpires' eyes, and summoned waiters by tossing dinner plates into the air; they just don't make 'em like that anymore, which is a good thing.

Mike "SuperJew" Epstein

When the Athletics won three straight championships from 1972 to 1974, Epstein was "SuperJew" to Ken Holtzman's plain ol' "Jew"; not politically correct times, the 1970s.

Carl "Crazy Eights" Everett

Everett was crazy and wore number 8; after he denied that dinosaurs had ever existed, columnist Dan Shaughnessy took to calling Everett "Jurassic Carl."

Johnny "The Crab" Evers

"The Crab" reference had nothing to do with seafood; multiple teammates, opponents, and umpires believed that Evers was the most irritable and irritating man they'd ever met.

(Charles) "Victory" Faust

In one of the more bizarre chapters in baseball history, Faust once showed up at a Giants practice claiming that a fortune teller had assured him that the club needed him in order to win the 1911 pennant; after John J. McGraw humored the flake by allowing him a couple mop-up innings late in the season, the Giants *did* make it to the World Series for the first time in six years.

(Dave) "Boo" Ferriss

The nickname originally came from a toddler's attempt to pronounce "brother"; ironically enough, "Boo" was one of the most popular (and cheered) Red Sox of the late 1940s.

Mark "The Bird" Fidrych

Most fans know that Fidrych got this one due to the way his tall, lanky frame and curly blond hair bore a resemblance to a certain *Sesame Street* character. The Bird posed beside Big Bird for *Rolling Stone* in '76, becoming the first (and, to date, last) ballplayer ever to grace the magazine's cover.

Cecil "Big Daddy" Fielder

Fielder got this nickname for his big smile and fatherly presence, long before anyone had heard of a kid named Prince Fielder.

"Disco" Dan Ford

While playing for the Angels from 1979 to 1981, Ford frequently went out clubbing; teammate Don Baylor hated Ford's flash surplus and hustle deficit. ("He had the reputation for being a hot dog and a dog at the same time," Baylor wrote.)

Whitey "Slick" Ford

This one has at least three possible explanations: 1) Ford was a "city slicker" from Queens; 2) He got "whiskey slick" while out on the town with Mickey Mantle; and 3) he tossed spitters. Yankees broadcaster Mel Allen preferred Ford's other notable nickname for his intros: "*Ladies* and Gentlemen, *the chair*-man of the *board,* Whitey *Ford!*"

Terry "Hoss" Forster

"I guess fat tub of goo," says David Letterman, "was too on the nose."

(Bob) "Fatty" Fothergill

This guy didn't miss many meals; according to Baseball-Reference.com, Fothergill weighed more than 230 pounds, which, coincidentally, is the size of C. C. Sabathia's typical lunch.

Art "10 to 2" Fowler

Sparky Lyle: "Because that's the way his feet point."

Jimmie "The Beast" Foxx

The nickname was based on the slugger's bulging muscles, not his sunny, outgoing personality. Vernon "Lefty" Gomez used to claim that when Neil Armstrong first set foot on the moon, the astronaut found a ball that Jimmie Foxx had hit off him in 1937.

Frankie "Fordham Flash" Frisch

Everyone loved the alliteration and Frisch did have a real interest in books, but as Leo Durocher once pointed out, the undergrad jock "majored in baseball, football, and soccer."

Oscar "2-8-5" Gamble

When Gamble went into the '78 free agent market, the Padres gave him the . . .completely! . . . outrageous! . . . sum of $2.85 million for six years; of course, nowadays, everyone but the batboy is pulling down 2-8-5 or more.

Rich "El Guapo" Garces

Red Sox teammate Mike Maddux came up with this one, from a character in *The Three Amigos* movie; it means "The Handsome One," a less-than-obvious label for a man with the physique of a Venezuelan potato.

BASEBALL MULTICULTURALISM

(RICHARD) "TURK" FARRELL: Irish.

(OLAF) "SWEDE" HENRIKSEN: Danish ancestry.

KEITH "MEX" HERNANDEZ: Spanish-American.

"BLACK" JACK MCDOWELL: White.

(EMIL) "IRISH" MEUSEL: Born of German immigrants.

HONUS "THE FLYING DUTCHMAN" WAGNER: German-American.

(STEVEN) "TURK" WENDELL: Originally from Mars.

Steve "The Senator" Garvey

It may seem completely ridiculous now, but back when the clean-cut Garvey was making perennial All-Star appearances for the Dodgers in the 1970s, there was serious talk of his running for high office one day; after he was hit with multiple paternity suits in the late 1980s, Garvey bumper stickers cropped up reading FATHER OF OUR COUNTRY.

Fred "Fred Flintstone" Gladding

Jim Bouton: "He doesn't look like a pitcher. He looks like a grocer who's been eating up a good bit of the profits."

(Vernon) "Lefty" / "El Goofy" Gomez

A natural tag for an off-beat Spanish-American, no? In the early days, he was sometimes called "The Gay Castilian," but that one was later phased out, lest anyone get confused about just how offbeat Mr. Gomez really was.

(Leon) "Goose" Goslin

Unlike Mr. Gossage, this Goose got the nickname because his big nose looked like a beak; also, supposedly, Goslin looked like a bird flapping its wings when he chased after fly balls.

Charlie "Jolly Cholly" Grimm

During his stints as Cubs manager from the 1930s through the 1950s, Grimm would sing, drink, and joke around with his players by the hour; he once snipped off his players' ties and made a team quilt out of the fabric. Another time, he played piano as they went through spring training warm-ups. He was jolly.

Ross "Scuzz" Grimsley

Grimsley sported long, greasy hair to aid his spitballing ways or, maybe, just because he was gross.

"Smilin'" Stan Hack

Hack really had enough positive attitude and enthusiasm to light up a small city; a reporter once said, "Stan has more friends than Leo Durocher has enemies."

Harvey "The Kitten" Haddix

When he came up with St. Louis in the 1950s, they said Haddix was a younger version of Harry "The Cat" Brecheen.

Travis "Pronk" Hafner

"Half project, half donkey," they said when Hafner arrived in Cleveland; hands down, the best baseball nickname since Frank "The Big Hurt" Thomas came on the scene in the late 1980s.

Mike "The Human Rain Delay" Hargrove

Hargrove flashed enough twitches, fidgets, and gestures to fill up an obsessive-compulsive's handbook, but it was worse than that. He also took practice swings before each delivery, fouled off pitches, and took multiple walks; assuming a very conservative three minutes per at bat, Grover's 5,564 career turns took well over 11 full days, all told.

Ken "Hawk" Harrelson

Harrelson's bent beak inspired the most moniker-obsessed ballplayer of all time: "Hawk" was embroidered, engraved, or otherwise printed on almost everything the man owned, including clothes, apartment tiles, uniform jerseys, and an autobiography. Frank Howard also called Harrelson "Fab," short for "The Fabulous Hawk Harrelson."

(Charles) "Gabby" Hartnett

This was a sarcastic nickname that eventually became accurate. Hartnett was unusually quiet when he first came up with the Cubs in the 1920s, but he later opened up enough to become truly gabby.

Richie "The Gravedigger" Hebner

If it was based on the way Hebner (metaphorically) dug his opponents' graves with late-inning hits and clutch homers, this would
have been one of the most awesome nicknames of all time; unfortunately, it was based on the fact that Hebner (literally) worked at
his dad's cemetery during the off-season.

Harry "Slug" Heilmann

Heilmann both ran slow and hit hard, ergo "Slug."

Tommy "Ol' Reliable" Henrich

Mel Allen reportedly came up with this one, after an Alabama
railroad that always ran on time; Henrich's teams did win every
one of his eight World Series, which was about as reliable as you
can possibly get.

Chuck "Dr. No" Hiller

In the summer of 1962, the Giants' Hiller led all National League
second basemen in errors, so his teammates nicknamed him
after a James Bond villain with no hands.

Burt "Happy" Hooton

Teammates called Hooton "Happy" for much the same reason
some would call a fat guy "Tiny."

Bob "Buddha" Horner

Whitey Herzog called Horner "Buddha" because he was over-weight and usually sitting down somewhere.

"King Carl" Hubbell

As in 1930s-era ERA royalty; teammates also called Hub "The Meal Ticket."

Rex "The Wonder Dog" Hudler

Nicknamed after the almost-canine sense of enthusiasm he's brought to his job as an Angels broadcaster, offering phrases such as "Vlad swings from his nose to his toes, where he hits it no one knows!" and "John Lackey, keepin' it on track-ey!" These are things puppies would say if they could talk.

Randy "Shucks" Hundley

Hundley never used profanity; whenever he got riled up, the catcher never exclaimed anything wilder than "Shucks!" and "Darn!"

(Jim) "Catfish" Hunter

Everyone knows that A's owner Charlie O. Finley made up the nickname to make his prize prospect more marketable, but young Jim Hunter really did enjoy fishing. And hunting, for that matter.

Bo "RoBo" Jackson

Jackson built a lucrative endorsement career out of the fact that he could outrun, out-slug, out-lift, and out-throw anyone anywhere. Pat Tabler said Bo must be a robot ("He's not human").

"Shoeless" Joe Jackson

Producers changed the *Shoeless Joe* book title to *Field of Dreams* because audiences would otherwise think the story was about a homeless man; legend has it that a young kid once met Jackson, elbowed his friend, and said, "I told you he wore shoes."

Reggie "Mr. October" Jackson

How good was he in his prime? Well, Jax was almost as good as he thought he was. That good.

Davey "Dumb-Dumb" Johnson

This one's a completely sarcastic, upside-down nickname, as Johnson earned a college degree in mathematics and often made managerial moves based on the theory of favorable chance deviation. As a Baltimore player in the early 1970s, Davey once wrote up a "How to Optimize the Orioles Offense" report that suggested he bat cleanup.

Randy "The Big Unit" Johnson

Probably a reference to his 6'10" height. Probably.

"Sad Sam" Jones

Jones had one of those faces that looked downcast no matter what he was feeling, but "Sad Sam" could crack a joke and have fun at parties, no problemo.

"Hot Rod" Kanehl

Finished his career with 192 hits and almost as many stories of early 1960s derring-do; after Casey Stengel offered a small bonus to any Mets hitter to get hit by a pitch, Hot Rod took one for the team, then used a magic marker to ink "$50" on the bruise.

Charlie "King Kong" Keller

Keller was unusually big, strong, and hairy, but, not surprisingly, hated the nickname; when Phil Rizzuto called him "King Kong" to his face, Keller picked up the little shortstop and stuffed him into an empty locker.

Harmon "Killer" Killebrew

The nickname was nothing more than an easy pun on his sur-name; apart from baseballs, the outgoing, genial Killebrew never hurt a thing in his life.

Ellis "Old Folks" Kinder

Kinder didn't have his first big year with the Red Sox until 1949, when he was already 35 years old; for his ability to drink himself senseless and recover in time to pitch, teammates also referred to him as "Superman."

"Sinister" Dick Kinsella

With his tall frame, thick black hair, bushy eyebrows, dark suits, and "an ominously quiet manner," Kinsella, who was John J. McGraw's scouting director for decades, was a stage villain to all appearances. His friends thought he was a nice enough guy, though.

Ray "Mr. Nancy Lopez" Knight

After he retired as a player, Knight briefly caddied for his wife, who knew how to play golf better than he knew how to play baseball; Nomar Garciaparra was sometimes referred to as "Mr. Mia Hamm," too.

"Handsome" Jack Kramer

The reference was to his face, not to any great-looking stuff; Mickey McDermott wrote that "when Handsome Jack threw his fastball, three birds s——t on it before it reached home plate."

Mike "Spanky" LaValliere

LaValliere resembled the ringleader of the Little Rascals and hit only 18 more career home runs than the other "Spanky."

Bill "The Spaceman" Lee

Lee, a dedicated baseball man who dabbled in Eastern mysticism, described himself as "equal parts Yogi Berra and Maharishi Mahesh Yogi"; due to his outspoken environmentalism, "The Spaceman" preferred to be called "The Earthman."

Johnny "Disaster" LeMaster

LeMaster once hit .254. It was a career year. It was that kind of career.

Jeffrey "Penitentiary Face" Leonard

Leonard may have looked as fierce and angry as any competitor anywhere, but Don Zimmer once described him as "one of the sweetest guys I ever knew."

Jim "The King" Leyritz

Don Mattingly and other Yankees veterans coined this sarcastic nickname when the swaggering, motor-mouthed rookie first came up in the early 1990s; they also called him "Jumbo Jimmy," only that one wasn't sarcastic.

Phil "SuperSub" Linz

Linz could play ball but couldn't play particularly well for particularly long, so he ended up as a spare part/jack-of-all-trades player for the Yanks and Mets; he once said, "They say you can't get rich sitting on the bench, but I'm giving it a try."

Eddie "The Junkman" Lopat

Overcame rag-arm velocity with superb off-speed guile and guesswork; read: junk.

John "Brother Lo" Lowenstein

Lowenstein was a combination of a Bill Lee and a Sparky Lyle: a nimble thinker with a prankster's heart. Whenever a little cake arrived in the Orioles' clubhouse in the late 1970s, teammates would chant "Lo! Lo! Lo!" until Lowenstein grabbed a bat and splattered the dessert, samarai-style.

Sparky Lyle

Lyle's nickname origin is about the same as that of Sparky Anderson and every other major league Sparky; he always insisted that his parents named him after the family dog, though.

Steve "Psycho" Lyons

This one gained currency when Lyons absentmindedly dropped his pants right after a particularly messy slide into second base. Lyons's autobiography was called *Psychoanalysis,* probably because the title was more memorable than "Mediocre Player and Worse Broadcaster."

Garry "Secretary of Defense" Maddox

Harry Kalas: "Two-thirds of the earth is covered by water and the other third by Garry Maddox."

Greg "Mad Dog" Maddux

A play off the future Hall of Famer's name and competitiveness, not his looks, which call to mind a male assistant librarian. When his brother was asked if Maddux's physique had changed over the years, he answered, "Yeah—it's gotten worse."

(Walter) "Rabbit" Maranville

. . . had a short, slight body frame to go with a pair of big ears. Just like a rabbit.

"Brawlin'" Billy Martin

Master of the unkind word and sucker punch against opponents, his own players, traveling secretaries, fans, cabbies, bar bouncers. . . . By one unofficial tally, Martin's amateur fistfighting record totaled 11 wins, two losses, and two draws.

(Johnny) "Pepper" Martin

Martin was also called "The Wild Horse of the Osage"; he once said, "I grew up in Oklahoma. Once you start runnin' out there, there ain't nothin' to stop you."

Pedro "El Duro" Martinez

"The Hard One" once said George Steinbrenner "might buy the whole league, but he doesn't have enough money to put fear in my heart." Red Sox fans are still swooning over that one.

Christy "The Christian Gentleman" Mathewson

If he didn't make it in the national pastime, Matty would have undoubtedly become a Presbyterian minister; as his completely serious nickname might indicate, it's almost impossible to overstate how revered Mathewson was during his 1900s to 1910s heyday.

Hideki "Godzilla" Matsui

As an MVP-quality player back home in Japan, he hit enough home runs to knock over the Tokyo skyline, but the nickname also referred to his not-quite-perfect facial complexion. Matsui once did a cameo in a *Godzilla vs. Mechagodzilla* remake.

Kaz "Little" Matsui

The "Little" apparently referred to his power production and on-base percentage in New York. In Japanese, "Kaz Matsui" can be roughly translated as "Rey Sanchez."

Gary "Sarge" Matthews

When Wrigley's Bleacher Bums started cheering his every appearance in left field during the Cubs' '84 playoff run, Matthews gave them an old-fashioned military salute in return; the media guys said he looked like a drill sergeant out there.

Don "Donnie Baseball" Mattingly

When Milwaukee fans call Bob Uecker "Mr. Baseball" they're joking, but when a generation of Yankees fans invoked "Donnie Baseball," they were completely serious.

Willie "The Say Hey Kid" Mays

When he came up to the big leagues, Mays had trouble remembering names, so his "Say hey" greetings basically translated into "Hey you, whatever your name is." While he was finishing out his career with the Mets, writers had a lot of fun with the "Shea Hey Kid" and the "A-Mays-ing" headlines.

"Marse Joe" McCarthy

One of the most famous managers in history had one of the more obscure nicknames; the "Marse" was a slang term for "master," as in "slave master." So much for the good old days, huh?

(Robert) "Maje" McDonnell

While growing up in Great Depression–era Philadelphia, McDonnell showed up at Shibe Park so often that his family and friends took to calling him "The Little Major Leaguer," which became "Maje." The moniker stuck with him for more than 60 years through McDonnell's career as a Phillies coach, scout, executive, and community ambassador.

"Sudden" Sam McDowell

McDowell's sudden fastball earned him Nolan Ryan–levels of strikeouts, but his bar-fight losses earned him another nickname: "Canvasback."

"Super Joe" McEwing

In 47 career at-bats against Greg Maddux and Tom Glavine, Super Joe was Superman (.333 batting average/.500+ slugging); against the rest of the league, he was Clark Kent (.251/.355).

"Iron" Joe McGinnity

McGinnity's nickname originally referred to his off-season job in an iron foundry, then to his eye-popping innings totals. As the story goes, a young player once took his naive young girlfriend to her first baseball game and, when she asked if he'd be pitching both games of a doubleheader, he replied, "Who do you think I am, Iron Joe McGinnity?"

John "Little Napoleon" McGraw

Kind of redundant, isn't it? For his pug nose, opponents called McGraw "Muggsy," and for his spirited play, Cuban fans called him "El Mono Amarillo" ("The Yellow Monkey").

Austin "Fireman" McHenry

A young Cardinals player living near St. Louis's Robison Field in 1919, McHenry smelled smoke within the old wooden ballpark one night, alerted the local fire department, and proceeded to join the brigade in dousing the flames. McHenry was surely the only position player ever to be nicknamed "Fireman."

"Trader" Jack McKeon

As Padres GM in the 1980s, McKeon was capable of trading away virtually any player, including his son-in-law, Greg Booker. And you thought *your* family's Thanksgiving dinners were awkward.

(George) "Doc" Medich

Medich actually attended medical school
during his off-seasons with the Yankees
and Rangers and, after retiring, Dr. George
F. Medich became a practicing orthopedist
back home in Pittsburgh.

Fred "Bonehead" Merkle

After his infamous baserunning blunder contributed to the
Giants' losing the 1908 pennant, Merkle must have feared that a
nickname like "Bonehead" would stick around long enough to be
mentioned in his obituary; 48 years later, it was.

(Carl) "Stump" Merrill

The future Yankees manager was an undersized and power-defi-
cient minor leaguer, but his sense of humor never left him; when
he hit his first homer after four seasons in the bushes, he made a
grand slide into home plate as his roommate swooped in to call
him safe.

Len "Boots" Merullo

On September 13, 1942, the Cubs' Merullo played the second
game of a doubleheader in Boston while nervously waiting for
his wife to give birth to their firstborn back in Chicago. Len Jr.
and his mom turned out fine, but Merullo was unsteady enough
to commit a record four errors in an inning, so the next day's
headline read "BOOTS" IS BORN/MERULLO BOOTS FOUR.

Stu "The Bullet" Miller

Miller was a changeup specialist, so the nickname was, obviously, sarcastic. Ron Luciano once said he pitched at four speeds, those being "slow, slower, slowest, and stopped."

Kevin "World" Mitchell

When he first came up with the '86 Mets, Mitchell logged time in six field positions and filled almost as many lineup slots; Gary Carter said he could play anywhere in the world.

Johnny "The Big Cat" Mize

Like most felines, the original "Big Cat" was respected more for his quick reflexes and great vision than for his brawn; when he slugged 25 homers at age 37, Dan Parker wrote "Your arm is gone/Your legs likewise/But not your eyes, Mize/Not your eyes."

Omar "The Out-Maker" Moreno

Not a reference to defensive skills. Moreno was a .250 hitter, struck out four times for every walk, and was thrown out in nearly half his steal attempts; in 1980 he set a single-season record for outs made (515 at the plate, 45 on the base paths).

Roger "Wrong Way" Moret

Moret was relatively effective when healthy and focused, but that was a rare combination; Bill Lee said his pal "was usually headed the right way, but had a habit of falling asleep while going there."

"Walpole Joe" / "Tollway Joe" Morgan

A Massachusetts native turned Red Sox organization man, Morgan really did hail from Walpole and once held an off-season job as a toll worker on the Massachusetts turnpike. Nowadays, he's sometimes called "the white Joe Morgan," much the same way that the Frank Thomas from the '60s is sometimes referred to as "the white Frank Thomas."

Jamie "The Ancient Mariner" Moyer

After a really rough start to his career, Moyer's changeup and changeup-on-his-changeup repertoire aged remarkably well in Seattle; at age 38, "The Ancient Mariner" became the oldest pitcher ever to win 20 games for the first time.

Don "Mandrake" Mueller

Back when the Mandrake the Magician stage act was popular in the 1940s and 1950s, Giants fans insisted that Mueller could wave his bat around like it was a magical wand.

(Hugh) "Losing Pitcher" Mulcahy

Chuck Tanner once said that the greatest feeling in the world is to win a major league game and the second greatest feeling is to lose a major league game; Mulcahy experienced the second greatest feeling in the world 76 times from 1937 to 1940.

Johnny "Grandma" Murphy

Murphy supposedly complained all the time, just like a team-mate's grandmother.

Tom "Murph the Surf" Murphy

As a member of the L.A. Angels from 1968 to 1972, Murphy had a habit of showing up at the ballpark in swimming trunks, T-shirts, and sandals, as if he was just making a quick stop on his way to the beach with Gidget and Moondoggie.

(Lynn) "Line Drive" Nelson

Great nickname for a hitter but, unfortunately for him, Nelson was a *pitcher.* The "Line Drive" nickname came from the hits he gave up.

(Louis) "Bobo" Newsom

Newsom constantly referred to himself (and everyone else) as "Bobo." He changed uniforms an astounding 25 times in a 25-year pro career, so maybe he wasn't around long enough to learn anyone's real name.

Bill "Swish" Nicholson

Nicholson finished at or near the lead in National League strikeouts seven times in the eight seasons from 1940 to 1947. Interestingly enough, another Nicholson—Dave, no relation—became the easiest strikeout victim in history 20 years later, with one K for every 2.5 career at-bats.

Hideo "The Tornado" Nomo

"The Tornado" derived from Nomo's jerky, twisty motion. When the hurler was washing out with half a dozen teams, Joe Posnanski took to calling him "Sadly He Can't Pitch" Nomo.

(Johnny) "Blue Moon" Odom

A's owner Charlie O. Finley supposedly bestowed this one because of Odom's downbeat ("blue") attitude and moon-shaped face, but it's more likely that he was simply thinking of the old doo-wop song title. Once, when Odom mixed it up with fellow Oakland starter Vida Blue, the fight was dubbed "Blue Moon vs. Blue."

Buck "Nancy" O'Neil

As the story goes, Satchel Paige once had one of his girlfriends set up in a hotel room just down the hall from where he was staying with his steady girl, then snuck out in the middle of the night, tapped on the unofficial girl's door, and whispered "Nancy? Nancy?" When Paige's steady girl woke up and angrily asked him "Who's Nancy?!" his buddy O'Neil opened his door in the adjoining room, quickly sized up the situation, and called out, "Yeah, Satch, what is it?"

Rey "Rey-Rey" Ordonez

Hitting coaches from New York to Chicago to Tampa Bay frequently muttered "Rey, Rey, Rey . . ."

David "Big Papi" Ortiz

Obviously, a very heavy hitter; obviously, a very heavy everything.

"Junior" Ortiz

Ortiz once told reporters that he'd named his newborn son "Junior Junior," but he was just putting them on; his birth name is "Adalberto Ortiz, Jr."

(Clarence) "Brick" Owens

Owens was the only major league umpire ever to be nicknamed after an object that was once thrown at him.

Paul "The Pope" Owens

Supposedly because the former Phillies general manager 1) resembled Pope Paul VI, and/or 2) was considered infallible.

Lance "Big Wheel" Parrish

Some thought that Parrish was the biggest gear in the '84 Tigers' engine. When his son Matt signed with Detroit, the kid was quickly dubbed "The Hubcap."

Carl "American Idle" Pavano

Pavano became a punch line after sitting out most of four seasons with injuries that included a sore butt; after "American Idle" got into an accident in his new Porsche, Johnny Damon asked if the car was OK.

Pascual "I-285" Perez

In August 1982, Perez missed a start for the Braves because he got lost on Interstate 285, which circled Atlanta Fulton County Stadium; he never heard the end of it.

Johnny "Mr. Red Sox" Pesky

After arriving in 1942, Pesky served as a Red Sox player, coach, manager, minor league instructor, scout, assistant GM, and broadcaster, not to mention stints in the team's marketing, community relations, and PR departments; no truth to the rumor that Pesky ever sold concessions or joined the grounds crew.

"Babe" / "The Blimp" Phelps

Ernest Phelps was one of the fattest catchers of his day, which was saying something; he once refused to travel by air, leading some to call him "The Grounded Blimp."

"Sweet Lou" Piniella

Once, in the minors, the temperamental Piniella kicked a right field fence, bringing a 15-foot section of it right down on top of him. Andy Messersmith noted that the "Sweet Lou" nickname "didn't describe his personality—it described his swing."

(John) "Boog" Powell

Short for a childhood connection to "boogers"; as most Orioles fans know, Boog(er) eventually became a restaurateur.

Bob "Gunner" Prince

The origins of this longtime Pirates broadcaster's nickname are shrouded in mystery—it was either based on his staccato on-air style or an incident in which an unhappy husband pulled a gun on him.

Albert "El Hombre" Pujols

The Cardinals' star slugger was seen as a Spanish-speaking, latter-day version of Stan "The Man" Musial, so local broadcasters took to translating the nickname into "El Hombre."

Dick "The Monster" Radatz

Mickey Mantle, who couldn't touch the fireballing Red Sox reliever in the 1960s, once exclaimed, "He's a monster." Radatz disliked the nickname because it scared kids.

Alexei "The Cuban Missile" Ramirez

Born 20 years after the Kennedy-Khrushchev showdown, Ramirez hailed from Pinar del Río, Cuba, and could run very, very fast.

BASEBALL GEOGRAPHY

DARYL BOSTON: Played for Chicago, New York, and Denver.

ROGER "DUKE OF TRALEE" BRESNAHAN: "The Duke of Toledo," was more like it.

REGGIE CLEVELAND: Not from Cleveland, not from Ohio, not even from America; Cleveland was from Canada.

TRUMAN "TEX" CLEVENGER: The nickname wasn't based on his home state but on his resemblance to teammate Tex Hughson; Tex Clevenger was actually from California.

JIM "MUDCAT" GRANT: When he came up with Cleveland in 1958, the organization thought Grant was from Mississippi, which was known to some as the "Mudcat State." If they had known he was born and raised in Florida, maybe they would've called him "Sunshine Grant."

ORLANDO HUDSON: Born and raised in Darlington, South Carolina.

JOHN MAINE: The pride of Fredericksburg, Virginia.

Pedro "The Cuban Cowboy" Ramos

Ramos learned English by watching western movies on TV and later adopted cowboy getups for his off-field clothes, complete with ten-gallon hats, studded belts, leather boots, and six-shooters.

(Calvin) "Pokey" Reese

Reese was apparently a plump infant, so his grandmother called him "Porky," which eventually became Pokey. He has a sister nicknamed "Peaches."

Phil "The Vulture" Regan

Sandy Koufax coined this one, based on the reliever's uncanny ability to come into the late innings of tie games, then "vulture" what could've/should've been the starting pitchers' wins.

"Pistol" Pete Reiser

The outfielder had a reckless habit of colliding into walls, which was nearly as dangerous as playing with guns; to the surprise of no one, "The Pistol" ran out of ammo by age 30.

Ken "Zamboni" Reitz

In his '70s heyday, Reitz, a third baseman, displayed superior fielding percentage and range, year in and year out; the "Zamboni" swept everything up, you see.

Edgar "Rent-an-Error" Renteria

During 2005's hellish (30-error) campaign in Boston, local radio stations took to calling Renteria "Rent-an-Error," "Rent-a-Wreck," and several names involving loose stool.

Rick "The Chubby Cubbie" Reuschel

. . . because, when Reuschel was playing for Chicago in the 1970s, he was tipping the scales at way over 250 pounds.

Allie "Superchief" Reynolds

For decades, "Chief" was the default nickname for any player of Native American ancestry, but not just any player can put up a .686 winning percentage and a 6–0 playoff record.

(Karl) "Tuffy" Rhodes

A career journeyman, Rhodes earned the nickname when he was six years old and refused to cry after being hit in the eye with a baseball. "Tough" became "Tough-y," which became "Tuffy."

Branch "The Mahatma" Rickey

In the 1930s, Mohandas Gandhi was once described as "an incredible combination of Jesus Christ, Tammany Hall, and your father" and the phrase seemed just as fitting for this longtime GM. It's one of life's little ironies that Rickey, one of the great Bible thumpers of all time, was tagged with the *Hindu* term for a holy man.

Mickey "Mick the Quick" Rivers

The "quick" reference was to his feet, not his head; once, in the late 1970s, Rivers tried to duck creditors by using the alias "Miguel Rivera."

Wilbert "Uncle Robbie" Robinson

As the "Daffy Dodgers'" skipper from 1914 to 1931, Robinson would discuss his starting rotation with waiters and debate hit-and-run calls with cabbies and doormen; Brooklynites called Uncle Robbie's wife "Aunt Mary."

Pete "Charlie Hustle" Rose

As the story goes, Whitey Ford gave Rose the derisive nickname after seeing him sprint to first base after drawing a walk in spring training, but Rose soon adopted it as a badge of honor; one dictionary definition of "hustle" is "participating in an illicit scheme, dishonest gambling game, etc."

(Carvell) "Bama" Rowell

A lot of major league infielders came out of Alabama, but few had Rowell's unique combination of slow feet and clumsy hands; after he failed to reach a single ball during a Dodgers doubleheader, he admitted that "maybe it's just as well."

(George) "Babe" Ruth

Like all kids, Ruth could be self-indulgent. When he saw food, he ate it. When he found alcohol, he drank it. When he had cigars, he smoked 'em. When he met willing women, he . . . the point is, the Babe was self-indulgent.

C. C. "C.G." Sabathia

After a midseason trade sent him from Cleveland to Milwaukee, Sabathia went through a string of complete-game ("CG") gems. "C.C." stands for "Carsten Charles."

Hank "The Mayor of Wrigley Field" Sauer

As a Cubs slugger in the 1950s, Sauer was so popular that the hometown faithful tossed packets of his favorite tobacco on to the Wrigley outfield. "The Mayor" would wave his thanks, tuck the chew into the ivy, then take it back to his dugout at the end of the inning.

Joe "Ol' S——— F———" Schultz

Somebody counted once, and Schultz was quoted in connection to the phrase "s—— f——" more than *200* times in Jim Bouton's *Ball Four*; not exactly "The Peerless Leader," is it?

George "Boomer" Scott

Probably the first sports figure to gain the nickname later adopted by the talkative guys named Esiason, Berman, Wells, et cetera, but this one was based on booming home runs; Scott also popularized the terms "taters" (homers) and "riding the pine" (benched).

"Tom Terrific" Seaver

When he first showed up in 1967, Seaver was supposed to be the kind of once-in-a-generation wunderkind to establish himself as a dominating number one starter, lead the Mets to championship glory, make the Hall of Fame, and establish world peace. He did not establish world peace.

Gary "Sheff" Sheffield

At one point in his Atlanta tenure, Sheff had his own little cheering section in the outfield, complete with multiple fans wearing Braves-logo chef hats.

William "Buck" Showalter

When Showalter was a minor leaguer, teammates noted his habit of hanging out in the clubhouse while buck naked.

(Harry) "Suitcase" Simpson

Simpson packed and unpacked his way through six teams in eight years in the majors, mostly because he fielded like Lisa Simpson.

Bill "The Singer Throwing Machine" Singer

In the decade from 1967 to 1976, Singer averaged 30 starts and more than 200 innings pitched per year; he was as reliable as an old Singer Sewing Machine, you see.

Doug "Risk" Sisk

While serving as a middle reliever for the Mets in the mid-1980s, Sisk always made it interesting—he'd consistently put up high walk/hit totals but managed to work out more-than-respectable ERAs, year in and year out.

Lou "The Nervous Greek" Skizas

Onetime teammate Mickey McDermott claimed that the skittish Skizas sometimes wore two wash-and-wear suits at the same time, one on top of the other. "Maybe his apartment didn't have a closet," he said.

(Bill) "Moose" Skowron

After his family gave him a buzz haircut as a kid, they joked that it made him look like a certain Italian dictator, so they started calling him "Mussolini," which was eventually shortened. Everyone else called him "Moose" because Skowron was kind of big and slow.

Lonnie "Skates" Smith

Due to a combination of speed and awkwardness, the outfielder sometimes, literally, fell on his face while racing after fly balls; Darrell Porter said Smith fielded like he was wearing roller skates.

Ozzie "The Wizard of Oz" Smith

A fairly obvious linkage between the defensive wizardry and birth name of "Osborne," no? When he was inducted into Cooperstown in 2002, Smith connected the messages within *The Wizard of Oz* to the lessons in his baseball career, then finished the speech by singing "Over the Rainbow."

(Esix) "Speed" Snead

Notice the nickname wasn't "Hit" Snead; as a cup-of-coffee guy, he supposedly inspired the expression "You can't steal first base."

(Edwin) "Duke" Snider

When the teenaged Snider proved himself a royal phenom, he became a "Duke." A song entitled "Mickey, Willie, and the Edwin" wouldn't have quite the same ring, would it?

Warren "Lucky" Spahn

Teammate Eddie Mathews called him this, short for "Lucky Bastard." Mathews said that was what opposing hitters muttered to themselves on the frequent occasions that they flied out to the warning track.

Don "Full Pack" Stanhouse

Earl Weaver said the flaky reliever's appearances made him so nervous that the manager had to smoke a full pack of cigarettes back in the dugout.

Eddie "The Brat" Stanky

Oh, to think back on all the little guy's history of racial taunts, vicious insults, fistfights, cheating schemes . . . there was only one Eddie Stanky. Who'd want another?

Fred "Chicken" Stanley

Stanley was called "Chicken" not because he was cowardly on double-play pivots, but because he had thin, chickenlike legs.

Willie "Pops" Stargell

As a Pirates veteran, Stargell was probably the most respected clubhouse leader of his era, a "Pops" anyone could love. In one *Three's Company* episode, Chrissy Snow called him "Willie Star Trek."

Casey "The Ol' Perfessor" Stengel

Stengel was once appointed honorary professor at the University of Mississippi, which naturally led to his being known as "The Professor," then "The Ol' Professor," then, via a Noo Yawk accent . . . Like any self-respecting academic, the Ol' Perfessor often referenced fact sources to back his views ("You could look it up").

Ron "Rocky" Swoboda

Short for "Rockhead"; Swoboda was nobody's idea of a rocket scientist.

Jeff "The Ozark Bear" Tesreau

Tesreau was, sure enough, a huge guy from southern Missouri, and they just don't make nicknames like this anymore. If they did, we'd be calling Roy Oswalt "Mississippi Slim," make references to "Big Jim" Thome, stuff like that. We live in nickname-impoverished times.

George "The Stork" Theodore

Tall and gawky, Theodore's nickname should have been "The Crane," but the early 1970s Mets already had Ed "Krane" Kranepool on the roster, so that never happened.

Frank "The Big Hurt" Thomas

One of the few great nicknames of the modern era, bestowed on Thomas by longtime White Sox announcer Ken "Hawk" Harrelson; several teammates were dubbed "The Little Hurt" over the years, but none really took.

"Stormin'" Gorman Thomas

As early '80s Brewers fans knew all to well, the rhyme didn't work out too well in the real world, as Thomas wasn't likely to storm his way to anything except a dinner buffet.

"Marvelous" Marv Throneberry

Throneberry hit 16 home runs in 366 at-bats for the '62 Mets, which wasn't too marvelous but wasn't chopped liver, either. Despite his famous initials, Marvin Eugene Throneberry pledged allegiance to his first major league organization, which is to say that M.E.T. always considered himself a Yankee.

Dick "Dirt" Tidrow

Sparky Lyle called Tidrow "Dirt" because of his habit of diving for balls during pregame pepper contests.

Cesar "Mr. Versatility" Tovar

Tovar lived up to the tag. In 1967, he divided his season between third base (70 games), center field (64), second (36), left (10), short (9), and right (5). He was also rumored to be simultaneously married to women in three different countries, which, if true, probably took the versatility thing to a new, unhealthy extreme.

(Harold) "Pie" Traynor

According to Bill James, there are at least a couple plausible explanations for this nickname, one of which has nothing to do with pies.

Jim "Milkman" Turner

Like many nicknames, this one's origins are cloudy; it might have been based on the fact that Turner 1) woke up early enough to see old-time milkmen do their rounds; 2) drank a lot of milk; or 3) actually worked as an off-season milkman at some point.

(Melvin) "B. J." Upton

Melvin Upton's dad was nicknamed "The Bossman," so Upton grew up as "Bossman Junior," or "B. J." for short.

Mo "Hit Dog" Vaughn

No one's really sure where this one came from, only that it sounded about right. After he retired, Vaughn opened up something called "The Hit Dog Baseball Clinic and Hot Dog Stand" at Tufts University.

Bob "Johnson" Veale

The lefty had a habit of calling everyone "Johnson" for some reason. During a stint with the Red Sox, Veale did play for Darrell Johnson.

Shane "The Flyin' Hawaiian" Victorino

While running high school track back home in Wailuku, Victorino set an Aloha State record in the 100-meter dash.

Leon "Big Daddy Wags" Wagner

When Wagner was playing for the Angels in the early 1960s, he opened up an L.A. clothing store with ads reading GET YOUR RAGS FROM BIG DADDY WAGS. Sportswriter Ross Newhan claimed that the motto was better than the merchandise.

Harry "The Hat" Walker

Walker had a habit of constantly adjusting his cap during his at-bats in the 1940s, just before batting helmets became mandatory; a few years later "The Hat" would've been "The Helmet."

Paul "Big Poison" Waner

As the story goes, the tag came from the Brooklyn-ese pronunciation of "person." But Waner was, indeed, muscular enough to murder fastballs, so "Big Poison" almost certainly meant "big poison."

(Harold) "Rabbit" Warstler

Steven Goldman: "The nickname applied both to his quick fielding and his soft, fluffy bat."

John "Way Back" Wasdin

Wasdin gave up more than 1.5 home run balls per nine innings pitched, some of them landing, yes, way, way back.

Earl "The Little General" Weaver

Ron Luciano called him a "belligerent midget," but give the Orioles skipper points for bossy ingenuity; when he went out to argue with Jim Palmer, Weaver always made a point of positioning himself at the very top of the pitching mound, then looking down.

David "Boomer" Wells

Wells, famously, refused to shut his big mouth up, whether it came to eating or talking; onetime teammate Roger Clemens referred to him as "Eli," "'cause if 'e talkin', 'e lyin'."

"Hard-Hittin'" Mark Whiten

He once hit four homers in a game but, based on a 108 OPS+ for his career, it was more like "OK-Hittin'" Mark Whiten.

Earl "Big Money" Williams

Williams hit 61 home runs in his first two full years, but a lack of effort and bad attitude soon caught up to him; after he hit .237 for the '73 Orioles, some started calling him "Small Change."

Mitch "Wild Thing" Williams

After the *Major League* movie came out in '89, Williams seemed like the closest real-life counterpart to Ricky Vaughn, so sure enough, the publicity-courting reliever began wearing number 99 and coming into games to the tune of a certain Troggs song; Joe Carter apparently never saw the film's happy ending, though.

Ted "The Kid" Williams

People started calling Williams this when he was a teenager and never stopped, even as he reached his exalted status as the game's grand old man; in 1993, *Sports Illustrated* put him on the cover with the headline THE KID AT 75.

Walt "No Neck" Williams

Also known as "Head and Shoulders." As Brendan Boyd and Fred Harris once pointed out, Williams's legs weren't particularly long, either.

Maury "Mouse" Wills

Vin Scully called him "Little Maury Wills, the Darling of the Dodgers." If you believe his autobiography, Wills was also— briefly—the darling of Doris Day, too.

(Howard) "Highball" Wilson

This one had nothing to do with Wilson's pitching.

(Lewis) "Hack" Wilson

No one seems to know where this came from. Take your pick: 1) Wilson moved like a ballplayer named Hack Miller; 2) resembled a wrestler named Hackenschmitt; 3) hacked at the ball; 4) had some kind of connection to a cabbie; or 5) something else.

(William) "Mookie" Wilson

Wilson never explained the nickname's backstory, but I'm relatively certain that it had nothing to do with Mookie Blaylock.

Dave "Mr. May" Winfield

After George Steinbrenner soured on his expensive free agent in 1985, he contrasted him with the departed Reggie Jackson, saying "I got rid of Mr. October and got Mr. May." Winfield batted just .208 in more than 100 career at-bats in the playoffs.

Gene "New Reliable" Woodling

When Tommy "Ol' Reliable" Henrich retired from the Yankees outfield, his replacement, Woodling, became . . .

Jimmy "The Toy Cannon" Wynn

Wynn stood 5'9"—if he was on his very tippy-toes—but spent five seasons on the National League's leader board for home runs.

Carl "Yaz" Yastrzemski

The family name is pronounced "Ya-STREM-ski," as if there was no "z," so, naturally, Red Sox fans took to calling him "Yaz" anyway. The player balloting for the 1967 American League MVP included votes for "Yaztremski," "Yastremski," "Yastrezemski," "Yastreszski," "Yastremzminski," "Yastrstrenski," "Yazstremenski," "Y'str'mski," and, simply, "Yaz—Boston."

Kevin "Greek God of Walks" Youkilis

Billy Beane coined this one in the course of the *Moneyball* draft process, but Terry Francona once commented "I've seen Youkilis in the shower, and I wouldn't call him the Greek god of anything."

Don "The Gerbil" Zimmer

Zimmer was a kind, beloved baseball man for nearly 60 years, but there's no denying his puffy-cheeked look; this one was coined by his longtime nemesis Bill Lee, who later said, "I should have apologized. To the gerbils. No sense insulting defenseless animals."

Joel "Zoom" Zumaya

After Zumaya developed a 100+ mph heater during his rookie year, he honored the zoom-zoom by having hot rod–style flames tattooed to his famed right arm.

The 20 GREATEST BASEBALL PRANKS EVER PULLED

It's only fitting that the baseball season kicks off right around April Fools' Day.

The major leagues have long been a prankster's paradise, so much so that ballplayers have long developed a standard repertoire ("The Classics"; page 325) and some well-understood guidelines ("The Rules"; page 316) throughout the sport's long, hilarious history. Here's a highly unofficial, highly subjective ranking of the most memorable mischief ever to take place before the players got to work.

20.

Jerry Reuss and the Autographed Ball Incident

Before a late 1970s Dodgers game umpired by Frank Pulli, the L.A. starter Reuss, apropos of nothing in particular, somehow got his hands on an official game ball and wrote out the inscription "To Frank, May God Bless You, Tom Lasorda." It was a pretty clever little dig on his glad-handing, autograph-a-minute manager, most would say.

Well, the ball did get into the game, but it was unnoticed by Pulli before being fouled off into the grandstand. What saved the stunt was the fact that the fan who caught the autographed ball was, indeed, named Frank. Divine intervention, maybe?

19.

Gene Michael and the Frog Incident

As a teammate, Gene Michael was well known for a couple of qualities: 1) he was skinny enough to be nicknamed "Stick"; and 2) he had a Phil Rizzuto-like aversion to little animals.

Enter prankster Mel Stottlemyre.

Just before the Yankees readied for an early '70s spring training game, Stott got his hands on a frog, then silently, secretly placed the little fellow in the pouch of Michael's jock strap. The pitcher somehow kept a straight face as his pal walked in . . . got dressed . . . startled for a moment . . . and suddenly screamed, "Something just kicked my d——!"

Sparky Lyle's book *The Bronx Zoo* described Michael's reaction: "I don't know how he did it, but in one movement he jumped right out of his uniform. As his pants and jock lay on the floor,

Gene was just walking around the club-house, looking down at them."

They say that afterward Michael developed a curious habit of poking his pinstripes before getting dressed . . .

18.

Buddy Lewis and the DC-3 Incident

Before the outbreak of World War II, Buddy Lewis was one of the Senators' top hitters. Afterward, he was a celebrated Air Corps officer. During the war, he became a celebrated prankster.

In June 1943, Lewis, who was undergoing flight training near the Senators' home ballpark, decided to "borrow" a DC-3 aircraft for an impromptu trip over Washington. Right in the middle of a game against the Tigers, Lewis's plane suddenly roared in over Griffith Stadium's center field, low enough to almost clip the flag pole, then soar over the diamond. As the plane maneuvered its wings to greet the stunned home crowd, Lewis's former team-mate, George Case, joyously tossed his bat into the air from the on-deck circle; he later called the event the most thrilling thing that ever happened to him in baseball.

Captain Lewis was reprimanded for breaking flight regula-tions, but all was forgiven after he later used his piloting skills to earn the Distinguished Flying Cross and Air Medal in the China-India theater. Plus, when he made it back to Griffith Stadium, in the last couple months of 1945, Lewis hit .333.

17.

The Thurman Munson Incidents

Thurman Munson angered easily and, when he was properly riled up, you could just see it in his reddened face and grumbling mouth. Naturally, clubhouse pranksters couldn't get enough of him.

Everyone knew that the Yankees captain carried on an intense personal rivalry with the Red Sox's Carlton Fisk, for instance, so Mel Stottlemyre stuck handsome Fisk pictures inside his locker, just so they could witness Thurm stumble across the photos, fume, and rip 'em all apart—worked like clockwork.

Everyone knew that "Squatty Body" was self-conscious over his weight issues, too, so Mike Kekich made a habit of reaching into his locker and strategically placing brochures for Overeaters Anonymous. Same explosion.

Once, Jay Johnstone drew Munson's likeness on a watermelon, placed a "NY" cap atop and a pair of cleats below, then positioned the melon on the catcher's locker. Sparky Lyle said it "had sideburns and a little fat face. Looked just like Thurman." Explosion.

The Yanks' most elaborate stunt, though, happened when the ever-temperamental Munson decided to order a custom-made gun holster through the mail. Big mistake.

Fritz Peterson intercepted the order form, changed the information from a righty's wide waist to a lefty's twenty-inch waist, then watched as Munson fumed over the tiny holster that arrived a few weeks later. Munson, naturally, re-sent the order form, and, naturally, Peterson intercepted it once again, eventually getting the same tantrum out of his catcher a couple more times. As a topper, Peterson had a "Thurman Munson" letter sent to the holster company, thanking them for their wonderful service and offering both free tickets and his contact information.

Now, if that poor company did call in asking for its free tickets, you can imagine how Thurm would have felt about that . . .

16.

Jay Johnstone and the Grounds Crew Incident

Was it a congenital allergy to benchwarming boredom? A lifelong interest in gardening?

No one in the Veterans Stadium crowd knew exactly what prompted the Dodgers' Jay Johnstone to dress up as a member of the Phillies grounds crew in the early 1980s. All they knew was that Johnstone and coconspirator Jerry Reuss donned overalls and helped drag the Veterans Stadium infield right in the middle of one fine ballgame in Philadelphia.

Johnstone was immediately spotted by the road crowd, prompting what may have been the first-ever groundskeeper ovation, but L.A. manager Tommy Lasorda had a slightly different reaction, fining his reserve outfielder $200 on the spot. Lasorda also had Johnstone pinch-hitting the next inning, apparently to show him up, but, if that was the case, Johnstone messed up his plan by smacking a clutch home run. As he gave a round of high-fives to his delirious teammates, he deadpanned, "Tommy, next time you need me, I'll be down in the groundskeepers' room."

15.

Jeffrey Leonard and the Crazy Crab Incident

The on-field Jeffrey Leonard absolutely perfected a deadly serious competitor's death glare, to the point that opposing players often referred to him as "Penitentiary Face." The off-field Leonard could be pretty ornery, too, especially when it came to the contents of his locker—he never threw anything away, so his locker was stuffed with dozens of socks, shoes, pads, and the like. No teammate was allowed anywhere near the stash.

The average person would see all sorts of tension and craziness in this situation. An inveterate prankster saw a challenge.

One day during the 1984 season, Steve Nicosia, seized by a moment of Leonard-centered inspiration, decided to break into the closet where the Giants' mascot uniform was kept. Newly dressed as "Crazy Crab," the reserve catcher sauntered into the area where his teammates were readying, messed up Duane Kuiper's perfectly coifed hair, danced a bit, and walked to and fro. Most of the guys couldn't get enough of the unexpected show.

Thus emboldened, the Crab/Nicosia made his way to Leonard's forbidden locker area. "Penitentiary Face" was, not surprisingly, not amused, but the renegade mascot didn't care—staring down the imposing slugger from behind his googly-eyed getup, Nicosia grabbed a pair of socks, raised them up for all the team to see, then tossed 'em across the room.

You could hear a pin drop.

Mike Krukow said he expected Leonard to start throwing punches right then and there, but the Giant was apparently too stunned to do a thing. After a long, silent few seconds, Nicosia decided to go all in, picking up and tossing locker item after item so that, within seconds, the team had witnessed most of Jeffrey Leonard's precious locker contents flying through the air, all courtesy of a 5'10" crustacean.

Realizing that he could either beat up Nicosia or go along with the gag, Leonard tensed up, gritted his teeth and . . . let out a loud laugh, almost in spite of himself. The rest of the room broke up, too, especially one very, very relieved catcher turned Crab.

THE RULES

1. **Publicity stunts aren't pranks.** Bill Veeck once decided his team's on-field moves through an organized fan vote and Charlie O. Finley used his pet mule for all kinds of player exhibitions in the 1970s, but those weren't pranks; they were owners' publicity stunts. A true prank isn't intended to drum up publicity or sell tickets or do anything other than feed the instigator's somewhat skewed need for amusement. Pranking must be its own reward.

2. **Show some wit.** Ralphing into someone's cap or hitting someone over the head with a frying pan might be the stuff of slapstick comedy, but real pranking calls for more original material. Rude and crude is fine—necessary, even—but put some cunning and planning into your work; take the time to think out a special stunt.

3. **Nothing too painful.** There's absolutely no need for a gotcha to bruise anything more than an ego, especially in an era when major league athletes can (literally) be worth their weight in gold. When it comes to modern legal liability, nobody has a good sense of humor.

4. **Nothing truly offensive, either.** Jokes based on the target's height, weight, haircut, personality—almost always OK. Anything racially based or sexually based—almost always verboten. Nobody wants to come off as an offensive, John Rocker–esque buffoon.

5. **Off-field downtime is the time for practical jokes.** Even would-be Ashton Kutchers have to be all-business competitors between the white lines, so they don't prank themselves into a benching, demotion, or trade.

6. **Losing's no laughing matter.** Levity may be especially needed after a bad loss or during a losing streak, but no one wants to look like he's goofing off when he should be working hard. Generally speaking, the better the ball club's doing, the more room for some good old-fashioned pranking.

7. **Keep a straight face.** Countless would-be pranks have been foiled when otherwise anonymous coconspirators gave themselves away with stray snickers, smirks, and giggles, so immaturity is to be avoided at all costs. Remember that, when it comes to monkey business, you've got to be serious.

8. **No snitching.** Don't rat out pranksters/culprits, at least until you're safely traded away from the ball club.

9. **Lie, deny, alibi.** When an instigator is confronted with (a completely true) accusation from his target, he's obligated to lie like an old rug; getting away with a prank is kind of an after-prank in itself. It adds to the mystique and, besides, there's no telling when a target might want payback someday.

10. **Play along.** And, speaking of payback . . . once you've been pranked, it's OK to growl and curse and maybe chase a prankster/suspect around the clubhouse, but you don't want to throw some kind of real arm-waving, screaming tantrum. You may never live that down—it's just the kind of thing a Kirk Gibson–, Jeff Kent–type hothead would do. Don't do it.

No, instead, you want to smile, nod, tell the boys that it was a good one, and, gosh, you'll get 'em next time. You'll get some brownie points for dignity under duress. And that's the moment you should start dreaming up a retaliation prank of your own.

14.
Steve Garvey and the Brownie Incident

The victims: Steve Garvey and Jerry Reuss.

The plan: Johnstone melted a brownie just before game time, then secretly placed the confection within the fielding glove of Garvey, a notorious neat freak. They said "Mr. Perfect" used to have his immaculate Dodgers uniform steamed and pressed before each ball game.

Johnstone got the brownie timing just right, as Garv didn't realize a thing until after he ran onto the field, reached into the mitt, and felt a certain brown, gooey something. He immediately dropped the glove like a hot rock, of course, but he already had melted chocolate all over his hands and wrists.

Garvey, naturally, called time and moved into the dugout for a towel, where—and this is the beauty part—he spotted an oblivious Jerry Reuss with some telltale chocolate smudges on his pants. You see, Johnstone had secretly smeared Reuss with the brownie right before the game, as a way to frame him for the Garvey prank.

The payoff: As the home Giants rolled and the Dodgers wondered what the heck was happening, an enraged Garvey began to thump on a completely oblivious Reuss.

13.

Babe Ruth and the Waiter Incident

Did any major leaguer ever enjoy himself as much as Babe Ruth?

Hardly a day of the Babe's adult life passed without countless backs slapped, hands shaken, pictures posed, autographs signed, smiles smiled, and chit chatted. Inside the clubhouse, he was known to slip a lit cigar into neighbors' uniform pants as they dressed and place pieces of cardboard into unattended sandwiches.

One time, though, the joke was on him.

During a black-tie dinner thrown by the New York Baseball Writers' Association at the swank Waldorf-Astoria Hotel in December 1924, a rude waiter ruined virtually the entire evening. He spilled soup on Yankees owner Jacob Ruppert, elbowed Commissioner Kenesaw Mountain Landis, bumbled and stumbled over others, and made rude comments to still others. When he finally came across Ruth, who was only the most famous athlete in America, the waiter poked him in the chest and asked, "Who ever told said you're a ballplayer?"

Well, that was about enough for the Bambino, who, along with Rosy Ryan of the Giants, shot out of his chair and proceeded to chase the offending server around the luxury ballroom, finally bringing the guy down with a flying tackle. Ruth was just about to throw a punch when chortling sportswriters rushed to intervene, explaining it was all a put-on. The "waiter" was, in truth, Vince Barnett, a comedian/actor they'd hired to mix things up for the evening.

Barnett was grateful for being spared a swing from the Yankee, but the Babe seemed half disappointed by the revelation. "And just when I had him by the neck," he shrugged.

12.

John Lowenstein and the Stretcher Incident

Almost all great baseball pranks are the result of careful preparation or, at minimum, a moment of inspired premeditation. John Lowenstein's stretcher incident was a notable exception.

It seems that, in a June 1980 Orioles game against the Athletics, "Brother Lo" stroked a clean hit to the outfield, only to slide into a hard relay throw that hit him right in the batting helmet. The poor guy was knocked out for 20 seconds or so, long enough to be carried off by the O's trainers, but he slowly regained consciousness as he heard the sympathetic applause of the home crowd.

Lo decided to play possum for a few seconds, then, just before the stretcher reached the dugout steps, he suddenly sprang up and threw his arms above his head in a defiant, *Rocky*-style salute to his supporters. After a stunned second or two, the theatrical move brought the house down.

11.

Luis Aparicio and the Cutoff Jeans Incident

What's it mean to be treated as a national hero? For perennial All-Star Luis Aparicio, it meant that his postseason return flights home were treated as Venezuelan state occasions, complete with airport greeting ceremonies, marching bands, wall-to-wall television coverage, and a "welcome home" handshake from the president.

The occasions were always memorable, but one of them was even more memorable than the rest.

On the last day of the 1971 season, with the Red Sox out of the running for the playoffs, Little Looie had his wardrobe flown home to Caracas, leaving his travel clothes locked up in a Fenway storeroom, safely tucked away from prankster teammate Carl Yastrzemski. Or so he thought.

As it turns out, Yaz was on to Aparicio's plan. He bribed his way into the storeroom, then ducked inside during Aparicio's at-bats, just so he could hack away at the clothes in secret. By the time the game's final pitch came around, the precious locked-up duds were in tatters.

Aparicio was, obviously, beside himself, not only for his lack of clothes, but because he didn't have a minute to lose before taking his plane back to Venezuela. He had no choice but to buy a club-house boy's clothes, which is why a national hero once showed up to his big arrival ceremony wearing . . . a pair of cutoff jeans, a T-shirt, and a pair of beat-up sneakers.

10.

Harry Caray and the Miracle Recovery Incident

The late, great soul singer James Brown had an incredible signature move for his stage act.

Late in an hours-long concert, just as it seemed like "The Hardest-Working Man in Show Business" had sung, danced, and sweated as much as any human possibly could, Brown would begin to stagger about. One of his assistants would cover him with a cape and begin leading him off the stage for some much-needed rest. As the crowd beseeched the seemingly spent super-star to come back, Brown, suddenly rejuvenated, would shoot back up, fling off the cape, then jump over to the microphone.

It was the power of soul, you see; the audience always went completely nuts.

Somewhere, Harry Caray must have been watching James Brown do his thing, because, on one very special occasion, he used much the same move.

After Caray was nearly killed in a car accident in November 1968, the beloved Cardinals broadcaster endured several long months of painful physical rehab for his legs. During his on-field introduction on Opening Day 1969, he still required two walking canes in order to move around.

Or so the fans believed.

In reality, Caray, like Brown, wasn't quite as bad off as he led the audience to believe, which is why, on that Opening Day, he was able to suddenly convert his injured hobble into a confident stride and quickly fling away one cane, then the other. "It's a beauuuuuuuuutiful day for a ball game!" Harry said as leaped to the mic.

It was the power of baseball, you see; the crowd went completely nuts.

9.

Rabbit Maranville and the Golf Shot Incident

Through the early 1920s, Charlie Grimm was Rabbit Maranville's favorite drinking buddy and, when the two pals were traded to the Cubs in time for the '25 season, Grimm also became Maranville's most unwitting accomplice.

A magazine had asked the duo to take a wacky publicity picture for their new team during spring training. In keeping with their flaky reputations, the photographer asked Grimm to lie down on a golf course with a tee clutched in his teeth while Rabbit stood above him with a club, pretending he was ready to strike at a ball set about one inch above Grimm's smiling face.

The photographer clicked on the fake pose but, just at that moment, Maranville, who rarely golfed, impulsively decided to take a real, full-force swing at the ball. Rabbit hit it cleanly, but when the startled Grimm sprang up from the turf, he was, understandably, about as white as a sheet. Too bad the photographer didn't get *that* shot.

8.

Vin Scully and the Ron Fairly Incident

Vin Scully's an L.A. institution on par with the hollywood sign, the Oscars, and suntanning, but the Hall of Famer is unique in another way—he's the only broadcaster to ever pull a prank against a major leaguer in the middle of a regular season game.

It happened in October 1965, the day after the Dodgers clinched the National League pennant. Without the knowledge of his players, manager Walt Alston decided to let Scully "manage" the team's meaningless finale against the Braves.

The first big surprise was that Ron Fairly would be starting. Like all the other L.A. regulars, Fairly had been out partying on the night before, anticipating that only the reserve players would be in the lineup on that Sunday afternoon.

The second surprise came in the Dodgers' half of the third inning, after Fairly singled his way to first base. Scully secretly signaled Alston to have Fairly steal. Now, the lead-footed, stocky outfielder had exactly two swipe attempts on the year, so Scully's blithe broadcast "prediction" of a Fairly steal attempt was a pretty shocking pronouncement.

At any rate, Fairly, seeing the sign from third base coach Preston Gomez, dutifully lumbered off to second base.

Unfortunately for him, teammate Lou Johnson fouled off Bob Sadowski's pitch. Nothing doing. Fairly, who was already hung over, tired, and sweating in the California heat, staggered back to first.

On the second pitch, it happened all over again: Scully secretly signaled from the booth down to the dugout, made another on-air "prediction," Fairly ran, Johnson fouled, and Fairly staggered back.

What's the French phrase for triple déjà vu? On the third pitch, it was . . . again . . . signal, prediction, run, foul, stagger.

After all that huffing and puffing, Fairly simply shook his exhausted head when he saw yet another "go" sign. "Manager" Scully chuckled and conceded, "All right, you're on your own."

7.

Rick Dempsey and the Rain Delay Incident

When you think about it, the theater biz and the majors have a lot in common. Both produce live dramas on an almost daily basis. Those who make it rely both on physicality and artistry to make difficult performances look easy. Both reward showmanship.

Rick Dempsey, whose mom and dad were both professional actors, knew all about the theater/baseball connection. That might be why he pulled off one of the greatest shows the national pastime's ever seen.

It was the last day of the 1977 season, when a meaningless Orioles–Red Sox contest had turned into a lengthy, exceptionally boring rain delay. Dempsey, no doubt thinking of his parents' old stage shows, decided to spring into action. He stuffed some towels into his shirt, waddled out onto the slick Fenway tarp, went into an elaborate pantomime of Babe Ruth's "Called Shot" homer, then started skating and sliding around the base paths, finally concluding with a lengthy belly flop across the home plate area.

The Boston crowd had never seen anyone treat a tarp like a giant Slip 'n Slide—no one had—and as soon as Dempsey made to leave the diamond, the fans started standing on their seats and clapping for an encore. Even his Orioles teammates urged a curtain call, so Dempsey dutifully came back out in front of the dugout and, as "Raindrops Keep Fallin' on My Head" came up on the PA system, led all of Fenway Park into a shower-soaked sing-along.

It was the stuff of instant legend, of course, one that called for several repeat performances in later years. The most notable probably came in 1983, in Milwaukee, when Dempsey replayed Robin Yount's heroic pennant race homers from the previous year; he prompted a standing ovation as he stripped off his Baltimore jersey to reveal a number 19 Brewers top, then took some pre-game hacks from home plate.

To this day, Dempsey still gets requests for a reprise of his rainy-day theater ("Every time it clouds up, the phone rings"), but nowadays, the 60-something broadcaster isn't quite up to anything more elaborate than Santa performances at the Orioles' annual holiday party. Still, his original stunt will never be forgotten. "It's amazing," he said. "There's always some young kid who's not a young kid anymore who comes up to me and says, 'I was there.'"

THE CLASSICS

As long as there have been pranks, prankees in every walk of life have experienced unwanted 3 A.M. wake-up calls, exploding cigars, redirected luggage, water balloon bombs, and phone messages from someone calling himself "Ben Dover." But baseball is its own special world, one with its own menu of standard high jinks, such as:

1. **Hot foots.** This is a gag predating Don Zimmer's grandpa: Carefully place a book of matches in a teammate's cleats while he's unaware, set a fuse or trail of lighter fluid, light the thing up, and then sit back and enjoy as the target does a sudden fiery little dance. (By the way, they're always "hot foots," for some reason, and never "hot feet." The grammar's as skewed as the humor involved).

2. **Clothes shenanigans.** Any and all off-field clothing is fair game—legs and bottoms can be cut out, knots can be knotted, dead fish can be placed, ties can be snipped, shoes can be nailed to the floor (or ceiling), sneakers can be frozen, shower flip-flops can be melted.

   Extra credit for cutting pant legs off at the knees, carefully taping them up from the inside, then having your victim watch the pants fall off as they're put on.

   Extra extra credit for forcing the victim to take the flight back home dressed in his game-day uniform pants and a team jacket.

3. **Shaving cream pies in the face.** Extra credit when a ballplayer's conducting a live interview on camera.

4. **Itching powders.** To be placed on unattended jock straps. Variation: analgesic ("red-hot") balm on jocks.

5. **Fake interview appointments.** Extra credit for convincing the victim that he's in line for something like a *GQ* cover shoot or a major product endorsement.

6. **Goldfish in the visiting clubhouse's water cooler.** Variation: sneezing powder in the air vents.

7. **Firecrackers.** To be used at decidedly unexpected times, such as when the target's in the toilet or nodding off in the bullpen. Variation: surprise appearances by smoke bombs, live snakes, and other critters.

8. Shoe polish on the hat brim. Extra credit if the gunk leaves a perfect black circle on the victim's head.

9. The gullible batboy gags: Give one of the newbies the urgent task of retrieving mystery items such as "the key to the batter's box," a "bucket of steam," "the foul line–straightener," "the lefty-hitter bats," or "the bat stretcher." (And make sure the confused kid eventually gets an extra tip for his troubles.)

10. What hit? Picture the scene: A fresh-faced young arrival from the minors finally achieves a lifelong dream, getting his very first major league hit, and, just as the kid peers back at his team-mates, seeking some acknowledgment and approval . . . the guys couldn't care less. Just to sell the nonchalant act, some of 'em might start yawning. Well, at least until they decide to break character and give the rookie a congratulatory slap on the back when he returns to the dugout.

11. Rookie cross-dressing: On the last road trip of the season, the new guys' street clothes have to disappear from their lockers while women's clothes mysteriously take their place. The rookies are then expected to cross-dress their way from the ballpark to the airport to the hotel. Extra credit for theme hazing, such as when the rookies get *Wizard of Oz* outfits or Hooters duds.

6.

Casey Stengel and the Sparrow Incident

Long before Casey Stengel became the most memorable manager in New York Yankees history, he pulled the most memorable stunt in New York City's baseball history.

Casey was playing outfield for the Pirates at Ebbets Field in May 1919 when he noticed a sparrow smack into a nearby fence, hitting the wood just hard enough to be momentarily dazed. Never one to pass up a potential trick, however unexpected, Stengel quietly picked up the bird and tucked it away.

A couple of minutes later, at the top of the next inning, Stengel was the leadoff man at the plate. He nonchalantly dug into the batter's box, called time, feigned some little adjustment . . . then removed his cap to reveal his little friend, which had just revived enough to flap off into the Brooklyn skies. Once the fans recovered from the initial shock, they burst into laughter; even umpire Cy Rigler broke up.

After the game, Stengel's former manager, Wilbert Robinson, quipped "Hell, he always did have birds in his garret," but Stengel noted that he did have three hits on the day. "I figure I'm showing a more serious attitude than players with no sparrows in their hats," he said, and who could argue?

5.

Moe Drabowsky and the Bullpen Call Incident

Many qualities are needed for a classic prank. An odd sense of humor. Daring. Ingenuity. In Moe Drabowsky's case, good working knowledge of Municipal Stadium's phone system came in pretty handy, too.

The incident took place in 1966, one year after Drabowsky was traded from the old Kansas City Athletics to the Baltimore Orioles. Gone though he may have been, Drabo still hadn't forgotten the stadium's extension numbers, including the number for the home team's bullpen.

Opportunity rang.

In the middle of the Orioles first road game in KC, Athletics coach Bob Hofman got an unexpected call. "Get Krausse hot in a hurry!" was the order from a voice dripping with the southern-fried accent of Alvin Dark, the Athletics' manager. Hofman dutifully told righty Lew Krausse to get up, despite the fact that starter Jim Nash was doing just fine through the early innings. As it happened, Nash noticed the bullpen activity behind him and, apparently unnerved, started getting shelled, at which point Hofman then took another hasty call, this one telling him "That's enough! Sit him down!"

The next day's newspaper stories revealed that the Athletics' bullpen call, and subsequent loss(!) came courtesy of a certain mimic from the opposing team's bullpen, which prompted a Kansas City complaint to the league—it was to no avail, of course, since no one had ever thought of a rule against bullpen coach fake-outs. For his part, Drabowsky "complained" that the official scorer should have credited him with the Orioles' win.

Oh, and one other thing . . . The next night, the sheepish Hofman got another call in the Athletics' clubhouse, this one carrying the voice of his team's ever-mercurial owner, Charlie O. Finley. "Mr. Hofman, this is Finley! I just got back in town and I saw that story this morning about the calls you got Friday night! I'd like to hear your version of the episode!"

An anxious Hofman began stammering, "Well, sir, although we didn't know it at the time, it was Moe Drabowsky who called. Sounded a lot like our skipper, though." The coach could only flinch and await a possible tongue-lashing, maybe a firing, but, after several long moments, he couldn't hear a thing on the other end of the line. That is, apart from some faint, smothered giggles.

Suddenly, Hofman realized he'd been had. Again. "Ok, Moe, it's you."

4.

Kyle Kendrick and the Japanese Trade Incident

Most ballplayers eventually get the same out-the-door feeling. Maybe it's because they're hurt or in a slump, or perhaps there is some reason known only to the front office, but, one way or the other, all of them are eventually traded, released, or cut. Whether they like it or not, one sad day, players must make their exit.

That happened to the Phillies' Kyle Kendrick during spring training 2008, as the second-year pitcher was solemnly called into the office of manager Charlie Manuel, where he met with Manuel and assistant general manager Ruben Amaro. The two told Kendrick that they'd decided to trade him for a player named Kobayashi, from the Giants.

The only twist was, the team on the other end of the deal was the Yomiuri Giants. The ones that play in Tokyo, not San Francisco. That would be the club from Japan's Central League, not America's National League.

Kendrick was so surprised that he'd soon be playing in another organization, let alone another country and continent, that he called his agent, Joe Urbon, who dutifully confirmed the deal and told him that he'd be expected in the Land of the Rising Sun the next day, on a 7 A.M. flight. As earnest reporters began to slowly crowd around Kendrick, seeking comment, all he could stammer was "Do they have good food in Japan? I don't know what to think right now. I guess it's going to be a whole new chapter, huh?"

Finally, after the 23-year-old Kendrick had contemplated his future for the longest few minutes of his life, Brett Myers let his teammate off the hook. "You've been punked," Myers said, letting on that the Japanese exchange had never happened. (He might have also mentioned that it would have been illegal for the

Phillies, or any other major league team, to ship a player off to a new country without his permission).

It was a pretty original stunt, by any measure, but what really sold it were the nice little details, the dramatic sales job involved. It was in the fact that "Kobayashi" wasn't the name of a Yomiuri Giants player, but a competitive hog-dog-eating champion. It was in Manuel's handing over paperwork that included an official-looking contract swap and a fax detailing a 20-hour, economy-class(!) flight to Tokyo. It was in the team's enlisting Urbon and the reporters to play along on the agent call and mock press conference. It was in Myers (the prank's instigator) playfully ignoring Kendrick's sense of shock, instead wondering aloud if the Phillies' newest "import" had a good fastball.

At the end of the day, of course, Kendrick's bated breath turned into an exhale, and his attentions turned to a *SportsCenter* news story and a *Today* show interview. When asked what it was like to find out he'd be staying put in Philadelphia, Pennsylvania, USA, the youngster said, "I've never been so happy."

3.
The Upright Citizens' Brigade and the "Rob! Rob! Rob!" Incident

Major league ballplayers get all the fame, the fortune, and the females. That may be inevitable, but they shouldn't necessarily get to perpetrate all the pranks, or so believed a New York–based comedy group calling itself the Upright Citizens' Brigade. They proved as much with an elaborately orchestrated ruse in August 2006.

The UCB's Rob Lathan was the main instigator and actor in the prank, one that was based on his real-life experiences in getting lost in packed ballparks. After Lathan and his coconspirators bought some seats in Yankee Stadium's upper right field deck, he headed out to the concourse for some midgame food and drinks. The fun began when Lathan, toting several popcorn boxes and beers, re-emerged among the sold-out crowd, seemingly puzzled over his seat's exact location. His fellow actors began calling "Rob! Rob! Rob!" so as to bring their "lost" compatriot back and, just as they expected, several helpful fans around them joined in the "Rob!" call. Unfortunately for them, Lathan carefully avoided eye contact as he wandered through the nearby aisles.

So far, so good.

In keeping with his prearranged plan, Lathan, still seemingly oblivious, still loaded down with the concessions, soon strolled over to sections just to the right and to the left of his original locale in such a way that several dozen fans were hopping, waving, and yelling in a (perpetually fruitless) effort to get the wandering fan back to his original seat. It wasn't long before virtually the entire right field deck was involved, though Rob kept on feigning some combination of deafness, blindness, or dullness.

Just to keep the gag stringing along, Lathan soon came up with new variations for the trick. He'd pop up in an entry point enticingly close to the right section, then quickly disappear. He'd cock his head and point to those who were pointing to him, as if puzzled over the fuss coming from a mass of strangers. He'd feign surprise as some New Yorkers decided to chant "ROB'S RETARDED! (Clap!) ROB'S RETARDED! (Clap!)." At other times, he'd pretend to take their hints, wandering in the right direction, only to overshoot it and prompt a new, adjoining section to get in the act. At one point, when nearly everyone was either on to the joke or otherwise tickled, Rob was spotted clear on the other side of Yankee Stadium, in left field's upper deck.

Of course, all good things must end, including the wandering fan's travels, and by the time Lathan "found" his seat in the eighth, several innings after he'd gotten lost, he'd attained celebrity status

among his fellow fans. As he settled in, a
loud cheer and "ROB! ROB! ROB!" chant
went up. ("I'd never received such an ovation in my entire life," he later admitted.)
Many of Lathan's would-be helpers smiled
and waved. Some others walked up to say
hello, land a high-five, and snap a photo; a
couple of them suggested taking it easy on
the beer or maybe getting a couple of tests done.
Seeing as how the Yanks ended up losing the game to the Tigers
in the ninth inning, Rob's unofficial helpers may have enjoyed his
plight in the stands more than they enjoyed the action on the field.

P.S. After Lathan managed to get on a first-name basis with
most of the stadium's upper deck, a couple of spectators spotted
him going home on an East Side subway line. "Wait, weren't your
friends going to some bar on the West Side?" they asked. Lathan,
perfectly in character, rubbed his chin and mused, "Oh, well.
Don't worry. . . . I'll find them."

2.

George Plimpton and the Sidd Finch Incident

In spring 1985, *Sports Illustrated* landed the story behind the
greatest baseball prodigy of all time.

To hear *SI* tell the tale, the eccentric Hayden Siddhartha
Finch spent much of his orphaned youth in England, dropped
out of Harvard after one semester, then traveled to the Tibetan
Himalayas, where he became a novice Buddhist monk. It was in
the process of Zen meditation, when his mind and body came
into perfect tantric harmony, that Finch discovered the ability to
throw a baseball at 168 miles per hour and, soon afterward, the
New York Mets discovered him.

No doubt about it, *Sports Illustrated* had absolutely nailed the story of the most unhittable pitch in history. The only problem: It was pure fiction.

Finch didn't wear one hiking boot or favor the French horn. Finch wasn't "a disciple of the great poet-saint Lama Milaraspa, who was born in the 11th century and died in the shadow of Mount Everest." Finch didn't have an invisible fastball. Finch didn't exist, even, except in the mind of magazine contributor George Plimpton.

The hoax started when *SI*'s managing editor, Mark Mulvoy, noticed that an upcoming issue's cover date would fall on April 1. He persuaded Plimpton, the Mets front office*, and Joe Berton, a young high school teacher, to play along with an elaborate April Fool's gag. The Mets organization went so far as to issue Berton a uniform (number 21) and permit full access to their spring training complex, all so they could convincingly sell Sidd as their new mystery man.

It was simply the most impactful prank ever. An unprecedented amount of reader mail, from the duped to the distraught to the delighted alike, poured into the *Sports Illustrated* offices. Plimpton put out a best-selling novella. The Mets staged a well-attended "Retirement Day" ceremony for the greatest player they ever/never had. More than 20 years later, Berton still poses for pictures and signs balls in the guise of his alter ego.

The *New York Times* said that the hoax "came to embody a piece of the game's eternal dreaminess, its belief that someday, someone might come out of nowhere with a pitching arm touched by the heavens." Right here it says that Sidd Finch was (almost) the greatest baseball prank of all time.

---

* Why the Mets? Probably because they'd come up with another ridiculously great phenom, Dwight Gooden, the year before, in 1984. Those pranksters, they think of everything.

1.

Wilbert Robinson and the Grapefruit Incident

When you think about it, the perfect prank has at least several elements:

1. It has to be based on something plausible. As plausible as, say, a sudden trade, a lost spectator, or a ridiculously great pitching phenom.

2. It has to be somewhat unexpected. As unexpected as, say, an outfielder/groundskeeper, a hidden sparrow, or a crank call to the bullpen.

3. It has to be slightly dangerous. As dangerous as, say, a traipse across a rain-slicked tarp, a golf swing just over a friend's face, or an in-game bomber overflight.

4. It has to be a little weird. As weird as, say, mistaking a national hero for a hobo or a reserve outfielder for a groundskeeper.

Wilbert Robinson and the grapefruit incident had 'em all.

It was plausible.

During spring training 1915, the Dodgers were in camp at Daytona Beach, Florida. At some point one of the players mentioned, in passing, that the Senators' Gabby Street had caught a ball dropped from atop the 555-foot Washington Monument a few years before; it was a well-publicized feat that supposedly, literally, couldn't be topped.

The club's veteran manager, Wilbert Robinson, respectfully disagreed, saying he could catch one from that height or even higher, if need be. As it happened, Daytona didn't have any structures that tall, but the area did have something even better: a female flyer named Ruth Law, who was offering locals rides on her new biplane, one of the first Florida had ever seen. It was quickly decided that Robbie would try to break the record by having Law drop a baseball from an overflight.

That was the (entirely conventional) setup: An aging manager made a hasty, macho bet to prove he could still teach the kids a thing or two.

It was unexpected.

Then things got a little weird. You see, Law didn't end up dropping a baseball from her plane. She dropped a grapefruit.

There are conflicting stories on how it all came about. Some say that the team trainer, Frank Kelley, came up with the substitute fruit. Some say the idea originated with the Dodgers' resident flake, a crazy kid named Casey Stengel. Some say Law decided on her own. Others insist that Law simply forgot to bring a legit horsehide to the airport, then borrowed from someone's lunch at the last minute.

One way or the other, as Robbie stood on the Dodgers' practice field that March afternoon, wearing his old catching gear, looking up to the sky and pounding at his mitt, he was about to get the surprise of his life.

It was dangerous.

Try to imagine a 52-year old man who hasn't caught a professional ball game in more than 12 years. He weighs in at 300 pounds or so. He's standing on a dewy, slippery diamond as his assembled team watches.

Suddenly, nearly 1,000 feet above his head, a tiny black sphere appears. The thing's accelerating toward the target at a rate of more than 32 feet per second, every second, until finally reaching a velocity in excess of 100 miles per hour. Suddenly the "ball" glances off the old man's glove and hits him flush in the chest. There's a loud splat/explosion. The team gasps.

It was weird.

Stengel later described Robbie's immediate reaction to the blow: He spun around, staggered for a couple steps, clutched at his chest, then fell over, as if he were a bad guy who'd just been shot in an old-fashioned Western movie. As a young onlooker remembered it, the manager also shouted, "Jesus Christ, I'm all in blood!"

It took at least a few seconds to realize that Robbie's fall and "blood" were caused by nothing more harmful than some very instant grapefruit juice, but when the realization did sink in, the Dodgers went into hysterics. The manager himself wasn't quite so tickled, of course, at least not at first, but it wasn't long before he was chuckling, too, and insisting he would have caught a real ball, if he only had the chance.

Stengel must have told and retold the grapefruit story a hundred times over the decades, most often with an expert, full-scale pantomime of Wilbert Robinson's pratfall, eventually transforming the routine into a classic on par with Abbott and Costello's "Who's on First?" It never failed. It was the greatest baseball prank of all time.

There's one in every crowd.

He's the joker in the deck, the gin in the tonic. Every office seems to have a wisecracking comedian around the water cooler, most schools have a class clown, and baseball clubs have a prankster in chief.

The role is almost as old as infield dirt—the prankster's the main suspect any time a teammate finds eye-black on the rim of his cap, unneeded mail orders at his home address, or uniform pants flapping from the ballpark flagpole. Flakes from Germany Schaefer to Jay Johnstone to Roger McDowell have all pulled those kinds of practical jokes and many more besides, but none were quite like the Orioles' Myron "Moe" Drabowsky.

What made Drabo special was his ability to put a twist on the classics. Others had used rubber snakes to startle oblivious teammates, but only Moe would take the time and effort to borrow live ones from pet stores, then wait for just the right moment to artfully place his slithering friends into Paul Blair's pants or Luis Aparicio's glove. Others tossed firecrackers, but only one ringleader went so far as to have his fellow relief pitchers paint their faces in camouflage, crawl past outfield fences, and toss cherry bombs into unsuspecting opponents' bullpens. Others have been known to give plentiful hot foots, too, but Drabowsky had the nerve to victimize countless reporters and friends, not to mention his own team owner and the commissioner of Major League Baseball. Anything to establish himself as a grown man with a six-year-old's sense of humor.

Beyond the tried-and-true gags, though, what set Drabowsky apart was the originality in his pranks. Like any great entertainer, the guy knew how to consistently top himself with all-new material.

One time, he used the bullpen phone in Anaheim to order Chinese takeout food, a relatively remarkable request considering that the restaurant involved was located in Hong Kong. Then, Moe used a knowledge of bullpen extensions and mimicry to target former Athletics teammates in an elaborate stunt described on page 328. Just a couple of years later, after being traded away from the Orioles, Drabo reached out to a former team once again: He rented a plane to circle Memorial Stadium during the 1969 World Series with a banner reading GOOD LUCK BIRDS. BEWARE OF MOE. No one ever knew what he was liable to cook up next.

Drabo never offered any deep, elaborate reasons for his admittedly juvenile ways, other than an amiable hankering for the unexpected. Maybe he got a bit stir crazy while waiting around to make a late-inning relief appearance. Maybe tricking his fellow ballplayers provided the same kind of kick he got from fooling opposing batters with curveballs.

The stunts may have indicated nothing more than a silly soul's grasp of the more serious part of life. Without the well-chronicled prank practice, it's doubtful that few would spell, much less recall, the name of Moe Drabowsky, but as it was, he was one of the most beloved Orioles of all time, a larger-than-life figure whose 2006 death was met with numerous obituaries and almost as many fond stories. It's the wise man who realizes that life's all about happy memories, and a few well-placed snakes and well-planned calls generated plenty of 'em.

Any of that might've explained it, but onetime teammate Boog Powell had his own theory on the greatest prankster in baseball history. "Obviously, Moe's parents never let him have toys when he was little," Boog said. "He had a lot of catching up to do."

ACKNOWLEDGMENTS

In my last book I thanked my fellow lawyers, for inspiring me to become a writer.

I was just kidding.

The real beginnings of this book were in the generous encouragement of many friends. There may be too many to mention, but some of the greatest support came from members of the DeVito, Diaconescu, Docimo, Handrinos, Katsaros, Musilli, Nanos, Nelson, and Rokanas families. I'm still in debt to the late Souli Nanos and Tony Soutos, who once advised me to follow my dreams.

Apart from those dear compatriots, the people who really made my work happen are thousands of strangers. I want to thank you, the readers, for choosing this book and coming along on this journey; I hope you enjoyed reading it as much as I enjoyed writing it.

Finally, I worked on this book with a special new friend in mind. My infant niece Sophia DeVito brought all of us so much happiness . . . she gets the final word: thanks.

—P. H.
Norwalk, Connecticut
November 2009